THE PROFESSIONALIZATION OF PUBLIC PARTICIPATION

The Professionalization of Public Participation is an edited collection of essays by leading and emerging scholars examining the emerging profession of public participation professionals.

Public participation professionals are persons working in the public, private, or third sectors that are paid to design, implement, and/or facilitate participatory forums. The rapid growth and proliferation of participatory arrangements call for expertise in the organizing of public participation. The contributors analyze the professionalization of this practice in different countries (United States, France, Canada, Italy, and the United Kingdom) to see how their actions challenge the development of participatory arrangements. Designing such processes is a delicate activity, since it may affect not only the quality of the processes and their legitimacy, but also their capacity to influence decision-making.

Laurence Bherer is Associate Professor of Public Administration and Policy in the Political Science Department at the Université de Montréal. Her research focuses on participatory democracy, local democracy, and urban politics in Canada and Europe.

Mario Gauthier is Full Professor of Urban Studies in the Social Sciences Department at the Université du Québec en Outaouais. His research work concerns urban and regional planning, environmental impact assessment, and sustainable development.

Louis Simard is Associate Professor in the School of Political Studies at the University of Ottawa. His research work focuses on public participation, instruments of public action, social acceptability, and organizational learning in the environmental and energy sectors.

"As public authorities and other institutions increasingly employ public participation processes, we are witnessing the emergence of a new cadre of actors: public participation professionals (PPPs). PPPs play a significant role in negotiating the design, application, and impact of participatory processes and yet our knowledge of their activities is limited. This timely collection opens up this novel field of activity to systematic and critical reflection."

> – **Graham Smith**, *Professor of Politics at the Centre for the Study of Democracy (CSD), University of Westminster*

"The last several decades have spawned an incredible resurgence of interest in public participation. As the field has grown, so too has the proliferation of public participation professionals—individuals working the public, nonprofit, or private sector who are paid to design, implement, and/or facilitate participatory forums. Anyone interested in public participation must read this book to understand how these actors are professionalizing the field, and how this professionalization is shaping (for better and for worse) the growth, development, and prospects of public participation in the 21st century."

> – **Tina Nabatchi**, *Associate Professor of Public Administration and International Affairs, Maxwell School of Citizenship and Public Affairs, Syracuse University*

THE PROFESSIONALIZATION OF PUBLIC PARTICIPATION

Edited by Laurence Bherer,
Mario Gauthier, and Louis Simard

Routledge
Taylor & Francis Group

NEW YORK AND LONDON

First published 2017
by Routledge
711 Third Avenue, New York, NY 10017

and by Routledge
2 Park Square, Milton Park, Abingdon, Oxon, OX14 4RN

Routledge is an imprint of the Taylor & Francis Group, an informa business

© 2017 Taylor & Francis

The right of Laurence Bherer, Mario Gauthier, and Louis Simard to be identified as the authors of the editorial material, and of the authors for their individual chapters, has been asserted in accordance with sections 77 and 78 of the Copyright, Designs and Patents Act 1988.

Library of Congress Cataloging-in-Publication Data
Names: Bherer, Laurence, editor. | Gauthier, Mario, 1965– editor. |
    Simard, Louis, editor.
Title: The professionalization of public participation / edited by
    Laurence Bherer, Mario Gauthier, and Louis Simard.
Description: New York, NY : Routledge, 2017. | Includes bibliographical
    references and index.
Identifiers: LCCN 2016044339 | ISBN 9781138638112 (hbk) |
    ISBN 9781138638129 (pbk) | ISBN 9781315637983 (ebk)
Subjects: LCSH: Political participation—Case studies. | Political
    activists—Case studies.
Classification: LCC JF799 .P755 2017 | DDC 323/.042—dc23
LC record available at https://lccn.loc.gov/2016044339

ISBN: 978-1-138-63811-2 (hbk)
ISBN: 978-1-138-63812-9 (pbk)
ISBN: 978-1-315-63798-3 (ebk)

Typeset in Bembo
by Apex CoVantage, LLC

CONTENTS

FIGURES

TABLES

ACKNOWLEDGMENTS

The starting point for this book was a symposium entitled "Developing expertise in the design of participatory tools: professionalization and diversification of the public participation field," held in the context of the Annual World Congress of the International Political Science Association (IPSA) on July 19–24, 2014, in Montreal. Some of the papers presented at the symposium were subsequently rewritten to become chapters for this book. The symposium was organized in partnership with the Institut du Nouveau Monde (INM), a Canadian NGO (non-governmental organization) specializing in citizenship education and public debate. We would like to thank Michel Vennes, director general and founder of the INM, and especially Malorie Flon, strategic advisor at INM, for her involvement in organizing the symposium.[1] Along with the three editors of this book, the academic committee organizers included Alice Mazeaud (Université de La Rochelle) and Magali Nonjon (Université d'Avignon), whom we would particularly like to thank for their help in organizing this event, which brought together researchers and practitioners from Canada and elsewhere. The publication of this volume was also made possible by grants from two organizations, whose contributions we most gratefully acknowledge: the Social Sciences and Humanities Research Council of Canada, through its program of "Insight grants," one of which was awarded to the editors of this book for their research project entitled "Expertise, champ et diffusion des pratiques de participation publique" ("The expertise, field and dissemination of public participation practices") (2012–2015); and the *Villes Régions Monde* network, funded by the Fonds de recherche Québec—Société et culture (FRQ—SC). We also offer our sincere thanks to Evelyn Lindhorst, for her work in translating and revising several of the chapters, and to Mathieu Labelle and Myriam Morrissette, for their involvement in the layout and formatting of this volume. Nor would this book have been possible without the trust in us on the part of Routledge, and especially Lillian Rand, who acted as editorial assistant from the beginning of the project. Parts of Chapter 3 have been originally published as "De la cause au marché de la démocratie participative," *Agone, 56* (2015): 135–154. Chapter 10 was originally published as "Learning to facilitate deliberation: practicing the art of hosting," *Critical Policy Studies, 8*(3): 300–322 (copyright © Institute of Local Government Studies, University of Birmingham, reprinted by permission of Taylor & Francis Ltd, on behalf of Institute of Local Government Studies, University of Birmingham).

Note

1 INM has published a summary of the round table discussions at this event, and of a survey of the participants involved, entitled "Professionalization of the Public Participation Field: Actors, Challenges, Opportunities" (also available in French). Available at https://inm.qc.ca/produit/professionnalisation-de-la-participation-publique-acteurs-defis-possibilites/.

1

INTRODUCTION

The Public Participation Professional: An Invisible but Pivotal Actor in Participatory Processes

Laurence Bherer, Mario Gauthier, and Louis Simard

Introduction

Participatory processes are generally viewed as a meeting between the sponsor of a participatory forum and citizens. In this equation, the sponsor is the one who initiates the participatory process and invites citizens to come and give their opinions on a specific issue that the sponsor has carefully defined. These citizens are individuals or groups that have shown their interest in the issue and that may have been selected through a variety of representation mechanisms (voluntary participation, random selection, a particular interest or involvement in an issue, etc.). Depending on the type of participatory setting, experts of various kinds (scientists, professionals, civil society groups, etc.) may also intervene to inform citizens about a particular aspect of the issue under examination so that they can give an enlightened opinion.

In this equation, there is also another actor who remains relatively invisible but who nonetheless plays an essential part in the conducting of participatory processes: this is the public participation professional (PPP), that is, an individual working in the public or private sector who is paid to design, implement, and/or facilitate participatory forums (Chilvers, 2013; Lee, 2015; Moore, 2012). Public participation professionals may have acquired their training in very different areas, but their professional trajectories and experiences have led them to become experts in the organizing of public participation. PPPs can be found not only in public administrations but also in NGOs and private firms.

In the last 20 years, many studies have been published on the growing use of public participation tools at every political level and in a variety of policy domains. Most focus on micro-sociological issues, that is, on the internal or immediate context of the participation mechanisms. This very prolific work has allowed us to map out a series of participation practices. But it has only given us a partial picture of public participation, as studies from this perspective have generally concentrated on a single participation mechanism or have compared isolated participatory arrangements. Public participation is, however, not limited to a series of isolated practices but is organized through a variety of networks of organizations and actors. We have only to think about the advent of specialized firms working in the field of public participation (Hendriks & Carson, 2008), about the creation of public agencies devoted to public participation—like the CNDP, or public debate commission, in France (Revel, Blatrix, Blondiaux, Fourniau, Hériard Dubreuil & Lefebvre, 2007) or the Bureau d'audiences publiques sur l'environnement (BAPE) in Quebec (Gauthier & Simard, 2011), and, of course, about the proliferation of participation mechanisms. This trend can be summarized in the notion of a participation movement, which refers to the growing number of participation mechanisms, some of which are very interesting from a democratic viewpoint, and includes other less sophisticated mechanisms which are nonetheless still part of the call for citizens to participate (Bherer, 2010). From this point of view, research on public participation must now investigate the interactions between participation mechanisms so as to understand the conditions involved in the production of participation as a whole and to better explain the factors that hinder or encourage public participation. In order to do so, this book proposes to analyze the role of the public participation professional, a public participation actor that, surprisingly, has until now been little scrutinized (see the pioneering studies by Chilvers, 2008a; Hendriks & Carson, 2008; Nonjon, 2005).

PPPs in fact interact with all the actors involved in participatory spaces (elected officials, civil servants, citizens, NGOs, public or private sponsors) in order to negotiate how the public participation will be carried out. Over time, and as public participation has become recognized, these professionals have developed a unique and rare expertise that they can now sell to clients or to potential employers. This pivotal role in the design of participation mechanisms also means that PPPs act as bridges between the different arenas in which public participation operates. In sum, participation professionals are well placed to play an important role in the implementation of public participation (Hendriks & Carson, 2008). They are at the heart of the supply of participation approaches and have to negotiate the design of participation mechanisms with public authorities. They thus reveal the nature of the field of public participation, and they are well aware of the tensions that shape this practice in a given political system.

What are the effects of this professionalization of public participation? Does it compromise or support the democratic aims associated with public participation? How does the approach that PPPs take affect their abilities to design effective public participation mechanisms? While the contributions in this book cannot fully answer all the questions raised by the professionalization of public participation, taken together, they provide a clearer profile of these actors in different contexts and help to explain the reasons for the rapid development of this profession, the role of PPPs in the dissemination of public participation practices, and the main day-to-day challenges that public participation professionals face in the pursuit of this new "craft." Because PPPs are invisible actors, they are not easy to "capture," methodologically speaking. The analyses gathered here are based on some of the first research programs in several areas (political science, sociology, management and leadership, urban planning, environmental studies) devoted to this new actor. In this brief introduction, we outline who the PPPs are, identify the main issues related to professionalization trends in this field, and present the various chapters of the book.

Who Are Public Participation Professionals?

Researchers use a variety of terms to designate public participation professionals—a fact that clearly reflects the wide range of activities performed by PPPs and the different approaches that they employ to do their work. To cite only some examples, PPPs have been called scribes (Escobar, 2014), facilitators (Moore, 2012), participatory process experts (Chilvers, 2008b), public engagement practitioners (Lee, 2014), professional participation practitioners (Cooper & Smith, 2012), participatory engineers (Bonaccorsi & Nonjon, 2012), deliberative organizers (Hendriks & Carson, 2008), or reflective practitioners (Albrechts, 2002). Forester is certainly the most imaginative author in finding several original names for this new profession, as he has also used "deliberative practitioners," "mediators," "facilitative leaders," "self-styled community builders," "coalition builders," and even "de facto peacemakers" (Forester, 1999, 2009). In this introduction and in several chapters of this book,[1] we have deliberately chosen to use the term public participation professional because it does not emphasize any single aspect of the PPPs' work. "Public participation" is used here as a term that encompasses many different approaches and forms of dialogue and collaboration.

The issue of the terminology and definitions used shows that there are all sizes and shapes of levels and forms of action, from the scribe who merely takes notes or facilitates communications to a limited extent to the expert who designs, regulates, and evaluates. This also indicates that this practice is characterized by a significant division of labour and a process of sub-specialization. Chilvers (2013, pp. 288–289) is the author who has gone the furthest in classifying PPP activities, using what he calls a mapping technique to generate PPP profiles in the UK science and technology sector. He identifies four areas of expertise: (1) orchestrating: commissioning, sponsoring, and guiding participatory arrangements; (2) practicing: designing, facilitating, reporting on dialogue processes; (3) coordinating: networking, capacity building, and professionalizing; and (4) studying: researching, theorizing, evaluating, and reflecting. We will now examine each of these four areas in turn in order to present an initial overview of the field of public participation, the variety of roles that PPPs play, and the different types of organizations in which they work.

First, we can find PPPs in organizations orchestrating participatory arrangements. These are the ones that initiate and sponsor such participatory arrangements. The most important sponsors are public organizations that initiate participation processes, such as government departments, public agencies, municipalities, and so on. Even if the majority subcontract the development of one-off participatory spaces to private firms, public organizations need some individuals on their staff who can design and evaluate participatory arrangements and also supervise consultants. Sometimes, they choose to hire civil servants that are completely dedicated to this task (Gourgues, 2012; Mazeaud, 2012). However, certain private proponents of development projects, community and non-profit groups, unions, industry trade associations, etc. are also increasingly becoming involved in orchestrating participatory arrangements (Lee & Romano, 2013). These one-shot sponsors usually outsource this expertise: they ask participatory consultants to implement a one-off participatory process. As such participatory arrangements increase, we can hypothesize that, as some public organizations are already doing, some of these other types of organizations that have very often dealt with participatory settings may sometimes, in the near future, choose to hire one or two professionals who can perform or monitor the work of participatory consultants.

Practicing includes the practitioners that we think of spontaneously when we talk about PPPs, because they are the most "visible" PPPs. "Practicing" PPPs are those who put the participatory arrangements directly in place by performing typical services related to the design and implementation of public participation processes: the production of informational materials, stakeholder outreach and process marketing, selection of process methods, design of the topical scope and coverage, recruitment of participants and small group facilitators, overall facilitation and "master of ceremonies" duties, event logistics, ongoing communication with participants, and evaluation of process efficacy (Lee, McNulty & Shaffer, 2013, p. 85). These kinds of PPPs do not initiate participatory processes (or only do so very exceptionally). They usually act as consultants in private firms or as freelancers (Hendriks & Carson, 2008) and sell their services to organizations that sponsor participatory arrangements. Some NGOs or think tanks that sell their participatory services as private firms also have hired PPPs.

The "coordinating" and "studying" sides of the profession are less well known. Coordination refers to emerging organizations helping to organize and professionalize the field, such as professional associations or organizations that disseminate best practices. There has been no systematic analysis of this kind of organization, but the best known of them are the International Association for Public Participation (IAP2) (which is organized on the basis of various regional area or country associations) (Mazeaud, Nonjon & Parizet, 2016), the National Coalition for Dialogue & Deliberation (NCDD) in the United States, the "Public Participation" section of the International Association for Impact Assessment (IAIA), the Institut de la Concertation in France, etc. These associations organize annual conferences and training workshops, produce guides and toolboxes, and generally promote public participation.

"Studying" is certainly the most ambiguous area of expertise from the point of view of the PPPs interviewed by Chilvers, because it involves academics who help to develop and legitimize the field by creating participatory spaces but at the same time take a critical stance (Chilvers, 2010, pp. 20–21). Lee & Romano refer to them as "pracademics" (2013, p. 744). Here we can think of such internationally known academics as James Fishkin, but there is also a myriad of academics involved in participatory arrangements at their community level or at a higher political level. Some "pracademics" are also true "stars" in specific domains but are not very well known in the sphere of democratic innovations, such as Lawrence Susskind, Professor of Urban and Environmental Planning at MIT. "Studying" also includes academic research centres, which are too numerous to list here (Carcasson, 2014). These research centres usually play an active role in publicizing and advocating for participatory arrangements, through the direct implementation of participatory settings, the evaluation of these settings, or the conducting of extensive experimental research. In tracing the history of research on participation and the development of participation mechanisms in France since the 1970s, Blatrix (2012) highlights several types of contributions from academics: (1) researchers help to give credence to the concept of a social demand for participation and the need for participation mechanisms, for which they become the main advocates; (2) they foster the dissemination of participation mechanisms by giving priority to specific mechanisms; and (3) they contribute to the development of a doctrine of participatory democracy by formulating rules and principles of use. While the professional activities of academics warrant more systematic study, it should nonetheless be noted that they are engaged in a "passive" type of consulting: they do not solicit clients directly but often wait for clients to come to them, and they are also freer than other types of consultants to decline invitations and requests (Hendriks & Carson, 2008). However, it is important to acknowledge that the "studying" role can also be performed by NGOs or think tanks, as the number of guidelines on public participation published by these actors shows.

These four areas of expertise are not mutually exclusive (Chilvers, 2013, p. 290). The boundaries between the various categories are considered very porous, and movement between them is seen as commonplace. As Chilvers and others among the few scholars who are interested in this new profession have said, the situation is clearly very complex (2013, p. 289). PPPs in fact form a strategic action field (Lee, 2011). A strategic action field is a system of actors and organizations in which the actors consider other members in carrying out their actions (Fligstein & McAdam, 2012). This concept implies that society is characterized by sectors of action that develop after the creation of organizations that mutually recognize that they share the same sphere of activities and interact among themselves in different ways (collaboration, conflict, domination, etc.). These interactions do not automatically involve collaborative relationships. On the contrary, strategic fields include conflict and domination. This is the case in the public participation field, which is far from being homogeneous. Not only are PPPs hired by several types of organizations that perform the four different roles that we discussed in the previous paragraphs, but they also do not share the same understanding of the aims of public participation, of the way to concretely put it into practice, or of their own role in this practice. Some have a very minimalist understanding of their role, whereas others develop an interventionist style of facilitation (Smith, 2009, p. 198).

In the past 10 years, a small group of pioneering scholars have begun to be interested in PPPs, in the organizations that hire them, and in what this reveals about the practice of public participation: that is, they are attempting to understand the strategic field of public participation. Several of these scholars are included in this book, which, for the first time, brings together analyses on the development of this new profession in different countries and on the issues raised by professionalization in the pursuit of participatory democracy. The following section looks at some of the risks associated with the professionalization of politics and how this can be applied to PPPs.

What the Professionalization of Public Participation Means

Public participation professionals can be understood as forming part of the new political professions that have been created in the last 20 years and that have assumed a growing importance in activities of political mobilization and influence, such as election campaign organizers, public affairs consultants, lobbyists, or public relations specialists (Medvic, 2006; Svallfors, 2016; Walker, 2014). All of these new professions reflect the professionalization of politics and, more specifically, the professionalization of advocacy. They all share the general objective of developing and putting in place methods to reach and mobilize political actors and citizens in order to achieve the aims of the organizations that hire them (Walker, 2014). However, among these new types of professionals, public participation professionals are certainly the ones with the most ambiguous role.

Campaign organizers want to get their candidates elected. Public relations specialists manage communications and messaging by targeting the general public or specific groups of actors and citizens in order to improve the image of their clients. Public affairs consultants (also called grassroots lobbyists) also strategically manage their client's political and social environment but employ grassroots mobilization techniques to target and recruit activists for their client's cause (Walker, 2014). They all work on behalf of their clients to help them to obtain what they want, on a political level. For them, politics is often a zero-sum game where someone wins (hopefully, their clients), and someone loses. Their work is also controversial: they are often seen as puppet masters who seek to manipulate people to achieve their clients' ends (Medvic, 2006).

In contrast, the aims of the PPPs' work are not only broader, but also clearly more abstract and more demanding. The professional activities performed by PPPs are supposed to reinvigorate democracy by increasing citizen engagement in decision-making processes and creating spaces of collaboration according to a transparent set of rules favouring inclusion, openness, and empowerment, no less! The democratic ethos of their profession means that it is not easy to define whom PPPs are working for. For the sponsors of the participatory process (who can be either their employers or their clients depending on their status), surely! However, PPPs also need to prove the civic nature of their work by being equally concerned with the citizens involved in the process that they are implementing (Lee, 2015). PPPs have to find mutually satisfactory solutions, or "win-win" solutions. In other words, in comparison with the other new political professions, the professional activities of PPPs are closely associated with the realization of positive democratic values.

However, this high ideal can be a heavy burden to bear when it is time to put it into practice. Furthermore, whereas PPPs have a broader democratic ethos to fulfill than the other recent political professions, they can often face the same criticisms as those associated with the professionalization of advocacy understood as the mobilization of members or citizens and funds from the top down (Walker, 2014). The dangers of the professionalization of advocacy have been extensively analyzed and can be summarized in the idea that professionalization increases the gap between citizens and decision makers by making the access to influence more costly (only actors that have enough financial resources can obtain services from political professionals that allow them to influence public authorities) (Walker, 2014). This criticism can be applied to the work of PPPs in a growing number of circumstances. The rise in the United States of private corporations or large advocacy groups that sponsor participatory settings with the hope of influencing decision makers (Lee, 2015) suggests that scenarios in which actors with considerable financial resources buy a participatory service in using citizens to influence decision makers are increasingly becoming a reality. However, the sponsoring of a participatory process by a private corporation could also be seen as a sign of openness: it may not only be a case of a corporation buying a participatory service to get what they want, but it could also show an authentic desire to change the traditional corporate approach to dealing with sensitive issues and citizens' requests for more information about the corporation's projects (Simard, 2008). In this case, PPPs can help the corporation to design a fair and open participatory space.

The main threat arising from the professionalization of public participation depends on the kind of participatory process that PPPs are willing to offer. If the sponsoring of a participatory event by a corporation, activist group, or public authority has only been used to enable these sponsors to look like "good guys" and get what they want, PPPs then become partners in the instrumentalization of public participation. In this context, participatory arrangements would tend to be poorly designed and facilitated, and would be far from following the ideals of inclusiveness, transparency, and reciprocity. PPPs do not play a positive role in this scenario because they do not help to improve the design of participatory arrangements. Participatory arrangements then become just another technique to "activate" citizens, that is, to stimulate the action of targeted citizens in order to convince the general public or public authorities of the worthiness of the sponsor's project or cause (Schier, 2000). Activation is not fake participation but rather a biased practice where sponsors, with the help of a professional, facilitate the participation of some citizens to the detriment of others, in order to achieve their aims. They thus "manufacture" participation. Activation encourages "'thin citizenship' in which democracy is reduced to short-term, transactional, and individualistic exchanges between citizens and leaders" (Walker, 2014, p. 205). In other words, whereas there are democratic virtues associated with participatory democracy and the work of PPPs, manipulation and instrumentalization can also be part of the equation.

The criticism of the "activation politics" that accompanied the professionalization of advocacy is echoed by certain concerns about the kind of participatory arrangements that have emerged in recent years. Despite the enthusiasm in several sectors of society and in many organizations about implementing participatory arrangements, these arrangements often fail to change anything or to actually affect the decision in question (Polletta, 2015). Empowerment and control, two values at the heart of the political project of participatory democracy that emerged in the 1960s, are becoming less and less of a concern. The expression of citizens' inputs in a well-designed participatory event has now sometimes become more important than having an equal opportunity to influence decisions. Participation could tend to become a grand spectacle in which citizens are "activated," while, behind the scenes, the decision-making arena remains unchallenged.

The risk of "activation" is a real challenge, which shows how important it is to better understand the PPPs' role. Do they have some power of political influence, or are they powerless actors? The first option is certainly closer to the truth: because sponsors generally in fact know very little about the purpose and use of participatory processes (Cooper & Smith, 2012), PPPs perform an important role in educating and influencing political actors in regard to the democratic promises of participatory tools. Furthermore, many PPPs are well aware of the risk of manipulation associated with their practice. The work of Caroline W. Lee (2015; see also her chapter in this book) shows that PPPs often try very hard to ensure the authenticity of the participatory arrangements that they design and to foster reciprocity between their sponsors and citizens. In other words, they are not naïve and are very conscious of the tensions connected with their profession. However, we cannot assume that all PPPs will in fact play this role, because they are far from being a homogeneous community with a shared understanding of public participation. They also have to deal with a number of tricky situations where there is strong pressure to follow the agendas of the sponsors of participatory settings. This book invites readers to learn more about the tensions and contrasts in the PPPs' motivations and practices, and to see how some PPPs can help to sustain unequal democratic dynamics, whereas others can increase the openness of decision-making processes.

Presentation of the Contributions

This book is divided into two parts. The first part looks at specific contexts and includes chapters that focus on the growing role of PPPs from a national or sub-national perspective. The objectives of this part of the book are to examine the history of public participation practices in these political contexts and to explore specific issues related to the professionalization of public participation. These issues are addressed in five chapters that present different pictures of the PPPs' work in Italy, France, the US, Quebec (Canada) and the UK. In the Italian case, Chapter 2, by Rodolfo Lewanski and Stefania Ravazzi, asks how the institutionalization of public participation (that is, the dedication of funds and the enactment of regulations that make participation processes mandatory in certain cases) impacts the work performed by PPPs. Italy is one of the countries that has gone the furthest in the institutionalization of public participation by creating, within the last decade, laws and special public authorities dedicated to public participation in two Italian regions, Tuscany and Emilia-Romagna. Lewanski and Ravazzi show how these two recent reforms have contributed to the recognition of the expertise of PPPs and of the legitimacy of participatory processes, but in different ways. This institutionalization also helped to reinforce a significant division in the PPP community between those who see public participation as a tool to regenerate communities and create better citizens, and those PPPs who are more concerned about the effects of participatory arrangements on decision-making processes.

The contribution by Alice Mazeaud and Magali Nonjon also considers the role of institutionalization in the growing professionalization of public participation, in this case, in France. The originality of their analysis lies in their underlining of the fact that PPPs, once recognized, have pushed the institutionalization process further. The two authors show how participation has become a top-down process marked by the strong involvement of the state in the proliferation of participation mechanisms at every level of the French political system. This top-down process has been accompanied by a strong process of specialization of the profession of PPP, where, in a first stage, former activists converted their past experiences in urban activism into public participation knowledge and expertise and, in a second stage, PPPs from different professional backgrounds then emerged, particularly in the areas of communications, public relations and urban planning. Over the years, French PPPs have developed various skills and tools to legitimize their expertise and to demonstrate the existence of a demand for participation in France.

Caroline W. Lee's chapter examines the complexity of the public participation field in the United States by emphasizing an important paradox: as public participation settings proliferate and PPPs gain in legitimacy, the field is nonetheless being undermined by the growing competition from public relations firms, by the elite profile of this profession, and by the dangers inherent in innovation and new technology where there is little interaction or reciprocity. Whereas PPPs, particularly in the US, are aware of the inequalities in their country and of the positive role that they can play in helping to reduce bias and inequity, the participation industry is continuing to grow as empowerment and democratization are becoming less of a concern.

The chapter by Laurence Bherer, Mario Gauthier, and Louis Simard looks at how PPPs see the ideal of impartiality associated with this profession in the context of the strong commercialization of participation services. Or, in other words, how do they balance their loyalty to their client with a commitment to help citizens by implementing fair and transparent participatory processes? Based on the depiction of four types of PPPs (the promoter, the reformer, the militant, and the facilitator), the chapter shows that impartiality is far from being a norm shared by all. The authors' survey of public participation firms and their study of the history of this field suggest that the strong divisions between PPPs have resulted from the rapid diversification of this industry, which has attracted firms with very different types of commitments to public participation.

The contribution by Jason Chilvers offers unique insight into the professionalization trend in public participation in the United Kingdom, with particular reference to the domains of science and the environment. His chapter shows how the UK public participation field has rapidly grown and become standardized due to the creation of organizations such as Sciencewise, a public resource centre dedicated to learning about and the diffusion of public participation mechanisms and to helping to implement participatory arrangements across various sectors of government and beyond. Whereas Sciencewise has contributed to the diffusion and legitimization of participatory arrangements, it has also helped to narrow the innovation process by focusing on certain specific settings and favouring some of the big players in the participation industry, to the detriment of many small firms or self-employed workers that have been actively engaged in this field for a number of years. The importance of Sciencewise in the field also tends to overshadow smaller cases of participatory processes emerging from civil society. Chilvers concludes by pointing to the lack of reflexive forms of learning in the UK public participation field.

The second part of the book deals with some other important issues related to the professionalization of public participation. Its objective is to further investigate certain categories of PPPs (civil servants, academics) and the specific process of dissemination and standardization in the public participation field. Based on the case of local governments in Scotland, Oliver Escobar's chapter offers access to the world of PPPs who are civil servants and who are referred to in the text as "official PPPs." If the analysis by Bherer, Gauthier, and Simard demonstrates how the context of commercialization interferes with the PPPs' work, Escobar's study shows that official PPPs also have to deal with a great deal of pressure—political pressure in this case—from other civil servants, elected representatives, and NGOs. They are in the uncomfortable position of having their expertise wanted because new participatory settings have been created, while in their daily work, they encounter a lot of resistance because their presence had triggered changes in rules-in-use and in the overall culture of the decision-making process. Facing considerable stress and often feeling powerless, some official PPPs adopt a more bureaucratic style, whereas others choose to be an inside activist nonetheless, dedicated to changing traditional working practices in local administrations.

The contribution by David Kahane and Kristjana Loptson also examines a specific category of PPPs that are rarely studied: that is, academics who are involved in the implementation, analysis, and evaluation of participatory arrangements. The chapter focuses especially on the relationships between academics and practitioners or, to put it another way, between the studying side and the practicing side of the public participation field (see the typology developed by Chilvers, 2013, as outlined above). With the rapidly growing academic interest in the effects of participatory settings, more and more academics and practitioners are collaborating in organizing participatory forums: academics want to observe the outputs for themselves, whereas practitioners would like to obtain an evaluation of the settings that they have designed. Kahane and Loptson show that even although both sides want this collaboration, it becomes a constant balancing act between the requirements of the research combined with the academics' role as independent critics and the practitioners' need to manage a fair process on a day-to-day basis and to lead the process to its completion. It can be particularly difficult to reconcile the non-collaborative habits and attitudes of academics, who see power relationships everywhere, with the practitioners' desire to concentrate on the experience of the participants and on bringing people together, with less consideration of political aspects.

The contribution by Nina Amelung and Louisa Grabner tells the very interesting story of the transnational spread and standardization across countries of three "universal bestseller" designs: the planning cell, the citizens' jury, and the consensus conference. In each case during this process, the initial mechanisms, conceived separately, were transformed and adapted by different networks of actors from academia, consulting, the media, activism, governments, foundations, etc. The authors' analysis shows that although PPPs are an important actor in the dissemination process, they do not act alone. They are part of the larger category of "public participation advocates" that make the travel of participatory arrangements possible. But public participation advocates did not foster the dissemination of the three designs through strategic action. The standardization of these three "universal bestsellers" is in fact the result of a muddling through, of mixed contingency and local adaptation.

In their chapter, Kathryn S. Quick and Jodi R. Sandfort continue to explore this process of dissemination in detail by looking at one of the main approaches to facilitation in the US: the art of hosting. They are interested in the effects of training programs such as the art of hosting on PPPs, who belong to a profession characterized by "learning-by-doing." The demanding skills required to be a good PPP, especially in the craft of facilitation (selecting the appropriate design, maintaining an inclusive context, managing conflicts and power relationships, creating a context of mutual understanding, staying focused on the objectives of the process, etc.) mean that learning in action is in fact quite a challenge. Quick and Sandfort explore the different stages of what PPPs learn and how they can or cannot (or choose not to) integrate this new knowledge into their practice. The chapter shows that this complex learning process depends on several factors, such as the PPPs' personality, past experiences and professional identity, and their sense of belonging to the art of hosting community.

In our conclusion to this book, we highlight some of the general issues emerging from the rich material in each chapter on the factors that explain the development of this new profession, the standardization and diffusion effects of the PPPs' work, and the paradoxical existence of weaknesses in this increasingly popular and rapidly growing field.

Overall, this book is designed for academics, public participation professionals, and political actors who are interested in the conditions involved in the production of public participation as a whole and in better understanding the factors that hinder or encourage public participation. PPPs are an interesting and challenging group of new political professionals that are at the same time witnesses of the tensions and controversies between sponsors and citizens, specialists who influence the ways that political actors collaborate, and active entrepreneurs who promote the legitimization, for good or bad, of the use of participatory processes. This book is intended to help these professionals emerge from the shadows.

Note

1 Some of the authors included in this book have chosen to use different but often very similar expressions: dialogue and deliberation practitioners, professional public participation facilitation, participation professionals and facilitators, facilitators and mediators of public participation, deliberative engagement experts, hosting practitioners.

References

Albrechts, L. (2002). The planning community reflects on enhancing public involvement: Views from academics and reflective practitioners. *Planning Theory & Practice, 3*(3), 331–347.

Bherer, L. (2010). Successful and unsuccessful participatory arrangements: Why is there a participatory movement at the local level? *Journal of Urban Affairs, 32*(3), 287–303.

Blatrix, C. (2012). Des sciences de la participation: Paysage participatif et marché des biens savants en France. *Quaderni, 79*, 59–80.

Bonaccorsi, J., & Nonjon, M. (2012). "La participation en kit": L'horizon funèbre de l'idéal participatif. *Quaderni, 79*, 29–44.

Carcasson, M. (2014). The critical role of local centers and institutes in advancing deliberative democracy. *Journal of Public Deliberation, 10*(1). Retrieved from http://www.publicdeliberation.net/jpd/vol10/iss1/art11/

Chilvers, J. (2008a). Deliberating competence: Theoretical and practitioner perspectives on effective participatory appraisal practice. *Science, Technology, & Human Values, 33*(2), 155–195.

Chilvers, J. (2008b). Environmental risk, uncertainty, and participation: Mapping an emergent epistemic community. *Environment and Planning A*, *40*(12), 2990–3008.

Chilvers, J. (2010). *Sustainable participation? Mapping out and reflecting on the field of public dialogue on science and technology*. Harwell: Sciencewise Expert Resource Centre.

Chilvers, J. (2013). Reflexive engagement? Actors, learning, and reflexivity in public dialogue on science and technology. *Science Communication*, *35*(3), 283–310.

Cooper, E., & Smith, G. (2012). Organizing deliberation: The perspectives of professional participation practitioners in Britain and Germany. *Journal of Public Deliberation*, *8*(1). Retrieved from http://www.publicdeliberation.net/jpd/vol8/iss1/art3/

Escobar, O. (2014). Upstream public engagement, downstream policy-making? The brain imaging dialogue as a community of inquiry. *Science and Public Policy*, *41*(4), 480–492.

Fligstein, N., & McAdam, D. (2012). *A theory of fields*. Oxford: Oxford University Press.

Forester, J. (1999). *The deliberative practitioner: Encouraging participatory planning processes*. Cambridge, MA: MIT Press.

Forester, J. (2009). *Dealing with differences: Dramas of mediating public disputes*. Oxford: Oxford University Press.

Gauthier, M., & Simard, L. (2011). Le Bureau d'audiences publiques sur l'environnement du Québec: Genèse et développement d'un instrument voué à la participation publique. *Téléscope*, *17*(1), 39–67.

Gourgues, G. (2012). Les fonctionnaires participatifs: Les routines d'une innovation institutionnelle sans fin(s). *Socio-Logos* (7). Retrieved from http://socio-logos.revues.org/2654

Hendriks, C. M., & Carson, L. (2008). Can the market help the forum? Negotiating the commercialization of deliberative democracy. *Policy Sciences*, *41*(4), 293–313.

Lee, C. W. (2011). Five assumptions academics make about public deliberation, and why they deserve rethinking. *Journal of Public Deliberation*, *7*(1). Retrieved from http://www.publicdeliberation.net/jpd/vol7/iss1/art7/

Lee, C. W. (2014). Walking the talk: The performance of authenticity in public engagement work. *The Sociological Quarterly*, *55*(3), 493–513.

Lee, C. W. (2015). *Do-it-yourself democracy: The rise of the public engagement industry*. Oxford: Oxford University Press.

Lee, C. W., McNulty, K., & Shaffer, S. (2013). "Hard times, hard choices": Marketing retrenchment as civic empowerment in an era of neoliberal crisis. *Socio-Economic Review*, *11*(1), 81–106.

Lee, C. W., & Romano, Z. (2013). Democracy's new discipline: Public deliberation as organizational strategy. *Organization Studies*, *34*(5–6), 733–753.

Mazeaud, A. (2012). Administrer la participation: L'invention d'un métier entre valorisation du militantisme et professionnalisation de la démocratie locale. *Quaderni*, *79*, 45–58.

Mazeaud, A., Nonjon, M., & Parizet, R. (2016). Les circulations transnationales de l'ingénierie participative. *Participations*, *1*(14), 5–35.

Medvic, S. K. (2006). Understanding campaign strategy: "Deliberate priming" and the role of professional political consultants. *Journal of Political Marketing*, *5*(1–2), 11–32.

Moore, A. (2012). Following from the front: Theorizing deliberative facilitation. *Critical Policy Studies*, *6*(2), 146–162.

Nonjon, M. (2005). Professionnels de la participation: Savoir gérer son image militante. *Politix*, *2*(70), 89–112.

Polletta, F. (2015). Public deliberation and political contention. In C. W. Lee, M. McQuarrie & E. T. Walker (Eds.), *Democratizing inequalities: Dilemmas of the new public participation* (pp. 222–246). New York: NYU Press.

Revel, M., Blatrix, C., Blondiaux, L., Fourniau, J. M., Hériard Dubreuil, B., & Lefebvre, R. (Eds.). (2007). *Le débat public: Une expérience française de démocratie participative.* Paris: La Découverte.

Schier, S. E. (2000). *By invitation only: The rise of exclusive politics in the United States.* Pittsburgh, PA: University of Pittsburgh Press.

Simard, L. (2008). Conducting projects in uncertain times: The case of electric power lines. *Public Works Management & Policy, 12*(4), 578–589.

Smith, G. (2009). *Democratic innovations: Designing institutions for citizen participation.* Cambridge: Cambridge University Press.

Svallfors, S. (2016). Out of the golden cage: PR and the career opportunities of policy professionals. *Politics & Policy, 44*(1), 56–73.

Walker, E. T. (2014). *Grassroots for hire: Public affairs consultants in American democracy.* New York: Cambridge University Press.

SECTION I
Specific Context

2

INNOVATING PUBLIC PARTICIPATION

The Role of PPPs and Institutions in Italy

Rodolfo Lewanski[1] *and Stefania Ravazzi*

Introduction

Public participation processes—that is, practices aimed at directly involving citizens in policymaking through informed discussion forums (Fung, 2003)—are spreading in many countries. Designing such processes, especially when they are organized as "mixed discursive spheres involving politicians, administrators, organized actors, experts and ordinary citizens" (Hendriks, 2006), is a delicate and relevant activity, as it affects the quality and performance of the processes and their legitimacy (Parkinson, 2006)—and therefore the diffusion of such practices—as well as their capacity to have an impact on policy decisions. However, notwithstanding its key role, the design of public participation processes has only recently begun to attract the attention of the scientific community (Chilvers, 2008).

Participatory processes are generally designed (and managed) by professional facilitators (Hendriks & Carson, 2008); also, new institutional frameworks are spreading with the aim of promoting and regulating the public participation field. Both factors (PPPs and institutional frameworks) seem to be crucial in explaining how and why the public participation field develops and changes. On the one hand, professionals "are at the heart of the supply of participation approaches" (Bherer, 2011, p. 13), and the challenge they face is typically to reconcile intrinsic quality according to their values and standards while taking into account and dealing with social and political pressures.

On the other hand, institutional frameworks increase the chances that participation will be influential and protect it from risks of misuse or outright manipulation. To institutionalize participation means to make it a routine practice (Pellizzoni, 2005, p. 484), incorporating it into the ways that public decisions are taken (Fagotto & Fung, 2009, p. 42). Moreover, as I. Budge notes (2000, p. 195), institutional frameworks can be especially important in promoting innovative forms of participation. Institutional frameworks can in fact offer guarantees of impartiality, can contribute to the legitimacy of such processes, and can allow citizens to get back political power (Rosanvallon, 2008, pp. 350–351). However, such frameworks carry the risk of excessive formalization and "ritualization" (Alluli, 2011, p. 446), and might also cause loss of support, especially from societal actors.

The aim of the chapter is to contribute to the exploration of the complex design activity that occurs within institutionalized contexts. The field of inquiry is Italy, one of the few countries where public participation has been partially institutionalized through ad hoc legislation, dedicated funds, and regulatory agencies. Italy today features a broad market of PPPs; also, in two Italian regions, well-established institutional frameworks have been in place for several years now.

The Italian context thus allows us to address two main research questions, which are connected to the factors that seem to be influential in generating shared visions of public participation and in fostering innovative approaches to citizen engagement. First, what does public participation mean in the perceptions and views of its designers and managers? Are Italian PPPs divided by competing and somehow opposed visions and practices, or do they form a sort of epistemic community? Our second question addresses the role played by institutional frameworks: do they foster innovation in the "public participation industry" (Hendriks & Carson, 2008)?

In order to tackle these questions, two surveys were conducted between 2013 and 2014. With the first survey, 21 PPPs, representative of the best-known Italian consulting firms active in public participation design and facilitation, were interviewed to trace the profile of the Italian public participation industry: that is, to obtain the PPPs' views and storylines (Hendriks, 2005) on public participation, on some of the tendencies in methods and strategies, and on common grounds and differences. Because of the absence of official registers, a snowball approach was used to identify the PPPs to be interviewed in order to ensure a degree of representativeness across the country (Table 2.1). In the second survey, another 20 interviews were conducted with PPPs involved in the design and management of 10 processes[2] in each of the two regions that have introduced specific legislation on public participation: Tuscany and Emilia-Romagna.[3] Cases were selected in order to obtain a broad sample of processes designed and facilitated by different practitioners.[4] Respondents were asked to explain the principles and strategies that they followed in designing "process x" (that is, the specific process funded under one of the two abovementioned institutional frameworks), and which factors affected their decisions. This survey in particular was aimed at understanding how the two institutional frameworks affected the PPPs' design activity. Both surveys were conducted through interviews based on in-depth semi-structured questionnaires (only one closed question was included in the second survey).[5] Also, documentary sources were used to highlight the main lines of convergence and the differences between the two institutional frameworks that have been introduced so far.

TABLE 2.1 Consulting Firms Included in the First Survey (2013)

Company name	Headquarters
ABCittà	Milan
Ascolto Attivo	Turin
Avanzi	Milan
Avventura Urbana	Turin
Cantieri Animati	Florence
Cantieri Comuni	Rome
Città Fertile	Galatina
Città Possibili	Milan
Conetica	Bari
ElaborAzioni	Bari
Focus Lab	Modena
Genius Loci	Milan
Laboratorio Città	Bassano del Grappa
L'Ombrello	Venice
Metodi	Milan
Poliste	Cagliari
Sociolab	Florence
Università di Firenze	Florence
Politecnico di Torino	Turin
Università di Catania	Catania

In order to address the second research question, we defined innovation as change from "shallow" traditional public participation practices along five dimensions loosely derived from deliberative democracy theory: participant recruitment, information, conversation format, decision rules, and empowerment (Dryzek & Niemeyer, 2008).

Deliberative theory proposes the equal inclusion of viewpoints (through random sampling)[6] as a more democratic alternative to the traditional "open door" model, which tends to unbalance the arena in favour of the organized stakeholders. However provided (written materials, hearings with experts), heterogeneous and detailed information on the issue at stake is considered essential in order to move from an instinctive and unaware mobilization to informed participation. Assembly formats are considered more traditional and less dialogical as compared with structured methods aimed at enhancing communicative interaction in an appropriate atmosphere of mutual trust, respect, and equal expression of all viewpoints. As far as decision-making is concerned, deliberative processes are aimed at reaching some form of final outcome; usually, consensus is sought, but voting is also considered acceptable (Fung & Wright, 2003; Setälä, 2014, p. 149) and often used. Finally, deliberative democracy theory insists on processes exerting at least some degree of influence on decision-making rather than on the first "steps" of the participation "ladder," that is, performing only an information or consultation role (Arnstein, 1969).

The chapter starts by framing the issue of public participation design. Then, the main features of the Italian participation "industry" and the profile of the two regional institutional frameworks are outlined. The main findings of the research are illustrated in the subsequent two sections: the first reconstructs what public participation means for Italian PPPs; the second highlights how institutional frameworks affected the design activity of 20 processes in Tuscany and Emilia-Romagna, and whether and how these different frameworks fostered innovation in the public participation industry.

Designing Public Participation

Participatory designs may vary, within a wide range of possible options, from standard formats such as participatory budgets, citizen juries, or 21st Century Town Meetings to hybrid processes that creatively combine public participation methods and facilitation techniques in a variety of ways (Bherer & Breux, 2012; Bishop & Davis, 2002; Cooper & Smith, 2012; Fung, 2006).

Among the few studies that address the issue of the participatory design in a comprehensive manner, the classification of "democratic innovations" proposed by Smith (2009) is a clear example of how different design dimensions can be intertwined in public participation processes. Smith identifies four different types of such innovations: (1) popular discussion assemblies, open to the general public and characterized by weak facilitation and almost absent deliberative traits; (2) popular forums composed of randomly selected citizens and usually organized as small discussion groups actively facilitated by professionals; (3) online discussion forums, which may swing from (1) to (2) depending on the characters of the online arenas and the approaches used by the online moderators; and (4) direct legislation, composed of popular referendums and initiatives, which taken alone do not require any management and facilitation, but which combined with other methods can contribute to the design of a participatory process.

Aspects emerging from other studies (Chilvers, 2008; Cooper & Smith, 2012; Lewanski, 2013b; Ravazzi, 2013; Steiner, 2012) also suggest that public participation design can be considered as the result of a number of procedural and substantive choices, such as the timing and location, the criteria used for recruiting participants, the definition of the agenda, the framing of the briefing materials, the role of experts, the integration between online and face-to-face arenas, the channels of communication between the forum and the general public, the communicative interactions between participants and non-participants, and of course the discussion formats themselves.

The specific combination of these dimensions and methods may be affected by a number of factors. This analysis focuses specifically on two such factors: the "culture" of practitioners and the influence of institutional frameworks.

Practitioners can be driven by shared participatory storylines, approaches, and meanings (Bherer & Breux, 2012), as well as by common non-competing commercial interests (Hendriks & Carson, 2008). On the contrary, they can also be driven by different participatory storylines, approaches, and meanings and by competing commercial interests. In the former case, we can consider them as an epistemic community, with shared beliefs and common practices. In the latter case, the public participation industry can be considered rather as a divided or even fragmented arena of competing actors.

This difference between the two is not only analytic, as it carries relevant implications. According to Bherer and Breux (2012), it is plausible that the goal of public participation may be defined by practitioners in different and even irreconcilable ways: from an instrumental perspective, public participation can be seen as a decision-making tool aimed at improving the policy process, reducing conflict, and producing more consensual decisions; from an ethical perspective instead, public participation can be considered as an opportunity to open up new spaces for the expression of different viewpoints and opinions and is not necessarily aimed at producing consensual solutions.

Furthermore, practitioner culture is influenced by the "commercialization" of public participation, which has led to a competitive market mostly composed of small-sized organizations (Hendriks & Carson, 2008). As in any market, consultants try to occupy a share that is as large as possible, in order to protect themselves against fluctuations and reduce competition. So public participation practitioners might well act in the same way, by selling specific formats or methods in order to secure their primacy in the market (Cooper & Smith, 2012). This fragmentation could lead to design choices that are driven more by the instrumental aim of beating competitors than by the substantive aim of designing "good" processes: in the end, clashing participatory storylines could undermine the quality of participation and its overall effectiveness. On the other hand, some professionals might choose to foster a high-standard "image" by accepting to work only for quality processes in order to access and protect specific niches of the consulting market.

Participatory design and PPPs' choices are also likely to be influenced by the specific requests made by clients, usually public administrations, that promote the processes and are responsible for the final policy decisions. The relationship with these actors is delicate and challenging for PPPs, as the former may be keen to embrace specific design choices that better fit their participatory storylines or suit their instrumental aims. This job, like that of any other consultant—especially in the public sphere—can potentially suffer from a tension between professional standards and client imperatives. If client pressures strongly affect the design of a participatory process, the process itself could be "derailed" to satisfy instrumental aims, while affecting its efficacy and quality (Hendriks & Carson, 2008). A survey by Cooper and Smith (2012, p. 23) concerning PPPs' relationships with their clients, for example, revealed that some British and German practitioners are frustrated because clients tend to "follow a particular fashion in public participation, often pressing for inappropriate designs rather than considering the best model for the particular issue."

Furthermore, pressures from the social context, especially in complex or particularly controversial cases, can significantly affect the design of a process, inducing practitioners to partially change it before or during its implementation. These pressures can be contentious since participatory practices are often perceived to challenge the established patterns of relations among politicians, civil society actors, and ordinary citizens (Bobbio, 2013; Pomatto & Ravazzi, 2012). Such pressures also raise the issue of the extent to which adaptation strategies are acceptable, or instead conflict with professional norms and standards as well as with process quality.

Institutional frameworks, the second factor that we consider, have for a long time not represented a major challenge for engagement in general; more specifically, PPPs have usually practiced public participation according to informal formats. However, since the 1990s, a number of governments (local, regional, and national) have undertaken steps toward the institutionalization of the public participation field through the introduction of regulatory frameworks. The institutionalization issue is not yet well developed in the participatory/deliberative literature, but it is plausible that specific institutional frameworks could both foster and broaden, as well as, on the contrary, "trap" and standardize the public participation field.

PPPs become, in this sense, not only designers of decision-making processes, but also mediators who have to deal with different and even opposing forces (Bherer, 2011). How do they manage to face all these pressures while designing and conducting public participation processes? Which approach do they use and which strategies and methods do they apply? Do they share common visions and beliefs, or are they split into different strands of thought and different communities of practice? The Italian case can offer some interesting insights into these questions.

The Italian Public Participation Field: Two New Institutional Frameworks and a Heterogeneous Market

Compared with other countries, Italy has traditionally not been a "front runner" in the field of public participation. Citizen engagement began entering the public arena in the 1970s, in connection with urban planning and development projects (Gbikpi, 2005; Moini, 2012). During the 1990s, participation practices touched other policy areas such as the environment, especially in connection with Local Agenda 21 (after the Rio Conference of 1991), budgeting, social and welfare policies, and local development (Moini, 2012). Generally speaking, whereas participation in the 1970s was more bottom-up, ideological, and conflictual, in the 1990s it became more top-down—that is, promoted by public administrations—with low levels of antagonism (Moini, 2012). Many European Union policies, requiring some form of participation, also contributed to the diffusion of such practices in Italy.

In more recent years, participation has spread more broadly in different parts of the country and has involved a number of topics and a variety of methodological approaches (Bobbio, 2007). This diffusion has been fostered in particular by local governments, but some regional governments have also made a significant contribution by introducing institutional frameworks to promote and regulate public participation in policymaking (Font, Della Porta & Sintomer, 2014). Apulia and Latium, for example, introduced public participation requirements in land use planning laws or budgeting procedures in the early 2000s (Cellamare, 2010; Font et al., 2014; Goni & Troisi, 2013; Troisi & Buonocore, 2010). In 2007 and 2010 respectively, two regions, Tuscany and Emilia-Romagna, took a step forward by introducing specific laws, dedicated funds, and public agencies to promote, sustain, and regulate the public participation field (Moini, 2012, p. 36).

Although similar in some respects, their institutional frameworks differ in a number of substantial respects. Both the Tuscan Law 69/2007 (later replaced by the similar Law 46/2013) and the Emilia-Romagna Law 3/2010 offer economic support to local communities to carry out participatory policymaking processes concerning issues of local or regional relevance: Tuscany offered support of approximately 650,000 euro/year from 2007 until 2013, and Emilia-Romagna started with smaller but gradually increasing funding (approximately 200,000 euro in 2012, and 350,000 euro in the following years). Also, by requesting that decisions concerning the object of the process be suspended until the process is completed, both laws formally recognize that participation is aimed at exerting at least some influence on decision-making. Both laws also indicate a number of criteria to be respected and other criteria that give priority in access to funding: for example, adoption of specific designs, timing, inclusion of specific actors (associations, citizen committees, women, immigrants, etc.). Finally, ad hoc regional "actors," called an "Authority for public participation" in the Tuscan case and a "*Tecnico di garanzia*" in the Emilia-Romagna case, are assigned the task of funding requests, providing technical guidelines, and offering methodological advice to the proponents.

Notwithstanding these similarities, the two laws appear to be substantially different in their underlying "philosophy" and in how this is translated into specific provisions. The Tuscan law seems to be one of the first attempts to translate the normative principles of deliberative theory into institutional practice (Floridia, 2008; Lewanski, 2013a; Steiner, 2012). In fact, the law explicitly refers to several deliberative milestones that we consider to be innovative traits of public participation practices, namely, inclusion of common citizens and equal expression of different viewpoints through structured dialogical processes; provision of impartial information on the issue at stake; and some degree of real empowerment of citizens. In connection with the latter, in order to gain access to funding, administrations are required to officially declare that they will enact the results of the participation process. Should they deem the outcomes to be less than acceptable, they can override the outcomes only on the condition that they publicly provide the reasons for their decision. Thus, the responsibility of making the final decision remains in the hands of the administration, but *at the very least* they are obliged to account to their citizens.

The Emilia-Romagna law appears to be less ambitious, as citizen participation is presented as a co-decision process in which an agreement is to be reached by "negotiation or mediation" among the main organized actors in the community; no reference is made to public debates, information provision, knowledge sharing, or equal expression of different viewpoints on the issue; and, finally, decision makers are not required to adopt indications emerging from participatory processes, but only to adopt an official document explaining the reasons for their final decisions. Moreover, whereas the latter legislation offers financial and methodological support mainly to public authorities, Tuscany's law is more "open" as it also funds processes proposed by groups of citizens, schools, and firms.[7]

Finally, the Tuscan "Authority" is an independent institution led by an appointed expert in the field, chosen outside the regional administration. The Authority enjoys considerable discretion in making decisions based on professional judgment and plays a pivotal role in developing criteria for participatory processes to be funded. The *Tecnico di garanzia* of Emilia-Romagna also has considerable power, as he can validate the process or, on the contrary, withdraw funding if the process does not respect the originally approved design. However, the *Tecnico di garanzia* has a status that is much less independent from political power, as the role is assigned to a regional civil servant.

Thanks also to these two new institutional frameworks, unprecedented growth has taken place in the public participation industry: tens of facilitation companies and private consultants[8] today compete for mandates to design and conduct participatory processes for local administrations, firms, public institutions, and third-sector organizations. As mentioned above, the regional authorities in question do not directly select the professionals in charge of processes, but rather offer the financial resources to the local administrations and other actors promoting these processes. As such, actors would otherwise lack the human and financial resources required to ensure quality participation; the availability of regional funding plays a very relevant role in developing a professional market in this field.

Our first survey (also confirmed by the second one focusing on the two above-mentioned regional contexts) highlighted quite a heterogeneous landscape in this market: most practitioners had entered the field over the last decade, and no "typical" pathway nor standard background for becoming a professional in the public participation field is identifiable. Indeed, the backgrounds of Italian PPPs appear to be quite diverse (architects, urban planners, political and social scientists, psychologists, trainers) and their training seldom presents a clear-cut connection with public participation.

Furthermore, their expertise has mainly been developed through "learning by doing" rather than through specific training programs: whereas some professionals (especially architects and urban planners; urban planning, as mentioned above, represents the field in which participation had been practiced since the 1970s) had encountered the topic of public participation during their university studies, the initial interest of many in this new topic stemmed, rather randomly, so to say, from the writings and real-world experiments of a small number of academic "mentors." Moreover, almost all of the professionals completed their education in the field through personal reading, by taking part in conferences and courses in connected areas, and in general by getting involved in participatory processes both as designers and as facilitators of group dialogues. Some small networks have contributed to the dissemination of ideas in this field (for instance, the Italian association of urban planners INU, the Italian affiliate of the International Association for Public Participation IAP2, and the Italian chapter of the International Association of Facilitators IAF), but this has occurred only quite recently.

What Does Public Participation Mean? Visions, Participatory Storylines, and Practices of Italian PPPs

This section is devoted to the first research question, which concerns the characteristics of the Italian community of PPPs. In looking in particular at the level of commonality of its values and visions, what kind of community do Italian PPPs form: an epistemic community, a community of practice, or a fragmented community? The analysis focuses on three main dimensions, which together allow us to trace the profile of this community: (1) the general conception of public participation and its role in representative democracies; (2) the PPPs' visions of the objectives of the participatory processes and the PPPs' "storylines" (Hendriks, 2005), which concern key issues, such as who should be involved, what role information should have, and whether and how the processes should be structured and facilitated; and (3) the practical strategies needed to effectively lead the participatory processes.

Both the first and second surveys reveal that the PPPs seem to be driven by a common conception of public participation goals but, at the same time, by partially different participatory visions and storylines.

Most of the professionals interviewed are strongly convinced that citizen engagement is of utmost importance as "an answer to the democratic deficit of politics" (I35 [Interviewee 35]): rebuilding trust and developing shared projects is one possible way of overcoming the present crisis in traditional representation and of re-establishing an acceptable level of democratic legitimacy. The words of two PPPs effectively synthesize a widely shared belief:

> Politics in itself no longer has either the credibility or the authoritativeness to carry out projects if not shared with citizens and social actors.
>
> *(I28)*

> Citizen involvement, if it is well done, is extremely important to rebuild a feeling of active responsibility, of civic engagement, in citizens who are increasingly detached from public institutions.
>
> *(I29)*

In the views of most PPPs, to "open up" to citizens does not mean to shift political power from representatives to the people but to build a shared responsibility in decision-making processes and in general in the public sphere. This would improve several aspects of public administration: there would be fewer conflictual relationships between institutions and citizens, better decisions would be made, and citizens would be more aware of the complexity and constraints of public decision-making.

However, a sizeable group of PPPs is more concerned about revitalizing society in keeping with a bottom-up perspective: participation is seen as a way of regenerating communities, of favouring horizontal subsidiarity and active citizenship, and more in general as a way of satisfying a desire for participation in the public sphere that could be expressed not only through mobilizations and protests. Others instead view public participation from a more policy-oriented perspective: participation is seen primarily as a way to generate more consensual, stable, and effective decisions. These two strands thus hold partially diverse participatory visions, and around them two quite different storylines also seem to take shape in regard to the specific dimensions that we have considered as defining the innovative traits of participation in line with a deliberative type of approach. In this connection, it is interesting to note that a recognized or official code of conduct for PPPs to follow or to refer to does not yet exist in Italy;[9] indeed, the PPPs interviewed were not even aware that such codes in fact exist in other countries, nor did they seem to feel the need for them, stating that they have more or less implicit personal ideas about appropriate behaviour for PPPs.

Generally speaking, the professionals believe that quality of participation means the inclusion of all viewpoints. This said, the PPPs appear to be divided in the ways that they pursue such an objective in practice. Those with a community-building vision of public participation prefer the traditional self-selection principle of the "open door" model. This approach privileges de facto organized actors such as associations, active citizen groups, and interest groups. On the contrary, the idea of using more innovative forms of recruitment, such as random sampling, targeted recruitment, or hybrids of the former, is increasingly attracting the attention of those PPPs with a more policy-focused vision. In the opinion of some respondents, "these methods increase the capacity of the process to reach ordinary people, who otherwise would never show up" (I32). These professionals are aware that involving organized stakeholder groups poses a serious risk of involving mainly the "usual suspects" or of the process outcome being strategically "derailed" in order to favour particular interests.

Moreover, although many respondents seem to agree with the statement that "participants should come out of the process more aware and informed than when they entered; also, the language used should be understandable by lay persons" (I36), the information provided to participants before and during the process does not in fact constitute a major concern for the community-oriented PPPs.

A sizeable group of respondents agrees that participation needs to be facilitated and structured by using ad hoc methods. In their words, "participation can produce personal and reciprocal enrichment provided it is structured, inclusive and there is a real dialogue" (I29), and provided that "it follows rules and has some principles" (I22), and that it is "defined in [its] timing, with specific goals" (I30). PPPs keep a number of methods in their state-of-the-art toolbox, which they tend to "mix and match" (Holman, 2007) in order to structure communicative interaction, favour an appropriate atmosphere of mutual trust and respect, and foster constructive policy-making processes. Some of them have also developed sophisticated frames in this respect, in, for example, distinguishing between "cold" (Open Space Technology or OST, Future Lab) and "hot" methods (storytelling labs, Theatre of the Oppressed). However, structured dialogue (facilitated through specific techniques and cognitive frameworks and driven by the same PPPs) seems to be less important for community-oriented PPPs. In several processes, there was no dialogue facilitation at all, or political and administrative personnel in the local administration acted as facilitators, a choice that carries considerable potential bias as they are directly involved as sponsors of the processes and thus cannot ensure the required level of neutrality.

The difference between the two strands also emerges in relation to another process aspect: "policy-oriented" PPPs place great importance on getting at some kind of outcome (a recommendation, a decision, a plan, etc.) whatever the rule used, be it a consensus or a vote. "Community-building" professionals appear to be much more interested in generating relationships and social capital among participants and within the broader community.

Finally, the influence actually exerted by engagement processes on decisions is clearly perceived as a central element by PPPs. In this respect, the professionals find themselves caught in the crossfire, so to say, between citizens and clients. They must assert their autonomy from the client if they are to ensure the trust of citizens, who, initially at least, tend to identify them with the administration. The risk of instrumental, symbolic, or manipulative uses of engagement processes, in which decisions are already made beforehand by the clients and citizens' opinions are not taken into account, is present in the minds of many professionals. However, PPPs deal with these risks by adopting different approaches. One group stresses the importance of focusing the processes on real and concrete aspects, which participants see as directly concerning their own lives, as well as the relevance of monitoring the implementation phase. Another group of respondents, on the contrary, emphasizes a different aspect, connected with a community-building vision: that is, that participation is influential insofar as it generates social capital; participation is meant to improve trust and understanding between the administration and citizens, and to enhance civic action.

While the participatory storylines seem to somewhat split the PPPs into two strands, they are actually not so far apart when it comes to practical strategies: neutrality, transparency, issue-focus, and outreach are widely considered by the PPPs as the most important design imperatives.

The practice of neutrality is recognized by all as the fundamental starting point in any participatory process. Neutrality does not imply ignorance or lack of interest in the issue. In fact, some PPPs are "substantive experts" in specific policy sectors, such as environmental policies or urban planning. Neutrality has more to do with a sort of "suspension of judgment" on the issue at stake or, as one PPP has described it, "equidistance from the issue and from the policy makers' opinions" (I34).

"Transparency" concerns the PPPs' relations with their clients. The tension arising from clients' imperatives is common in any consulting activity, and many Italian PPPs are well aware of this. Public participation can give rise to difficulties in dealing with public authorities and civil servants, because these are processes that the latter are not used to, that are generally perceived as appropriate or fashionable, but that are also seen as threatening their turf. Many PPPs admit that the focus for many political actors is mostly on gaining consensus and visibility for themselves, rather than reaching a consensual and fair decision on a controversial issue or empowering citizens in order to strengthen democracy.[10] The PPPs' strategy in this respect thus consists in making the public authority explicitly clarify its real commitment, and in verifying the real boundaries of the issue at stake in the process (what is the real objective of the process, which options are really available and which are not); their aim is to build trust and create the appropriate climate for an autonomous design activity and process management.[11]

The words of one of the PPPs interviewed are typical of the comments made by many of the professionals in this respect:

> The aim is always to clarify beforehand with the Administration what stakes they are willing to make available in the processes, and which they are not, and the reciprocal engagements of the involved parties.
>
> *(I31)*

Although some skepticism may remain, in the end this strategy seems to be sufficient to reduce clients' pressures concerning the design and management choices made. According to the PPPs, public authorities in fact usually have limited knowledge about participatory methods and approaches and confused ideas of how to design public participation processes other than petitions or referenda.[12] Also, in the second survey it was found that PPPs had to deal with such problems in only four of the twenty processes, and, even in these cases, they managed to deal with them without deviating too much from the original process design.

A third common strategy is to design the process starting from the specific characteristics of the issue at stake. One practitioner summarized a widely shared practical imperative with these words:

> [T]he key task of the facilitation activity primarily concerns the formulation of the right questions to address the specific issue at stake and the choice of the right methods and techniques for that issue. And the type

TABLE 2.2 Participatory Processes Included in the Second Survey (2014)

Region	Name of the process	Policy area	Topic
Emilia-Romagna	Fiumana partecipa!	Culture and leisure	Planning of activities in a public space
	Rigenerare il sociale	Social policy	Services for disabled people
	Comune Par Tot	Culture and leisure	Summer activities in a city neighbourhood
	Crev.Azione agire per costruire	Urban restructuring	Public works for a town centre after the earthquake
	Nessuna scossa fermerà il nostro cuore	Seismic risk	Rules to prevent seismic damage to buildings
	Qui c'entro	Sustainable mobility	Bicycle paths between a town centre and its suburbs
	Brisighella Comune ospitale	Economic development	Local tourism services
	Empowerment e qualità lavoro	Social policy	Labour policies for unemployed residents
	Uno più uno uguale a tre	Culture and leisure	Planning of youth activities in a public space
	Laboratorio partecipativo per il Progetto Urbano integrato	Urban restructuring	Public works for a town after the earthquake
Tuscany	Biogas a Buonconvento? Parliamone!	Energy policy	Citing criteria for an energy production plant
	Barberino fa 100	Urban planning	Public works for a municipal territory
	Contiamo nell'Unione	Urban planning and public service evaluation	Public works for a municipal territory and evaluation of local public services
	Il Comune siamo noi	Urban planning	Public works for a municipal territory
	Cascina partecipa	Urban planning	Public works for a municipal territory
	Insieme per capire insieme per decidere	Land use policy	Planning of a new waste disposal plant
	Una Protezione Civile Partecipata Comunico	Disaster prevention	Reform of the municipal disaster prevention plan
	Bilancio in "Comune"	Urban planning	Public works for a municipal territory
		Urban planning and public service evaluation	Public works for a municipal territory and evaluation of local public services
	Programmiamo Insieme la Salute	Public health policy	Local public health plan

of issue does not have to do with its policy area, such as environmental or social policies, but with the type of population affected by the issue and with its level of conflict and complexity.

(19)

In the 20 processes considered in the second survey, the issue at stake was the most important variable that the PPPs interviewed took into consideration in process design (Table 2.2).

Finally, all the PPPs use some type of "outreach" method: that is, an ethnographic approach that requires preliminary qualitative inquiries (interviews, analysis of local media) in the communities where a participatory process is meant to take place and consisting mainly in reaching people in their everyday life places instead of inviting them to come to ad hoc meetings. According to the practitioners interviewed, outreach is useful insofar as it allows them to map active conflicts, the existing or potential stakeholders, the public discourse on the issue, and the way that the issues are framed by the actors. As one professional recalled:

> You understand which aspects interest them more. Maybe you find out that people have no clear ideas or that their ideas are too clear (rigid, fixed, stereotyped), yet this is extremely important, because you understand which things are most cited, which lexicon they use, and so you begin to be part of that community, at least to some extent and for a short time.
>
> *(16)*

Outreach is also considered essential because it allows PPPs to get acquainted with people and to involve those who are usually absent in the public and political spheres.

In summary, although driven by a shared vision of the role that public participation should play in our representative democracies, the Italian PPPs do not form an epistemic community whose members share common beliefs and imperatives. Instead, they seem to be divided into two different strands of thought: on one side, PPPs oriented toward community building, and on the other, more policy-oriented PPPs. These two sub-communities seem to have somewhat opposite participatory storylines, with the second group being closer to the deliberative ideal of public participation. At the same time, in the Italian case the public participation industry does not appear as fragmented, but rather as a community of practice, as most PPPs share a number of practical strategies in designing and managing processes.

Fostering Innovation or Standardization in the Public Participation Field? How the Two Institutional Frameworks Have Affected PPPs' Design Activities

The main differences between the two institutional frameworks have been traced in detail, but it may be useful to briefly reprise them here: (a) the Tuscan framework shows a clear commitment to deliberative democracy, through references to structured public debates, knowledge sharing, equal expression of different viewpoints, and citizen empowerment, while the Emilia-Romagna framework is closer to the traditional stakeholder mediation model; (b) the Tuscan Authority is chosen among experts in public participation and deliberative democracy[13] and has a pivotal role in developing deliberative criteria for participatory processes to obtain funding, whereas the *Tecnico di garanzia* is not properly an authority (although we occasionally refer to both regional entities with this term), since its role, assigned to a regional civil servant, is more technical and bureaucratic and less independent from the administration.

In the light of these characteristics, we can expect that the two institutional frameworks affected the PPPs' design activities for the 20 processes in different ways: the Tuscan framework could have fostered more innovation and diffusion of the deliberative model, while the Emilia-Romagna framework could have opened the way for both the models, thus reproducing the differences within the PPP community.

According to the 20 practitioners interviewed in the second survey, both institutional frameworks generally helped to create trust among citizens and stakeholders thanks to a number of elements: (a) the setting out of some precise rules for the public administrations that wanted to carry out a process; (b) the attribution of an official status to the participatory processes; and (c) the official recognition of the role of professional skills in the public participation field.

Both the laws and the two "authorities" also affected the processes by framing the PPPs' design activities. As a Tuscan PPP and an Emilia-Romagna PPP effectively summarized:

> The process was necessarily designed to take into account the official or informal requirements that increased the chances of obtaining funding from the [Tuscan] Authority.
>
> *(I26)*

> The [Emilia-Romagna] law was a reference point while we were designing the process. We paid particular attention to some aspects like the formal agreement with the local political authorities, the legal act to temporarily suspend any official decisional process on the issue by the municipal council and so on, in order to increase the probability of getting funding.
>
> *(I37)*

However, according to the PPPs, the two institutional frameworks affected the process designs in different ways and led to different outcomes.

In Tuscany, the law was more explicit in setting out a specific approach, and the Authority in fact played a strong role, in exerting considerable influence (and even "interfering," according to some respondents) on aspects such as participant recruitment, evaluation, the use of specific methods, impartiality guarantees, etc., and often changing the original projects presented by proponents. Formally, proponents (usually local authorities, but also schools and groups of citizens) requesting regional funding to support their processes were required to contact the Authority and discuss the projects with him/her, but usually, the proponents—lacking knowledge and previous experience in the field—were assisted by professionals, and sometimes completely delegated to them the task of interacting with the Authority. As a result, the professionals had to consider the requirements of both the law and the Authority, and to broker them to their clients. The Tuscan PPPs recognized that they had been pushed toward some innovative approaches that were usually applied in deliberative processes, and which in some cases were being applied by the PPPs for the first time. One practitioner summarized a consideration that was shared by all the other Tuscan PPPs interviewed:

> The regional law influenced the design of the process, giving it a general framework. . . . The Authority has systematically affected methodological aspects and the structure of the processes since the beginning of his mandate.
>
> *(I29)*

All the processes did in fact contain all of the following deliberative elements: stakeholder committees with a steering, supervising, and guaranteeing role, provision of information material and hearings with experts, at least partial random sampling to recruit ordinary citizens, and structured dialogical sessions. Also, all of the processes were designed to reach a defined outcome, either by consensus or by voting.

According to several Tuscan PPPs, the more binding nature of the Tuscan law and the stronger steering role of the Authority as described above led to the widespread practice of applying the innovative deliberative model, but at the same time, this driving force also led to some extent to the homogenization and standardization of the participatory processes. As one Tuscan PPP stated polemically:

> If you look at the design of the processes that were financed under the law and the supervision of the Authority, you find mostly random sampling arenas with a preliminary information session, no matter what kind of issue they have to face. Do you think this is the right way to design participatory processes?
>
> *(I27)*

These pressures were felt to be particularly strong especially by those PPPs who had a community-building vision of public participation, because they were apt to leave more room for spontaneity and to place less importance on the structuring of the process.

The Emilia-Romagna law and its *Tecnico di garanzia* were perceived as somewhat "softer" intervening factors in the PPPs' design activities. In particular, the law introduced some general methodological criteria, such as the use of preliminary inquiries about the issue at stake and the involvement of the stakeholders. On the whole, as all the Emilia-Romagna PPPs recognized, the law was useful mostly in providing financial resources and in monitoring such aspects as aligning the participatory process with existing administrative rules and procedures. Also, the *Tecnico di garanzia* was perceived as mainly being concerned about the respecting of formal requirements, rather than being substantively oriented toward specific models of public participation. Some PPPs never even contacted the *Tecnico*, and when the latter did intervene, he usually did so by suggesting only marginal changes in regard to the timing and the bureaucratic requirements.

Thanks to the "soft" and mainly formal role of the regional *Tecnico*, the 10 processes in Emilia-Romagna were able to resort to a very broad spectrum of participatory methods, ranging from OST to Planning for Real, from FutureLab to Sato laboratory, from World Café to Samoan Circle. However, the format of all of the processes except one was clearly closer to the traditional model of public participation, in mostly involving associations and interest groups while neglecting aspects such as the involvement of ordinary citizens and the building of shared knowledge on the issue at stake. Within this framework, the more policy-oriented practitioners also generally neglected to apply innovative approaches suggested by deliberative theory. So why did policy-oriented PPPs, who in general proved to be more attached to the deliberative ideal, also follow the traditional self-selection and uninformed participation model? The size of our sample does not allow us to provide a firm answer to this question, but a plausible explanation was offered by one of the interviewees: applying the deliberative approach requires much more effort and resources, in terms of personnel, time, expertise, coordination, and money. The only professional in Emilia-Romagna who focused on making adequate information available to participants in fact described this as an extremely time- and energy-consuming activity:

> The information phase was fundamental for the process . . . but the effort to find the right experts, to gather them together and to make them explain difficult matters in comprehensible language was huge . . . and everything went fast and all the material had to be transcribed and put on the website!
>
> *(I36)*

In summary, the two institutional frameworks not only exerted a function of legitimizing the public participation field and the PPPs' role within it, but also had an influence on the PPPs' design activities. However, this influence varied significantly in the two cases and led to different outcomes. In Tuscany, the institutional framework in fact fostered an innovative approach to the participation model traditionally used in the region before Law 69/07, in pushing the processes in the direction of the deliberative model; but it also constrained the field by to some extent homogenizing and standardizing the designs. In Emilia-Romagna, the institutional framework has had a weaker substantive influence, favouring heterogeneity among the methods used; but it has hardly encouraged innovation in the direction of the deliberative model.

Conclusions

Our initial research questions concerned two broad factors capable of influencing the design of participatory processes: first, the practitioners' culture, that is, their general vision of public participation and the specific participatory storylines implemented in practice; and, second, the role of institutional frameworks—specifically in the form of legislation and the public authorities in charge of implementing this legislation—in fostering innovation in the field. The case of Italy, one of the few countries where public participation has been institutionalized to some extent through ad hoc legislation, offers some interesting insights, as it appears to confirm the relevance of such factors in promoting innovative practices, as opposed to "shallow" traditional participation.

Concerning the first aspect, the picture that emerges from the surveys seems quite clear: in process design, the culture of practitioners, including their visions and storylines, plays a key role. Our findings show that the design of participatory processes is affected by a divided PPP culture. Although diversity is by no means negative per se, in this case there is an evident lack of common ground due to the absence of ad hoc "channels" (such as training or official codes of practice) through which practitioners can share professional norms and standards; this cleavage may undermine the quality and effectiveness of public participation and, in the long run, its fate as an innovative approach to collective governance.

Professionals in the field do share some basic concepts of public participation, in seeing it as a way to integrate and enrich representative democracy. They view their role as being that of independent and impartial consultants. They also share the use of some practical strategies, such as neutrality, transparency, and the early definition of the issue at stake with the clients, as well as the need for "outreach" to the social and political context in order to identify conflicts, interests, discourses, and stakeholders.

However, in their participatory storylines, Italian professionals are divided into two quite distinct strands, which we label as "community-building" and "policy-oriented": while some of them mainly consider public participation processes as a means of regenerating communities and making better citizens, others are much more concerned about the role that public participation can have in increasing policy effectiveness and legitimacy. This diversity to some extent confirms the hypotheses of Martin (2009) and Bherer and Breux (2012), according to which some practitioners may hold a more instrumental view (the policy-oriented vision), whereas others hold a more ethical one (the community-building vision). If we look at the criteria which these professionals state that they usually apply, this polarization emerges even more strongly.

Although only a few respondents say that they use a "standard technique" (thus confirming Cooper and Smith's findings on the British and German contexts), community-oriented practitioners mostly use less-innovative designs insofar as they adopt an "open door" approach (sometimes combined with an opinion poll), pay less attention to participant information aspects, and rarely use structured dialogue methods; all in all, respondents in this group seem to be hardly aware of the variety of options and approaches available and of the implications involved in their use.

Practitioners with a more policy-oriented vision are instead more likely to experiment with innovative approaches: they avoid the "open door" or at least integrate it with other recruitment criteria, provide information through documents and presentations by experts and stakeholders, totally reject the assembly model in using a variety of methods to structure dialogue, and are keen to ensure that processes actually reach an outcome, either by consensus or by voting (although only a few PPPs seem to have reflected on this aspect and to be aware of the implications of these diverse options).

The institutionalization of participation has proven to be very influential, as it in fact favours the proliferation of participatory processes which, in the dire financial situation presently experienced by local governments, would never take place without the financial contribution of the regions; in the first place, without the availability of such resources, the enhancement of process quality would indeed be quite impossible, and, in the second place, it seems unlikely that a professional market could develop. Furthermore, it can be noted that institutionalization acts as a "shield" in protecting PPPs from pressures from clients (however weak these may be); it also favours social learning and "memory maintenance" of the processes (features, outcomes, weaknesses) thanks to the "tracks" that processes leave behind, such as websites containing the final reports that PPPs are required to produce.

Institutionalization promotes innovative public participation models, in particular along the lines of deliberative democracy theory, and does so more in Tuscany than in Emilia-Romagna due to the different features of the laws passed by the two regions and of their implementation policies.

Both regions created an institutionalized framework context in which, while promoting engagement, they also framed it, insofar as their laws set out specific requirements and insofar as the "authorities" exerted a certain amount of "steering" (issuing guidelines, criteria, and priorities, giving methodological advice, and controlling funds). In this regard, the Tuscan institutional context seems to have been far more influential than that of Emilia-Romagna in pushing toward the diffusion of innovative approaches inspired by deliberative democratic theory. This pressure was exerted both by Law 69/07, which contained explicit deliberative features, and by the Regional Authority himself, who had an academic and practical background specifically in the deliberative democracy field.

These differences between the two regions produced different outcomes. The Tuscan framework certainly fostered the spread of deliberative designs, in innovating the traditional public participation model through the use of stakeholder committees as supervisors of the processes but not as participants, the use of random sampling to recruit ordinary citizens, emphasis on the relevance of the information (for example, written materials and experts' presentations) provided to participants, and structured dialogical sessions in order to encourage dialogue and reach some sort of final recommendations. However, the strong pressure toward the deliberative ideal also had the effect of homogenizing and standardizing process design to some extent.

The Emilia-Romagna law and the *Tecnico di garanzia* focused mainly on formal requirements, thus leaving more room for PPPs to make design choices; this indirectly favoured the experimentation with participatory methods, some of which were new in the Italian landscape, such as the Sato laboratory or the Samoan Circle. However, this "soft" and almost uniquely technical steering de facto did not favour innovation in the direction of the deliberative democracy model. Also, financial support was on average considerably lower in Emilia-Romagna (the *maximum* regional funding was 20,000 euro, whereas the *average* regional funding for processes in Tuscany was 31,500 euro); as deliberative participation is demanding in terms of efforts and resources, external support is a relevant factor in stimulating innovation.

The conclusion that emerges from our evidence is that the presence of an institutional framework can contribute to innovation; however, how and the extent to which innovation occurs largely depend on the specific traits (rules, implementing agencies, resources) of such frameworks.

Notes

1 Rodolfo Lewanski was the Regional Authority for public participation in Tuscany from October 2008 to March 2013. In order to avoid any "conflict of interest" with his past position, he did not carry out interviews in Tuscany, but only in Emilia-Romagna.
2 Out of a total of 25 processes funded in Tuscany and 12 in Emilia-Romagna in 2012.
3 Four of the PPPs selected for the second survey had already been interviewed in the first survey.
4 All of the processes were promoted by local administrations and focused on different issues, ranging from local development to urban planning, from sustainable mobility to natural disaster prevention, from social policies to project siting (Table 2.2).
5 To maintain confidentiality, we have omitted the identities of the respondents, to whom we refer only by a letter and a progressive number.

6 Although random sampling is the approach most often used, J. Dryzek and S. Niemeyer (2008) propose an original technique based on Q Methodology.
7 Out of 116 processes funded during the years of this law's implementation, 11 were promoted by citizens and 14 by schools (Lewanski, 2013a).
8 Of the three different kinds of professionals found in the market of PPPs, as indicated by Chilvers (2008), Italian PPPs mostly belong to the category of dialogue practitioners, although some of them work in academic institutions.
9 The Italian chapter of IAP2 has only recently translated the Core Values and Ethical Code of the IAP2 into Italian and made them available on its website: www.aip2italia.org.
10 This tendency seems to be common to other political systems as well; see Mendonça and Cunha (2014, p. 95).
11 This strategy is even pursued by some PPPs by having public authorities sign official "mutual declarations of intent."
12 In this respect, the Italian case appears to be similar to the case in other countries (Cooper & Smith 2012).
13 At present, under Law 46/13, which replaced Law 69/07, the Authority is now composed of three (rather than only one) appointed (academic) experts in public participation and deliberative democracy.

References

Alluli, M. (2011). Pratiche partecipative e istituzionalizzazione. Tra ritualità e decision-making. *Rivista Italiana di Politiche Pubbliche*, (3), 443–475.

Arnstein, S. R. (1969). A ladder of citizen participation. *Journal of American Institute of Planners*, *35*(4), 216–224.

Bherer, L. (2011). *Designing public engagement mechanisms: The role of professionals in the public participation field*. Paper presented at the 2011 European Consortium of Political Research Joint Sessions, St. Gallen.

Bherer, L., & S. Breux. (2012). The diversity of participation tools: Complementing or competing with one another? *Canadian Journal of Political Science*, *45*(2), 379–403.

Bishop, P., & Davis, G. (2002). Mapping public participation in policy choices. *Australian Journal of Public Administration*, *61*(1), 14–29.

Bobbio, L. (Ed.). (2007). *Amministrare con i cittadini. Viaggio tra le pratiche di partecipazione in Italia*. Soveria Mannelli: Rubbettino.

Bobbio, L. (Ed.). (2013). *La qualità della deliberazione. Processi dialogici tra cittadini*. Rome: Carocci.

Budge, I. (2000). Deliberative democracy versus direct democracy—plus political parties! In M. Saward (Ed.), *Democratic innovation: Deliberation, representation and association* (pp. 195–212). London: Routledge.

Cellamare, C. (2010). Percorsi di economia partecipata nella regione Lazio. *Contesti*, *1*, 111–114.

Chilvers, J. (2008). Deliberating competence: Theoretical and practitioner perspectives on effective participatory appraisal practice. *Science, Technology, & Human Values*, *33*(2), 155–185.

Cooper, E., & Smith, G. (2012). Organizing deliberation: The perspectives of professional participation practitioners in Britain and Germany. *Journal of Public Deliberation*, *8*(1). Retrieved from http://www.publicdeliberation.net/jpd/vol8/iss1/art3/

Dryzek, J. S., & Niemeyer, S. (2008). Discursive representation. *American Political Science Review*, *102*(4), 481–493.

Fagotto, E., & Fung, A. (2009). *Sustaining public engagement: Embedded deliberation in local communities*. East Hartford, CT: Everyday Democracy.

Floridia, A. (2008). Democrazia deliberativa e processi decisionali: La legge della Regione Toscana sulla partecipazione. *Stato e mercato, 82*(1), 83–110.

Font, J., Della Porta, D., & Sintomer, Y. (Eds.). (2014). *Participatory democracy in southern Europe: Causes, characteristics and consequences*. London: Rowman & Littlefield.

Fung, A. (2003). Survey article: Recipes for public spheres: Eight institutional design choices and their consequences. *The Journal of Political Philosophy, 11*(3), 338–367.

Fung, A. (2006). Varieties of participation in complex governance. *Public Administration Review, 66*(s1), 66–75.

Fung, A., & Wright, E. O. (2003). *Deepening democracy. Institutional innovations in empowered participatory governance*. London: Verso.

Gbikpi, R. (2005). Dalla teoria della democrazia partecipativa a quella deliberativa: Quali possibili continuità? *Stato e mercato, 73*(1), 97–130.

Goni, A., & Troisi, R. (2013). La costruzione di una "casa di vetro," ovvero una regione libera, aperta, condivisa. In A. Giangrande, R. Troisi, A. G. Mazzitelli, D. Festa & L. Angeloni (Eds.), *Democrazia emergente: La stagione dei Bilanci Partecipativi a Roma e nel Lazio* (pp. 17–38). Rome: Gangemi.

Hendriks, C. M. (2005). Participatory storylines and their influence on deliberative forums. *Policy Sciences, 38*(1), 1–20.

Hendriks, C. M. (2006). Integrated deliberation: Reconciling civil society's dual role in deliberative democracy. *Political Studies, 54*(3), 486–508.

Hendriks, C. M., & Carson, L. (2008). Can the market help the forum? Negotiating the commercialization of deliberative democracy. *Policy Sciences, 41*(4), 293–313.

Holman, P. (2007). Preparing to mix and match methods. In P. Holman, T. Devane & S. Cady (Eds.), *The change handbook: The definitive resource on today's best methods for engaging whole systems* (2nd ed., pp. 44–58). San Francisco, CA: Berrett-Koehler.

Lewanski, R. (2013a). Institutionalizing deliberative democracy: The "Tuscany laboratory". *Journal of Public Deliberation, 9*(1). Retrieved from http://www.publicdeliberation.net/jpd/vol9/iss1/art10/

Lewanski, R. (2013b). Valutare la partecipazione: Una proposta theory-based e user-oriented. In L. Bobbio (Ed.), *La qualità della deliberazione: Processi dialogici tra cittadini* (pp. 277–322). Rome: Carocci.

Martin, G. P. (2009). Public and user participation in public service delivery: Tensions in policy and practice. *Sociology Compass, 3*(2), 310–326.

Mendonça, R. F., & Cunha, E. S. M. (2014). Can the claim to foster participation hinder deliberation? *Critical Policy Studies, 8*(1), 78–100.

Moini, G. (2012). *Teoria critica della partecipazione: Un approccio sociologico*. Milan: FrancoAngeli.

Parkinson, J. (2006). *Deliberating in the real world: Problems of legitimacy in deliberative democracy*. Oxford: Oxford University Press.

Pellizzoni, L. (2005). *La deliberazione pubblica*. Rome: Meltemi.

Pomatto, G., & Ravazzi, S. (2012). Deliberazione e conflitto: Evidenze da un'analisi comparata. *Partecipazione e conflitto, 5*(2), 79–105.

Ravazzi, S. (2013). Facilitare la deliberazione: il ruolo dei professionisti. In L. Bobbio (Ed.), *La qualità della deliberazione* (pp. 149–180). Rome: Carocci.

Rosanvallon, P. (2008). *La légitimité démocratique: Impartialité, réflexivité, proximité*. Paris: Seuil.

Setälä, M. (2014). The public sphere as a site of deliberation: An analysis of problems of inclusion. In S. Elstub & P. McLaverty (Eds.), *Deliberative democracy: Issues and cases* (pp. 149–165). Edinburgh: Edinburgh University Press.

Smith, G. (2009). *Democratic innovations: Designing institutions for citizen participation*. Cambridge: Cambridge University Press.

Steiner, J. (2012). *The Foundations of deliberative democracy: Empirical research and normative implications*. Cambridge: Cambridge University Press.

Troisi, R., & Buonocore, M. (2010). Il Lazio: Un laboratorio di processi partecipativi. In U. Allegretti (Ed.), *Democrazia partecipativa: Esperienze e prospettive in Italia e in Europa* (pp. 263–274). Florence: Firenze University Press.

3

THE PARTICIPATORY DEMOCRACY MARKET IN FRANCE

Between Standardization and Fragmentation

Alice Mazeaud and Magali Nonjon

Introduction

Participatory democracy is presented as a desirable—and today, even an inevitable—evolution of contemporary democracies. Moreover, it is seen as the only possible response to a whole series of structural changes that are affecting our societies today, which in turn are considered to have become more and more "complex," "divided," "reflexive," "intractable," "distrustful," and largely "ungovernable" [our translations] (Blondiaux, 2008). Without disputing the objectivity of these changes, we however see this democratic and modernizing rhetoric as hampering an analysis of the conditions involved in the institutionalization of the participatory norm. In particular, it obscures the role that public participation professionals play in this process. That is why, in our research on participatory engineering, we focus not on participation mechanisms but rather on the actors described as participation professionals, that is, those whose professional activities consist in organizing, facilitating, and evaluating participation.[1]

In France, as elsewhere, these professionals have been little studied. The meager interest shown in their work is undoubtedly as much due to the overriding attention paid to participation procedures as it is to the substantial methodological difficulties involved in analyzing this new profession. Rather than being similar to a conventional "profession," participation professionals form a disparate and nebulous entity with shifting contours (consultants coming from the spheres of urban planning, communications, or design, civil servants, actors from civil society organizations, staff paid by private firms, etc.) that can only be mapped by considering various intersecting levels (the macro level of evolving demand for participatory processes from the public sector, the meso level of the structuring of the consulting market in the participation field, and the more micro level of public participation professionals' individual career trajectories) and by employing survey techniques. In order to assess this broad range of participation professionals in France, this chapter is based on a number of empirical studies carried out within the past 15 years. On the one hand, our study integrates the results of two doctoral dissertations—one on the emergence of a participation consulting market (Nonjon, 2006) and the other on the political and administrative uses made of the theme of participation in a particular region of France (Mazeaud, 2010)— along with original empirical data obtained from research conducted together on these professionals since 2011. On the other hand, our work combines the use of classic techniques for interviewing consultants, civil servants, and heads of public participation professional associations primarily,[2] observation in spaces of professional socialization, and the analysis of more original material (the qualitative and quantitative analysis of public organizations' calls for tender in the area of public participation, the creation of a database on specialized doctoral research concerning participation, an examination of handbooks on participation, an analysis of professional networks, and, in particular, of the network associated with the Institut de la concertation (ICT),[3] the existence of which since 2008 is itself a reflection of the solidity of the process of professionalization, etc.). The combination of these various materials enables us to show that, in France at least, professionalization is not only the outcome of the institutionalization of the participatory norm, but also actively drives this norm (Mazeaud & Nonjon, forthcoming).

Although there is still a need for a more systematic international comparison, in France the institutionalization of the participatory norm is directly linked to a growing public offer of participatory arrangements, which in fact reduced the contestatory scope of participatory democracy as promoted by the militants of the 1960s. Broadly speaking, in scientific terms as well as in the militants' discourse, the history of participatory democracy in France can be said to be divided into three main periods (Blatrix, 2012; Mazeaud & Nonjon, forthcoming). The first period extends from the 1970s to the end of the 1980s, when there were no real participatory public policies yet, as the approaches were primarily experimental and were being proposed by a militant avant-garde. Two main characteristics marked this period. On the one hand, elected officials and leftist movements were at that time converting the initial participatory project into concrete participatory tools and were experimenting, at a local level, with what they viewed as an alternative to the conventional political system. These experiments were, however, short-lived and were mostly abandoned after the 1977 elections. On the other hand, the conception of the general interest was evolving under the pressure of the increasingly conflictual nature of megaprojects, which resulted in particular in 1985 in dialogue and consultation becoming mandatory in the sphere of town and country planning. From this point of view, the 1980s marked the beginning of the institutionalization of participation, including the emergence of the "neighbourhood revitalization policy" ("Politique de la ville," or literally, the public policy for the city), which made citizen participation one of the main instruments of this project of urban renewal.

The second period, from 1992 to 2002, is characterized by a major promulgation of laws making participatory processes compulsory in some cases, the unprecedented development of participatory mechanisms, and a demand for participatory expertise, particularly in the areas of urban renewal and environmental policies. During this period, the French government reinforced the legal obligation of dialogue in development projects, especially those with a potential impact on the environment. Particularly significant was the creation of the Commission Nationale du Débat Public (CNDP) stemming from the Bianco Circular of 1992.[4] At the same time, from the 1992 legislation on the "Administration territoriale de la République" (local administration of the republic) to the 2002 Act on "la démocratie de proximité" (2002 Neighbourhood Democracy Act), citizen participation became enshrined as a natural component of local democracy, which led to the creation of new participatory bodies: the mandatory setting up of neighbourhood councils in cities with more than 80,000 inhabitants, the creation of consultative councils in counties (rural areas) and at the metropolitan scale, etc.[5] The right to participate gradually evolved from the "neighbourhood revitalization policy" to urban megaprojects, and then to development projects with an environmental impact. The final period, from the early 2000s until today, celebrates the advent of a "government of participation" (Gourgues, Topçu & Rui, 2013) characteristic of the institutionalization of this public offer of participation. Between political voluntarism and legal constraint, public authorities, and particularly local governments, have developed a broad range of participatory arrangements. First introduced in the area of urban planning and development, participatory procedures have become so common as to be integrated into administrative departments' everyday practices. The institutionalization of neighbourhood councils[6] has also led to the creation of administrative departments devoted to participation. Finally, we should mention that, at this same time, many local elected officials have invested in the theme of participation in an effort to re-legitimize themselves. They use the discourse on the "crisis of representation" as proof of the need to revitalize representation through the introduction of an offer of participatory arrangements (Le Bart & Lefebvre, 2005) and continue to experiment with participation in various sectors of policymaking (education, social policies, etc.), including in domains where no particular group has necessarily come together to call for the opening up of such spaces. These participatory experiments are not completely new. As far back as the 1970s, some local elected officials had set up consultative councils (made up of children, wise persons' committees, etc.) or neighbourhood councils. On the other hand, during the contemporary period, the number of participatory innovations has mushroomed, and the theme of participation has become a regular element of local marketing. Ultimately, we can say that, as of the mid-2000s, participatory policies have emerged as a truly public field in France. They have become largely independent from other public policy sectors. In this sense, we can talk about a public participation "offer" in order to emphasize that the production and circulation of participatory mechanisms follow logics exogenous to the transformations in democratic systems (Gourgues, 2012).

It should be pointed out that, although the social history of the institutionalization of the participatory norm that we have briefly outlined here has of course
included episodes of conflict, where more or less organized groups of individuals
have called for the opening up of decision-making processes, these mobilizations have rarely fostered the creation of participatory arrangements. The public
debate procedure under the aegis of the CNDP is the only case of a participatory
arrangement stemming directly from demand from civil society (Fourniau, 2011).
So, we can say that participatory democracy in France has emerged not so much
from initiatives from civil society or the economic sector as it has from initiatives
proposed by government actors. But, in political discourses, participatory democracy is legitimized by the supposed existence of a social demand for participation,
to which such initiatives claim to respond. In this chapter, we will show that, in
France, the contemporary success of participatory democracy is based on the
construction of a social demand for participation more than it is explained by
the existence of a genuine demand. The increasingly recurrent use of surveys as
a means of authenticating this demand in the sphere of participatory democracy
is quite emblematic of this process. An example of this can be found in the 2012
development of the first "barometer of dialogue" by the Respublica firm,[7] specializing in assisting public or private proponents in creating dialogue and participation tools, and the Harris Interactive survey firm, which claimed that "The
French people widely support dialogue as guaranteeing good decision-making."[8]
For these actors, the figures speak for themselves: "90% (of the French people)
feel that dialogue is a good thing, and 80% think that dialogue practices should be
developed and citizen participation should be encouraged" [our translations]. The
speech by the chairman of the CNDP, published in the press after the organization of the international conference on "citizens and public decision-making" in
July 2014, is equally exemplary on this topic:

> More and more, citizens want to directly participate in public decisions.
> This profound evolution of society, which now wishes to fully participate in
> democratic life, is clearly evident in the most recent survey on the subject,
> conducted by TNS Sofres for the CNDP: for example, more than 90% of
> citizens want to have better means of obtaining information as well as better
> means of direct expression at both the local and national levels. A change
> of this kind appears to be essential today, to respond to the three quarters
> of French citizens who feel that public authorities today do not take their
> views into account before making decisions any more than they did ten
> years ago.
>
> *(our translation)*[9]

An important part of the participation professionals' work is to authenticate and
highlight this demand for participation, which in itself shows the extent to which
the existence of these actors cannot be seen as the simple consequence of the

institutionalization of a participatory norm. They are also one of the main driving forces of this institutionalization. To support our hypothesis in this chapter, we will first show how, largely based in France on demand from the public sector, the participatory democracy market has grown considerably over the past decade as a result of the expansion and diversification of participatory policies. As the market strengthened, this led to a dynamics of standardization and homogenization of the profiles and practices of participation professionals and ultimately of the experiments with participatory democracy. Another consequence was however a fragmentation of this market, which led to the existence of a range of different specializations in participatory expertise and thus to a "division of labour" between professionals. An understanding of the structuring of and changes in this market will enable us to emphasize the impact of the dynamics of the professionalization of participation on the development of a public offer of participatory arrangements in France. We will then go on to show that, in order to exist, and for their position to flourish, participation professionals must in fact foster an artificial social demand (Blatrix, 2012) and become intermediaries between citizens and elected officials. This means that they must show proof of the success of participation by using techniques and procedures that are today less related to the activist sphere than to the sphere of public relations specialists and marketing experts. In this sense, the growing sophistication of the means of objectification of the demand for participation underlies the professionalization of participation and is associated with the consolidation of a participatory democracy market.

The Participatory Democracy Market: The Evolution of Demand from the Public Sector and the Changing Offer of Participation Services from the Private Sector

Due to the extreme variety of their profiles, it is very difficult to establish the number of participation professionals in France. They cannot be listed based on their holding of a specific degree or on their membership in any particular professional association or organization.[10] Given the extent to which the participation market is mainly sustained by the public sector, the number of public calls for tender related to mandates in terms of assisting with the organization, facilitation, or evaluation of participatory approaches can be seen as an initial indicator of the vitality of the participatory democracy market. According to our estimates, participation professionals chose their mandates from a series of about 150 requests for proposals in 2012 and from roughly 850 different public calls for tender between 2008 and 2013.[11] These requests for proposals were issued by various kinds of sponsors (local governments, large public development corporations,[12] decentralized state agencies, regional planning committees, etc.) in numerous sectors of policymaking (the environment and sustainable development, megaprojects, urban development, the "neighbourhood revitalization policy" and urban renewal, urban transit and transportation facilities, local development, scenario projects, and what could be called participatory democracy policies). The monetary value of these mandates can vary enormously depending on the sponsor, the duration of the contract, and the type of provision of services expected:[13] these contracts thus range from several thousand euros (the creation of advertising signs and the organization of public meetings to revise the local urban planning scheme for a small municipality) to one million euros for a global mandate in the context of a public debate organized by the CNDP.[14]

In terms of private service providers, the picture of this group of participation professionals is that of a vaguely defined sphere where actors from a wide range of different backgrounds co-exist: former social workers, architects, urban planners, management or marketing consultants, academics acting as consultants, etc. Another important point is that, in France, these participation professionals can work both in local governments[15]—as civil servants responsible for implementing participatory democracy, heads of a local democracy department, communications and participation facilitators—and in the private sector, in consulting firms, public relations agencies, and various kinds of associations that provide participatory services. The proportion of their professional activities that these actors devote to the particular theme of participation can also vary greatly. Over and above this myriad of profiles, the services and activities provided by these professionals are also extremely diverse, so that they can be said to offer participation "à la carte" (Nonjon, 2006), in response to the different kinds of situations in which potential sponsors may find themselves: "an offer to provide, ahead of the project, an overview of the context, impacts, and issues involved in the proposed development," "determining citizens' needs and evaluating their satisfaction," "setting up tools for citizens to communicate their views," "training discussion moderators." All of these types of service provision represent an opportunity for the professionals to develop disparate participation tools: "barometers" of dialogue, urban workshops, exploratory urban walks, deliberative meetings, forum theatre, citizens' conferences, self-mediation mechanisms, etc.

Market Consolidation and Standardization of Profiles

The existence of this nebulous participatory group of actors providing various services and presenting diverse professional profiles should not however suggest that there have been no dynamics fostering the structuring and standardization of practices since the 1970s (Nonjon, 2006). By centering participation around issues of methods, the first generation of "militants," those involved in urban protests in the 1970s, helped for example to disseminate a type of participatory know-how that was not essentially based on their past or present militant experiences but rather more on intellectual skills (the capacity to theorize about their practices and design them) and techniques (the production of tools) that were easier for professional milieus to use (Nonjon, 2012; Tissot, 2007). These pioneers of the early urban struggles also raised the question of how to translate what citizens were saying into a key issue to be considered in participatory forums. By concentrating on perfecting methodologies that would enable these citizens to express their views and to be heard, the militants facilitated the arrival of people with more technical professional profiles in their milieu to help them move from the stage of "gathering opinions to formulating proposals," in order to reveal the citizens' "social knowledge" and "expertise as users." Architects and urban planners, for example, were able to show their mastery of the language of urban planning, their capacity to translate needs into spaces, and their ability to draft or read plans. In the words of the director of an architectural and urban planning firm, "the architect is a person that has their place in a participatory approach as an enlightened intermediary between elected officials/professionals and citizens." The architect "has acquired notions of time and scale and knows the technical terms. He or she can consequently best translate these notions for people who lack such technical expertise" (Auxent, 2002) [our translations].

Professionals from the fields of communications and journalism have also been able to quite easily position themselves on this issue of translating technical terms and people's views. An example of this can be seen in the words of one of the founders of a public relations agency specializing in promoting audiovisual qualitative surveys[16] who explained in the early 2000s how he entered the niche of consulting in the sphere of participation and dialogue:

> I do exactly the same thing as I did on TV or in the written press. . . . I created a talk show, one of the biggest, where my idea was to have the public ask the question directly, without going through journalists. . . . When that was no longer possible because the public service provider gave up on all that by opting for reality TV . . . we then privatized that approach. Today, we are paid for doing much more effectively what we liked to do the most, that is, to give people the opportunity to express themselves on decisions that affect their fate, their future. For me, this is a key principle.
>
> *(our translation)*[17]

Finally, by reinvesting in the management sphere the knowledge acquired during trial experiences in the 1970s and 1980s (Nonjon, 2012), the militants of the early years legitimized the arrival on the market of specialists from the area of management consulting. The story of the founder of a consulting agency specializing in participation is emblematic of such a dynamics. Even in his choice of vocabulary, this consultant readily links the knowledge and know-how he gained during his experience as a marketing consultant to his current practice in the sphere of participation. He tells the story of his arrival in the "dialogue industry" as follows:

> Myself, I came out of a business school. Then I went to work for an international consulting firm. So I'm clearly a consultant. A consultant in what? In the past, I was a marketing consultant. . . . Then I went from consumer marketing to "user" marketing . . . and then, I moved into "citizen" marketing. But

I always moved on with the same philosophy, the same state of mind. Which means that, from my point of view, it was an approach targeted to quality.

(our translation)[18]

In a context of heightened competition, the first-generation "militants" of participation, like the more contemporary ones, have been obliged to professionalize their know-how and to follow an increasingly more managerial approach to the offer of participation services as proposed by the newer arrivals: the development of communication tools, the sequencing of interventions, the introduction of "à la carte" choices, the organizing of events, etc. This transition from "militancy" to "consultancy" is moreover characteristic of the changes happening among urban development professionals as of the late 1980s in the area of participation (Nonjon, 2012). More recently, because of the rise of e-democracy and open government, new professional specialists from the industrial design sector have entered the market. A large number of independent consultants from the sphere of collective intelligence are also starting to carry out dialogue mandates offered by public authorities, in addition to consultants from the marketing sector directly trained in participatory management. The successive reconversions of former "militants," as well as the advent of newcomers in the participation market, have thus made it easier to transfer and import models from private enterprise in particular and have helped to induce a process of homogenization of participatory engineering.

Competitive Dynamics and Fragmentation of the Market

Although we can identify certain dynamics of homogenization and standardization of practices over time, the participation market is nonetheless no less fragmented and competitive. First of all, there is considerable segmentation in terms of the services offered. Thus, although the number of firms benefiting from the public offer of participatory arrangements is growing, it is interesting that the number of firms providing entirely participatory services is not that large (there are only about 10 such organizations in France). Most of the firms that obtain public contracts to provide participation services are not in fact specialized in this area and tend to develop services based on another activity that is central to their trade. So it is particularly interesting to analyze the profiles of members of the ICT as of January 1, 2015, as this is one of the most visible professional networks in France associated with the sphere of participation. More than a third of ICT members are consultants and, for 75% of the latter, participation is only a secondary activity.[19] This diversification of the dialogue and participation consulting industry can also be seen in the dynamics of fragmentation of the professional activity sectors of engineering and research firms that have moved into this niche of service provision since 1990. As the following figure shows, there has been a growing fragmentation over time, among ICT members, in the positioning of consultants (158 firms and associations listed in 2015).

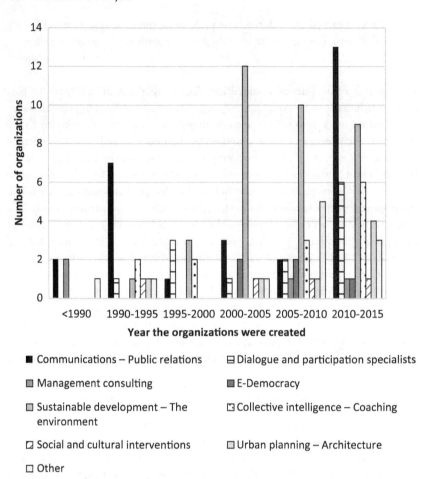

FIGURE 3.1 A Growing Diversification of Activity Sectors Among Regular Consultants in the Dialogue-Participation Industry: The Example of the Membership of the Institut National de la Concertation (N = 120)[20]

Whereas, in 1990, firms providing dialogue and participation services mostly attracted consultants from the communications and public relations sectors, as well as a smaller proportion from other specialized firms, the organizations created more recently that provide services in the area of participatory expertise are much more diverse in their professional positioning (sustainable development/the environment, collective intelligence, social and cultural interventions, e-democracy). So, the sphere of participation professionals remains a highly competitive one. Participatory work is strongly divided and hierarchized between participation consulting firms based on the types of services provided and the dialogue niche targeted. Without going into detail here, due to lack of space, it is also interesting to note that the proportion of services labelled as "participation" or "dialogue" services in no way indicates how solid a position the various firms or agencies occupy in the participatory democracy market. An analysis of public calls for tenders and an in-depth examination of the documentation of firms currently involved in the niche of participation suggest that it is more often the consultants' capacity to legitimize the production of expertise in the area of participation (publications, production of methodology handbooks, teaching in specialized academic training settings, contributions in conferences, the capacity to show academic expertise) that enables about 10 or so firms to occupy a central and leadership position in professional networks. It was in fact some of these private consulting firms that took the initiative of setting up the ICT network in 2008. Organizations that readily demonstrate their specialization in the niche of participation consulting and make this a trademark of their work may sometimes devote more than a third, or even a little less than half, of their services to contracts that have nothing to do, strictly speaking, with participation (organizing events, communications activities, expert reports, etc.).

In general, the type of services offered is what organizes or at least reflects the hierarchy in terms of size in the sphere of participation professionals. This is especially evident in the public relations sector between agencies that are able to sell strategic participation consulting services largely due to the academic networks that they have built up and firms that are confined to the logistics of the participation process (facilitating meetings, producing communication aids, etc.) in dialogue mandates. This distinction is clearly visible in mandates associated with public debate procedures, where there is a very strong segmentation between mandates to provide assistance to the Commission Particulière du Débat Public (CPDP), that is, in organizing public debates, and contracts to provide assistance to private or public proponents. An analysis of the 68 public debates organized between 2001 and 2013 suggests that it is not always the same services that are requested nor the same actors that are called upon (or that feel that they can compete for the contract). More generally, the analysis shows how closed the public debate market is, with only about 10 different service providers involved in all of the public debates. The entrance costs are very high for service providers. These mandates are "big" ones (in terms of the size of the contract, the duration of the project, and the type of resources that service providers are asked to supply) compared with other mandates in the area of participatory expertise (and especially urban planning projects), but they are "small" mandates compared with the usual contracts in the communications field (particularly in terms of the size of these contracts) (Picqué, 2012). Public debate mandates do not present any interest for large, non-specialized communications agencies—the costs would be too high—but they are also inaccessible for many service providers specializing in dialogue/participatory democracy—the communication skills expected and the logistical resources that would need to be mobilized are too great. Also, although public relations firms represent the majority of the service providers for public debate mandates, the niches of activity are mostly quite segmented (between logistics and strategic consulting services) and the dependence on public debate mandates is quite varied. Here again, the capacity to legitimize quasi-academic expertise in participation is still what determines the obtaining of certain contracts associated with assistance to project proponents, especially in terms of public relations expertise and strategic consulting.

Our research thus tends to show, on the one hand, the existence of distinct, and more or less open, mandates of participatory expertise, but for which not all participation professionals have the same opportunities to bid. On the other hand, the current structuring of the mandates and of the group of participation professionals is affected by both a trend toward greater specialization and a tendency toward diversification, which can be interpreted as testifying to the dissemination of the participatory norm to all public policy sectors. For 2012, among all the calls for tender listed in the official report of invitations to tender in the public sector[21] where the word "concertation" appeared (N = 106), a very small proportion of the organizations terming themselves specialists in "dialogue and participation" were ultimately chosen (see Figure 3.2).

More than a third of these past mandates were overseen by engineering firms that did not necessarily have skills in dialogue in the context of a project management mandate, where dialogue was only one task within a larger overall mandate. Moreover, when dialogue–public participation specialists were chosen to carry out these mandates, they were very rarely asked to act as the principal agent.[23]

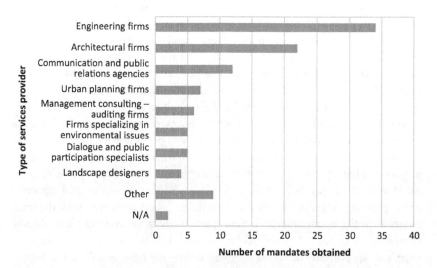

FIGURE 3.2 Dialogue and Participation Mandates That Do Not Necessarily Attract Specialists[22]: Type of Service Providers Selected Among 106 Calls for Tender Identified in the BOAMP (Official Report of Invitations to Tender in the Public Sector) for 2012 Involving Dialogue and Participation Mandates

These data show an important tendency in public participation mandates toward integrating and even merging communication and dialogue services. They also indicate how common "participation" services have become in some public policy sectors, such as urban planning. Figure 3.3 shows how, in dialogue mandates associated with urban planning operations, public participation specialists[24] are not as well positioned as urban planning firms or communications and public relations agencies that are not specialists in this area.

While this dual tendency toward the specialization and diversification of service providers in the public participation field in part explains the competitive dynamics in and fragmentation of the dialogue industry, the desire—on the part of both buyers and sellers of participation—to stand out from their competitors with innovative approaches also plays a key role. The participatory mechanisms that they promote are thus always said to be the first of something—"first digital participatory forum in Europe," "first participatory budget in a major capital city," etc.—or the only mechanisms that ensure that those citizens who usually do not have a voice will be heard, or that foster collective intelligence in a large group, etc. This game of innovation is largely shaped by both sides. Private service providers that need to stand out by creating niches for themselves help to influence the sponsor's expectations, and sponsors, by controlling the factors involved in their requests for proposals (timetable, price, ability to reach a large number of citizens, etc.), compel service providers to permanently adjust their service offering.

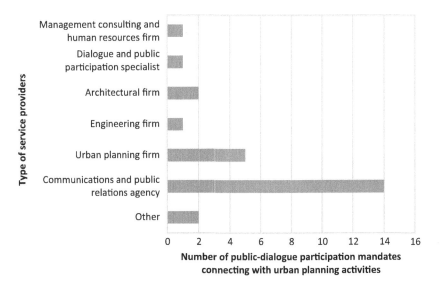

FIGURE 3.3   Dialogue-Participation Mandates in the Sphere of Urban Planning: A Competitive Market: Public Mandates Listed for the Cities of Nantes, Strasbourg, and Paris, 2009–2013 (N = 26)[25]

This dynamics of "co-construction" is particularly strong in France, where the institutionalization of participatory democracy has resulted in a growing internalization of participatory expertise within the administrations of those producing the demand for services in participation (local governments, large public corporations, etc.), which is leading to situations of both competition and collusion between professionals working internally and externally. It is in the interest of those working within administrations to emphasize their own expertise and thus limit the recourse to outsourcing but, at the same time, in order to obtain certain positions and to enhance their own reputations, they also need to collaborate with recognized experts. Far from being antinomical, the processes of the internalization and externalization of participatory expertise are thus largely intermingled. There may be internalization or externalization of the strategic dimension or, on the other hand, of the logistical dimension: it all depends on the resources that local actors have and on the structuring of the local field of expertise. Broadly speaking, our research has led us to distinguish between three main configurations of sponsor/service provider relations.[26] The first is that of local governments with few internal resources, which are dependent on the expertise of private service providers. If they are open to participatory processes, they call on dialogue specialists in order to develop new participatory strategies, and if they do not really believe in dialogue, they call on project management experts or communication specialists instead to help them meet the minimal obligations of dialogue. The second configuration involves local governments that have invested in the theme of participation by developing recognized internal expertise in this area and that only call on external service providers in situations when the use of an outside expert would help to legitimize them or when they lack a specific type of skill. The third case is that of local governments that have invested in the theme of participation and developed real internal participatory expertise, and that call on external service providers to increase their innovative capacity or when they need to demonstrate the independence of a particular participatory process. They may call on academic experts, especially to evaluate a particular mechanism or to act as guarantors (a "guarantor" in France is a person who supervises a participatory process to ensure that citizens can present their opinions to the proponent). In other words, consultants are sometimes dominated by public actors and limited to the role of service providers, whereas, in other cases, they have all the expertise and can impose their view of how the public policy process in question should be carried out. This difference in situations is especially evident in invitations to tender. Some local governments have real participatory expertise and call on service providers to help them manage the participatory process (organization and facilitation of the participatory process, the format of which has already been defined), whereas others expect the service provider to design the overall strategic participatory approach. This kind of "co-construction" underscores the fact that professional and commercial relations are determining factors in the institutionalization of participatory democracy. Far from being dictated by the question of democratic quality alone, the institutionalization of participatory democracy is largely dependent on the ongoing changes within this professional group and aspects involved in the shifting boundaries of this profession that affect it. Participation professionals need first to be able to justify their existence and thus legitimize the need for them to provide participation services.

From a Political-Driven Logic to a Market-Driven Logic: Legitimization of the Demand for Participation and Recognition of the Figure of the Professional

The history of participatory democracy can be seen as a shift from a bottom-up process, where participation arose from protests on the part of community groups, to a top-down trend of the ordering of participation by government authorities. This shift is said to at the same time explain the changing of the project of participatory democracy from a political-driven process to a market-driven process, and thus the movement from militancy to professionalism. We feel that, without completely challenging this vision, it is important to emphasize that such a history tends to maintain a commonly held representation, in the history of democracy, of citizens as demanding participation, whereas the few studies conducted on this issue tend to add significant nuances to such an interpretation.[27] It also prevents one from understanding the dynamics involved in the social construction of this demand for participation, and thus the role played by participation professionals in this process.

First, such a representation obscures the sometimes isolated and very localized character of the participatory experiences of the 1970s. And here we are thinking of such experiments as that of the Alma Gare group in the municipality of Roubaix[28] or the Petit Séminaire experiment in Marseille.[29] An analysis of the participatory experiments carried out by some socialist municipalities after the 1977 municipal elections—which were said to be a response to the demand for participation that had been expressed in these urban struggles—suggests that the demand was weak and localized and came from the most intellectual factions of the population (Lefebvre, 2011; Paoletti, 1997). The demand for participation can thus be seen as first and foremost arising from and maintained by spokespeople from various political, community, and academic spheres, who helped to create it, whereas in municipal participatory forums, it was often very hard to find participants, especially those from working-class neighbourhoods.

Second, this stylized history, largely supported by the proponents of participation, tends to associate the participatory tools of today with the myth of a militant heritage: the legal codification of participatory arrangements in the 1990s is thus seen as the victorious outcome of the earlier struggles (urban or environmental). If the end of the 1980s in fact marked an overturning of participatory mechanisms in France—as participation was institutionalized, especially as a result of the new urban renewal policies ("Politique de la ville") (Tissot, 2007)—it is important to note that since the 1990s the existence of a demand for participation, expressed in the form of protests, has no longer been questioned. The participatory rhetoric, backed by the social force of the underlying discourses that support it, is enough to make such a demand exist. So, in the discourse, the explicit function of the participatory approaches promoted by public authorities has become to enable those without a voice to be heard. The issue has been reduced to that of how to mobilize citizens and to ensure that they are heard in the context of procedures that are supposed to allow them to finally become visible and to publicly express their views (Carrel, 2014).

But such a representation ultimately conceals the process through which some actors have created and objectified the existence of this demand for participation. And here it is worth examining the particular role played by French academics in the social construction of this demand. Without being able to go into detail here, we can say that there in fact exists in France a process of an intersecting institutionalization and legitimization of the sciences and policies of participation that clearly illustrates the correlation between the development of a public offer of participation and the creation of an academic space devoted to this subject (seen, for example, in the creation of the research team "Participation, décision et démocratie participative" in 2008 and of an academic journal in 2011 called *Participations*). More broadly speaking, we can point to the many ways in which the professional and academic worlds of participation move between and mutually influence one another. The theme of the conference held by the research team "Participation et démocratie" in Paris in January 2015—"Chercheur.es et acteur. es de la participation: Liaisons dangereuses et relations fructueuses" (Researchers and actors of participation: dangerous liaisons and fruitful relationships)—shows the emphasis that researchers give to the question of their contribution to the legitimization and dissemination of a "participatory imperative." And outside the academic sphere, to act as though the demand for participation was self-evident also obscures all the work of the professionals who began in the 1990s to take on the responsibility of facilitating the participatory processes imposed by law, first mainly in the areas of urban renewal and the environment, and then in an ever-widening range of public policy sectors: these professionals came to work both in local governments as well as in private consulting firms mandated to assist public authorities in this task (Nonjon, 2006). Making the existence of this social demand for participation visible would become a defining and crucial phase of their professional activities.

The Sophistication of Strategies for Authentication of the Demand for Participation

This process of authentication of the demand for participation has involved setting up a variety of different strategies that are adapted to the project sponsor's expectations. So, it was the participatory processes themselves that first certified the existence of such a demand. It was through the implementation of participatory mechanisms that the success of participation was confirmed. But this was on one condition: the public had to become involved. Without any citizens to participate, there could be no participatory mechanisms. To counteract the threat of the absence of the public, which could jeopardize the existence of both the mechanisms and the professionals that were creating these mechanisms, participation professionals began to devise a series of different techniques. We can therefore see why the mastery of communication and mobilization techniques is today a central element in the participation professionals' practical approach. This ability to mobilize people is in fact equally valued in the sphere of community and cultural action, where the focus is on the practitioner's skill in mobilizing networks, as it is in other areas more closely related to the communications sector, where it is the professional's marketing know-how that is emphasized.

Participation professionals tend to concentrate on two dimensions: to attempt to involve people who are far removed from political life and to get as many people as possible to participate. The development and use of techniques for mobilizing potential participants are moreover a recurrent theme in professional workshops and colloquiums. And here, the professionals' interest in mini-publics and random selection is significant. If they cannot mobilize vast numbers of people from lower-income categories, the use of random selection[30] means that they can be sure of obtaining a more diverse range of participants than they would have by using mechanisms based on voluntary participation.[31] However, in France, mechanisms along the lines of citizen juries attract limited interest from local elected officials, whereas they are seen as very attractive by academics, who are inclined to value deliberative quality, and by professionals, who find in them a way of overcoming the uncertainty of public participation through a focus on quality and diversity. While elected officials may see citizen juries and the like as an opportunity to highlight their innovative capacity, they cannot actually use them to legitimize new proposals. Indeed, the strength of the argument of deliberative quality pales in the face of the force of numbers. In response to this, participation professionals try to reconcile the logic of numbers with that of deliberation. They have developed an entire series of collective intelligence techniques in large groups (the world café, electronic town meetings, etc.) in order to increase the number of participants, but without renouncing their belief in the value of small numbers, as seen in mini-public procedures.

And here we should add that it is not only a matter of attracting a large number of participants but also of showing that the participants were in fact numerous and actively involved. Some of the many examples of this include the reports on public debates, which invariably list the number of participants in the meetings or of contributors to the website, the "file on the 11,000 citizen participants"[32] from the Rhône-Alpes region (Gourgues, 2010), or the emphasis on mass participation in the participatory budget for lycées (high schools) in Poitou-Charentes.[33] Participatory procedures are now indissociable from counting operations. But the figures that are reported often mask the social characteristics of the publics involved and the fact that all the people present do not necessarily participate or adhere to the proposals made by sponsors. Quantitative success may hide the small number of adherents and enable the organizers to disseminate an aggregated interpretation of participation: "If they're there, it means they agree." The number of participants confirms the symbolic value of the participatory mechanisms and is seen as evidence of the massive local support for their sponsors. Ségolène Royal, a candidate defeated in the 2007 French presidential elections who was known for her considerable efforts to promote the model of participatory democracy,[34] claimed "more than 2 million" participants during her 2007 campaign.[35] She pointed to her extensive social support as attesting to how well her political platform met citizen "demand" and in rejecting the explanations given for her defeat. As she affirmed: "I should have explained my approach more clearly. But the grass roots . . . all those men and women who came out in huge numbers, understood perfectly well. And I didn't need to explain very much to them, either!" [our translation] (Royal, 2008, p. 304). Along with this activity of counting participants, there is also an array of tools mainly designed to highlight participation, or to attest that there was in fact participation. This tendency emerged with the arrival on the market of a nebulous group of service providers focusing on producing and selling a range of turnkey— and largely digitally based—participatory tools. Depending on the particular sponsors concerned, participatory products may now involve the publication of a website (forum, blog, etc.) or of web journals. With this glut of digital supports and spaces for electronic debate, the authentication of the participatory process has acquired an automatic dimension (Badouard, 2014; Bonaccorsi & Nonjon, 2012; Mabi, 2013) and meets the expectations of sponsors who have become increasingly fond of preformatted means of evaluation. From this point of view, the creation of the "barometer" of dialogue[36] or the case of the CNDP asking the survey firm TNS Sofres to conduct a survey can be seen as the outcome of a process of growing objectification of participatory democracy: participation professionals devote a large portion of their time and resources to authenticating the success of the participatory approach put in place by public authorities. Attesting to this success has itself even become one of the services provided.

Another argument often heard in the sphere of participation also merits discussion: namely, that the social demand for participation has to be "shaped." According to many experts, this demand cannot be expressed spontaneously. It needs to be brought to light and invigorated by the participatory strategies that they have developed. The purpose of these strategies is in fact to create this demand by channelling the expression of dissatisfaction or the desire for participation that may be expressed in other, often more contentious forms. The words of a local civil servant mandated to implement participatory democracy show this clearly:

> The question isn't to take for granted that there is no demand for participation. It is rather to ask why there isn't a demand for participation.

I personally think that if there isn't a demand for participation, it's because people aren't used to it . . . to having an offer of participation. . . . I refuse to say that the offer of participation does not meet a demand. The offer of participation will create the conditions for a demand to arise.

(our translation)[37]

The social demand of citizens/the governed is fostered by the public offer of participation developed by elected officials/governing authorities as much as this social demand helps to reinforce such an offer. Nor is it a question of trying to determine whether the social demand pre-exists the interplay between the social demand and the public offer of participation, because they are largely dependent on the work of the participation professionals. The authentication of this social demand for participation, or at least of this potential demand, is in fact the condition required for the conversion of the project of participatory democracy into professional outcomes.

The Process of Legitimization of the Figure of the Participation Professional

To establish their legitimacy, participation professionals focus on promoting participatory democracy and put a lot of effort into lobbying the local governments that are their main potential clients (or employers). The ICT, created in 2008 to facilitate debates between professionals, practitioners, and sponsors on effective approaches to dialogue, clearly indicates that its objective is "to improve their [mechanisms for dialogue] visibility in the eyes of public decision makers and especially local governments as well as the firms concerned" [our translation].[38] Established professionals moreover remind those who had entered the profession once the industry was developed about their role in promoting participation. One expert in dialogue in a large public corporation, who had in the past headed a project to put participatory democracy mechanisms in place in two local governments, and who is now involved in a number of training mandates focussing on dialogue, openly claims a role in promoting the theme of participation in discussion spaces such as the ICT, of which she is a particularly active member:

You can be quite happy doing this job when there are invitations to tender. Everything depends on the demand from public authorities. But the next day, if there aren't any calls for tender . . . I'm very conscious of working to develop and expand such demand. As much as you're comfortable when you're in the private sector [as a consultant, as opposed to working in the more vulnerable institutional position of a civil servant dedicated to public participation], it still depends on whether the demand is there. Until quite recently, it was really a form of political activity . . . whereas today, it may be more a question of emphasizing the need for participatory arrangements in the social sector and in public service, so that the field broadens in terms of the subjects dealt with and the content.

(our translation)[39]

But such lobbying activities are of course not enough to establish the participation professionals' legitimacy; it is also important that the latter present themselves as indispensable intermediaries between elected officials and citizens, and indeed as the only legitimate actors able to assume this role of "facilitator," "translator," "developer," or "intermediary guarantor of participation." In this role, they must attest to their skills in developing and leading the participation services offered. Also, while there are no selective, accredited, and unique diplomas or degrees regulating access to the sphere of participation professionals, the proliferation of qualifying professional training courses,[40] as well as academic courses,[41] in this field shows that participation is indeed considered in France today as an affair for specialists that calls for specific know-how and tools. For Loïc Blondiaux, one of the academic specialists most involved in promoting participation, who is the head of the professional master's degree program in "participatory engineering" at Université de Paris 1–la Sorbonne, professionalization has become a "decisive issue" in participatory democracy. He notes that the setting up of this master's degree program was based on "the wager that it is possible to train specialists in democratic participation and deliberation at the highest level who are able to combine a high degree of political and intellectual knowledge with practical qualities that make them immediately effective when working in professional organizations." This will enable them "to play a part in improving dialogue and citizen debate, and to ensure that there is real participatory democracy, which is more than just a slogan" [our translations].[42]

Participatory democracy is today at the heart of many professional networks and specialized meeting spaces. The launching of the first series of "meetings for participatory democracy professionals" in 2011 (the second series was held in November 2014) testifies in its very description to a recognition of the figure of the professional in the participation field. The publication of many handbooks on good participation practices, often produced by participation professionals themselves, also shows the vitality of reflections on the building of participatory know-how.[43] And, while participation professionals certainly do not yet represent a profession with clearly defined characteristics and boundaries, today they nonetheless form a professional group "that has acquired social visibility, that enjoys a fair degree of identification and recognition, that occupies a distinctive position in the social division of labour, and that is characterized by a symbolic legitimacy" [our translation] (Demazière & Gadéa, 2009).

Conclusion

The shift in focus from the political project of participatory democracy to the entrepreneurs of this project has thus enabled us to show, first, that the public offer of participation cannot be seen as the response to a pre-existing social demand; rather, the demand for participation is socially constructed. Second, this shift underscores the idea that the existence of participation professionals and of an offer to provide participation services cannot be considered as simply reflecting the institutionalization of participatory democracy; it is today also one of the main drivers of the development of the participation field. Third, this look at the world of the entrepreneurs of the participatory democracy project encourages us to think of participatory democracy, a cause initially promoted by the radical leftist militants of the 1960s, as an industry in which the issues of competition and professional legitimacy are important factors.

More broadly, the study of the structuring of the industry of participatory expertise in France induces us to think of certain variables as key to this development: the predominance of a public offer of participation mainly proposed by local governments, the process of the intersecting legitimization of academic and professional expertise, the expansion of professional development and academic training courses offered in this field, the strengthening of networks of actors and of spaces of socialization, the importance of the "Politique de la ville" (neighbourhood revitalization policy) in fostering the professionalization of participation, etc. In this respect, this study on the professionalization of participation in France raises the question of the possible singularity of these variables in the French context. Given the strong position of the state and public authorities and the limited autonomy of civil society organizations in France, it is ultimately not that surprising that citizen participation in France is more often organized by public authorities than by private actors. But beyond this observation, there is still a need for a more systematic international comparison of the mechanisms of the institutionalization of participation if we are to understand both the similarities and the differences in what some have called the global participatory turn.

Notes

1 Part of this chapter has already been published, in French, in the journal *Agone*. See Mazeaud and Nonjon (2015).
2 A total of more than 130 qualitative and/or oral history interviews were conducted with civil servants, elected officials, paid professionals from the private sector, consultants, and researchers working in the field of participation during the course of our individual (60 and 40 interviews respectively) and joint (35) research.
3 The Institut de la concertation, or ICT, was created in 2008 to promote participation and to encourage and organize discussion among professionals. It is the most active network of its kind in France and has the largest number of members. The term "concertation," which is extensively used in France, has no exact English-language equivalent. It has generally been translated in this text as "dialogue," and sometimes as "dialogue and participation," or simply "participation."
4 Created subsequent to the Barnier Act of 1995, the CNDP oversees public debate processes in France concerning major public development projects of national interest. To obtain an idea of the criteria for the submission of a project for debate and of how these criteria have evolved, see in particular Revel, Blatrix, Blondiaux, Fourniau, Hériard and Lefebvre (2007).
5 For more information on this series of participatory mechanisms in the area of metropolitan planning, see Scherrer (2008).

6 Local democracy bodies made obligatory in municipalities with more than 80,000 inhabitants by the 2002 Act on "la démocratie de proximité" (2002 Neighbourhood Democracy Act).

7 Respublica was created in 2004. It is a firm specializing in participation consulting strategies. It sets up dialogue processes based on the management of stakeholders' methodology. See http://www.respublica-conseil.fr.

8 *Baromètre de la concertation*, Respublica/Harris Interactive, 1st edition, 2012. A second edition was published in 2013 and a third in 2014. This indicator of the level of dialogue, based on quantitative surveys, claims to provide an objective measurement of participation supply and demand. See http://www.respublica-conseil.fr/barometre-de-la-concertation-de-la-decision-publique-edition-2014/.

9 Survey entitled "Le citoyen et la décision publiques," TNS Sofres for the CNDP, June 2014.

10 One indication of this is that nearly 180 organizations offering to provide assistance in the area of dialogue and participation were found by combining an Internet search using key words and an analysis of lists available to us of participants in professional meetings and specialized training on participation between 2000 and 2015. This figure is however far from being exhaustive, as there are clearly a significant number of independent consultants working in the niche of participation that are difficult to find, as well as many firms not necessarily specializing in participation but active in these markets. We will come back to this point a little later on in the paper.

11 Because of the wide range of potential key words that could be used to find mandates connected with participatory democracy and the limited advertising of smaller calls for tenders, it is difficult to make an objective assessment of the participatory democracy market. To get around this difficulty, we worked with a service provider who had been specializing in this market for more than 10 years. He sent us the list of calls for tender that he had found over the past six years, which enabled us to roughly map out the demand for participation services.

12 It is important to note that large development corporations such as the RTE (Réseau de Transport d'Electricité) (electric power transmission), RFF (Réseau Ferré de France) (railroads), and STIF (Syndicat de Transport d'Ile de France) (transportation), which are major sponsors of participation processes, are not obliged to publish a list of their invitations to tender.

13 All public administrations (the state and local governments) are required to publish a list of their mandates valued at over 15,000 euros.

14 Mandates related to the work of the CNDP involve a number of tasks that may be assigned separately or as part of a single contract: staffing the specific public debate process, strategic consulting, communications, and logistics.

15 Given the wide range of job titles, it is difficult to accurately estimate the number of civil servants working in the field of participation. The data that we do have suggest that the existence of civil servants (and of administrative services) devoted to participation has been spreading, at least in municipalities with over 50,000 inhabitants, and enable us to estimate the total number of civil servants whose activities mainly consist of implementing participation at around 1,000 to 1,500 people.

16 The qualitative surveys are administered to large and significant samples of the populations concerned (80 to 500 people). An open and unstructured questionnaire is used to elicit spontaneous responses, which are then analyzed in order to obtain an exact and dynamic representation of the views of the population considered on a particular topic. The agency shows a film to help to stimulate people's responses during the interviews. See http://campanaelebsablic.com/notre-offre/nos-activites/.

17 Extract from an interview with the director of a public relations agency specializing in participation and dialogue, Paris, 2004.

18 Extract from an interview with the director of a consulting firm specializing in partici- pation and dialogue, Paris, 2002.

19 In 2014, according to certain of its founding members, 33% of the ICT network was made up of consultants, 17% of civil servants working in local governments, 15% of NGOs and foundations, 12% of students and unemployed individuals, 6% of academics, 4% of public and quasi-public organizations, and 4% of private companies and boards of trade. But a more detailed examination of the ICT members' profiles suggests that there may be a larger proportion of members performing paid consulting work in the participation field, given that some NGOs and academics now carry out this type of activities.

20 We are focusing here on the 120 organizations (among the 158 listed in 2015 by the ICT) for which information on their date of creation was available to us.

21 In France, firms can use a website, www.boamp.fr (BOAMP = Bulletin Officiel des Appels d'offres de Marchés Publics français, or Official report of invitations to tender in the public sector) to help them find public calls for tender issued by the state, the army, local governments, and regional planning committees. We used this website to identify calls for tender involving "dialogue–public participation" mandates.

22 We should specify here that, in most cases, several service providers jointly respond to invitations to tender in the public participation field. Since the early 2000s, succes- sive reforms in the regulations governing public mandates in France have encouraged this type of joint approach. In these cases, one organization is chosen as the principal organization in charge of the mandate and has the important role of subcontracting out the different tasks in the mandate. In other cases, and less frequently, a single service provider may bid for the mandate. This is why, for each type of activity sector, the total number of mandates coming from calls for tender includes the mandates where the firm in question acted as the principal agent or sole service provider.

23 Of the 106 calls for tender identified for 2012, public participation specialists were chosen for 14 mandates. They acted as the principal agent or sole service provider in only five of these mandates.

24 These professionals are referred to in the figures as "dialogue and participation specialists."

25 The data shown in this figure are derived from information directly obtained from these three cities for the years from 2009 to 2013.

26 The typical profile of service provider/sponsor relations described in this text is based on that in local governments, as they account for about 80% of participation mandates. But it is possible to observe these three configurations in the case of large development corporations and state services.

27 This is a classic controversy in the participation literature (Hibbing & Theiss-Morse, 2002; Neblo, Esterling, Kennedy, Lazer & Sokhey, 2010), although few studies have attempted to empirically analyze the existence of a demand for participation. On the case in France, see Gourgues and Santy (forthcoming) and Mazeaud and Talpin (2010).

28 We are referring here to the more than 15-year-long conflict, from 1966 to 1983, between the municipality of Roubaix and a community group (the peoples' urban planning workshop of Alma-Gare) concerning urban renewal in a working-class neighbourhood. On this topic, see, among others, Hatzfeld (1986).

29 We are referring here to one of the first experiments in allowing the public to voice their views on a neighbourhood revitalization project, launched by Michel Anselme in the late 1970s in a low-income district of Marseille called Le Petit Séminaire. For a more detailed description of this experiment, see Anselme (2000).

30 The participants are sometimes paid for their participation.

31 It is interesting that a proposal of this kind can be found in the latest report on the reform of urban renewal policies (Bacqué & Mechmache, 2013).

32 This file was created by using the list of participants in the two-year-long series of meetings in regard to the project "construire Rhône-Alpes ensemble" (Let's build the Rhône-Alpes region together). It makes it possible to identify, trace, and mobilize a specific number of individuals for other professional participatory events.

33 The Budget Participatif des Lycées (BPL) (high school participatory budget) tested out by the Poitou-Charentes region starting in 2004 is recognized as one of the most innovative participatory experiments in France, given the large number of participants (tens of thousands each year) and the huge financial sums involved (10 million euros per year) (Mazeaud, 2012).

34 Ségolène Royal's promotion of "participatory democracy" was a key element of her political strategy. It was even said to be the main new political proposal that she offered (Mazeaud, 2010) and the distinctive mark of "royalism" (Lefebvre, 2008). During the 2007 presidential campaign, she set up participatory forums and proposed in her platform to establish citizen juries.

35 Speech given in Rennes on February 20, 2007.

36 In 2012, the Respublica firm created a "barometer of dialogue." For more details on this new tool, see Note 8.

37 Extract from an interview with a civil servant mandated to facilitate participatory democracy, Poitou-Charentes region, 2007.

38 Institut de la concertation. (2014). Qui sommes nous? Retrieved from http://www.concerter.org/.

39 Observation notes, meetings of ICT professionals, December 2012.

40 It is impossible to determine the number of training sessions or courses offered in the niche of participation. One indication is that the ICT reports at least three training sessions a month given by members of its network. Another indicator, among many, of the recognition of specific participatory know-how is that the Centre National de la Fonction Publique Territoriale (CNFPT) offers specialized training modules on participation to civil servants working in local governments.

41 There are not that many academic training programs where the teaching content and potential employment opportunities are clearly and mainly oriented toward participation (a master's degree program in participatory engineering at the Sorbonne, a master's in public communications and participation at Université de Lille-II, a master's in evaluation- and participation-related occupations at Université de Toulouse). Nonetheless, France seems to be one of the few countries to offer degree courses in this professional activity sector. The number of training programs where a large proportion of the courses are oriented toward participatory management and with professional outlets associated with participatory work is much greater. For more information, see http://www.comedie.org/formations.php.

42 Université Paris 1 Panthéon Sorbonne. (2012). Parcours affaires publiques – Ingénierie de la concertation. Retrieved from http://www.univ-paris1.fr/ufr/ufr11/scolarite-master-2/m2-pro-affaires-publiques/parcours-ingenierie-de-la-concertation/.

43 We found more than 60 handbooks on good participatory practices, and this list is far from being exhaustive.

References

Anselme, M. (2000). *Du bruit à la parole. La scène politique des cités.* La Tour d'Aigues: Éditions de l'Aube.

Auxent, B. (2002). L'architecte dans la démarche participative de projet: atouts et déficits. In B. Declève, R. Ferray & M. Michialino (Eds.), *Coproduire nos espaces publics: Formation-action-recherche* (pp. 95–87). Louvain: Presses universitaires de Louvain.

Participatory Democracy Market in France 63

Bacqué, M. H., & Mechmache, M. (2013). *Pour une réforme radicale de la politique de la ville*. Paris: Ministère de l'Égalité des territoires et du Logement.

Badouard, R. (2014). La mise en numérique des projets politiques. Une approche "orientée design" de la participation en ligne. *Participations*, (8), 31–54.

Blatrix, C. (2012). Des sciences de la participation: Paysage participatif et marché des biens savants. *Quaderni, 79*, 59–80.

Blondiaux, L. (2008). *Le nouvel esprit de la démocratie*. Paris: Seuil.

Bonaccorsi, J., & Nonjon, M. (2012). "La participation en kit": L'horizon funèbre de l'idéal participatif. *Quaderni, 79*, 29–44.

Carrel, M. (2014). *Faire participer les habitants? Citoyenneté et pouvoir d'agir dans les quartiers populaires*. Lyon: ENS Éditions.

Demazière, D., & Gadéa, C. (2009). *Sociologie des groupes professionnels: Acquis récents et nouveaux défis*. Paris: Éditions La Découverte.

Fourniau, J. M. (2011). L'institutionnalisation controversée d'un modèle français de débat public. *Téléscope, 17*(1), 70–93.

Gourgues, G. (2010). *Le consensus participatif: Les politiques de la démocratie dans quatre régions françaises*. Doctoral dissertation in political science, Université de Grenoble, Grenoble.

Gourgues, G. (2012). Avant-propos: Penser la participation publique comme une politique de l'offre, une hypothèse heuristique. *Quaderni, 79*, 5–12.

Gourgues, G., & Santy, J. (forthcoming). La démocratie participative peut-elle convaincre la population de participer? Analyse d'une enquête par sondage. In L. Blondiaux, J. M. Fourniau, L. Monnoyer-Smith & C. Neveu (Eds.), *La démocratie participative pour quoi faire*. Bruxelles: Peter Lang.

Gourgues, G., Topçu, S., & Rui, S. (2013). Gouvernementalité et participation. *Participations*, (6), 5–33.

Hatzfeld, H. (1986). Municipalités socialistes et associations. Roubaix: le conflit de l'Alma-Gare. *Revue Française de Science Politique, 36*(3), 374–392.

Hibbing, J. R., & Theiss-Morse, E. (2002). *Stealth democracy. Americans' beliefs about how government should work*. Cambridge: Cambridge University Press.

Le Bart, C., & Lefebvre, R. (Eds.). (2005). *La proximité en politique: Usages, rhétoriques, pratiques*. Rennes: Presses Universitaires de Rennes.

Lefebvre, R. (2008). Opinion et participation: La campagne présidentielle de Ségolène Royal. *La Vie des Idées*. Retrieved from http://www.laviedesidees.fr/Opinion-et-participation.html.

Lefebvre, R. (2011). Retour sur les années 70: Le parti socialiste, l'autogestion et la démocratie locale. In M. H. Bacqué & Y. Sintomer (Eds.), *La démocratie participative: histoire et généalogies* (pp. 65–81). Paris: Éditions La Découverte.

Mabi, C. (2013). Inclusions des publics et matérialité des dispositifs. *Participations*, (7), 201–213.

Mazeaud, A. (2010). *La fabrique de l'alternance: La "démocratie participative" dans la recomposition du territoire régional, Poitou-Charentes 2004–2010*. Doctoral dissertation in political science, Université de La Rochelle, La Rochelle.

Mazeaud, A. (2012). Administrer la participation. L'invention d'un métier entre militantisme et professionnalisation de la démocratie locale. *Quaderni, 79*, 45–58.

Mazeaud, A., & Nonjon, M. (2015). Construire la demande de participation pour asseoir le marché de la démocratie participative. *Agone*, (56), 135–152.

Mazeaud, A., & Nonjon, M. (forthcoming). *Le marché de la démocratie participative*. Bellecombe-en-Bauge: Éditions du Croquant.

Mazeaud, A., & Talpin, J. (2010). Participer pour quoi faire? Esquisse d'une sociologie de l'engagement dans les budgets participatifs. *Sociologie, 3*(1), 357–374.

Neblo, M. A., Esterling, K. M., Kennedy, R. P., Lazer, D. M. J., &, Sokhey, A. E. (2010). Who wants to deliberate—and why? *American Political Science Review, 104*(3), 566–583.

Nonjon, M. (2006). *Quand la démocratie se professionnalise: Enquête sur les experts de la participation.* Doctoral dissertation in political science, Lille, Université Lille-II.

Nonjon, M. (2012). De la "militance" à la "consultance": Les bureaux d'études urbaines, acteurs et reflets de la "procéduralisation" de la participation. *Politiques et management public, 29*(1), 79–98.

Paoletti, M. (1997). *La démocratie locale et le référendum.* Paris: L'Harmattan.

Picqué, A. (2012). *La fabrique de la concertation sur les grands projets: Études de cas.* Doctoral dissertation in political science, Université Picardie Jules Verne, Amiens.

Revel, M., Blatrix, C., Blondiaux, L., Fourniau, J. M., Hériard, D. B., & Lefebvre, R. (Eds.). (2007). *Le débat public: Une expérience française de démocratie participative.* Paris: Éditions La Découverte.

Royal, S. (2008). *Ma plus belle histoire c'est vous.* Paris: Grasset.

Scherrer, F. (2008). Planification métropolitaine et débat public urbain en France. In M. Gauthier, M. Gariépy & M. O. Trépanier (Eds.), *Renouveler l'aménagement et l'urbanisme: Planification territoriale, débat public et développement durable* (pp. 83–108). Montréal: Les Presses de l'Université de Montréal.

Tissot, S. (2007). *L'État et les quartiers. Genèse d'une catégorie de l'action publique.* Paris: Éditions du seuil.

4

PUBLIC PARTICIPATION PROFESSIONALS IN THE US

Confronting Challenges of Equity and Empowerment

Caroline W. Lee

Introduction

On January 3, 2014, dialogue and deliberation (D&D) practitioners in the United States received an alarming email about AmericaSpeaks, a flagship deliberation non-profit with one of the most recognized methods in the field, the 21st Century Town Meeting:

> AmericaSpeaks has an unparalleled record of organizing more than 100 major citizen deliberations in all 50 states. After 19 years of working as an independent, national, nonprofit organization—sustained exclusively by grants and contracts—AmericaSpeaks will close its doors for good today.

Founded in 1995, AmericaSpeaks was not just an early and important leader in major regional and national deliberative events, including initiatives to engage citizens in rebuilding Lower Manhattan after 9/11 and New Orleans after Katrina. Under the guidance of Carolyn Lukensmeyer, a senior stateswoman and veteran of non-partisan deliberation efforts from the Clinton to the Obama eras, AmericaSpeaks had led innumerable national collaborative efforts in service of advancing research and practice in the dialogue and deliberation field.

Reactions from the D&D community of practice on the web ranged from sadness to shock to dismay at the loss of a trailblazing organization when a national government so deeply tangled in partisan gridlock seemed to need rational public voices for change more than ever. The grief was palpable on an "AmericaSpeaks legacy" Tumblr site that organization staff, ever the masterful facilitators, had set up for former volunteers, discussion participants, and facilitators to "share your perspective on how AmericaSpeaks impacted you." On the National Coalition for Dialogue and Deliberation listserv, practitioners alternately expressed hope that the model developed by AmericaSpeaks would continue and laments about the problem of competition among D&D organizations at a time of shrinking philanthropic giving and government retrenchment.

Some prominent bloggers and leaders in the field placed blame elsewhere. They acknowledged that AmericaSpeaks had led the field for years, but that making change in the contemporary political context of the United States in the 2010s—an environment remade by the promise of deeper participation in politics, media, and social institutions over the last two decades, even as troubling signs of inequality were deepening—was a tall order. Peter Levine, a civic studies scholar, AmericaSpeaks board member, and author of a hopeful book on the "promise of civic renewal in America," reflected on his blog that AmericaSpeaks' closing carried grim lessons for the field:

> In essence, the people and organizations that really care about nonpartisan, open-ended citizen deliberations don't have a lot of money to pay for it, and that is a problem that affects more than AmericaSpeaks. . . . the ultimate failure of the business model raises serious questions about elites' support for civic engagement in America. . . . AmericaSpeaks leaves an inspiring legacy of examples and knowledge. But on its last day, I am worried that the demand for public deliberation is so weak.
>
> *(Levine, 2014a)*

Joe Goldman, a former staffer at AmericaSpeaks and later a funder of the organization through the Democracy Fund, reflected in a blog post that the larger field should take a deeper look at its commitments in light of the contemporary political and media culture of the US: "While we should not give up on our principles, we need to acknowledge that not enough progress has been made in institutionalizing the practices that we have spent so many years developing and defending" (Goldman, 2014).

The soul-searching experienced by the dialogue and deliberation community in the wake of AmericaSpeaks' demise described an uncertain future, characterized by alternating currents of hope for what the field had achieved and frustration that gains could be lost so quickly and change was so slow to arrive. In the 2000s and 2010s in the United States, at a time of deep apathy and cynicism about national politics, the value of demonstrating genuine public voice and citizen engagement grew. But "fake" participation had also exploded, whether from consulting firms soliciting public engagement on behalf of well-heeled clients or industry groups masquerading as the voice of the people (Bonnemann, 2010; Kuran, 1998; Levine, 2009; Snider, 2010; Walker, 2014). AmericaSpeaks itself faced criticism in 2010 for perceived partisanship from both the right and the left in its "Our Budget, Our Economy" national dialogues (Lee, 2015). Even the terminology of America's voice was deeply contested—with the Republican Party sponsoring a sound-alike interactive website called "America Speaking Out." By February 2015, the "americaspeaks.org" domain was occupied by an electronic cigarette industry-sponsored blog advocating "vaping for a strong economy."

For a volume concerned with the professionalization of deep democracy, this moment at the beginning of 2014 is useful to examine in detail, because it marks the uneasy status of the institutionalization of professional dialogue and deliberation facilitation in the United States at present. On the one hand, dialogue and deliberation experts have been invited into the halls of power as collaborators on federal Open Government initiatives and have achieved significant cultural gains in terms of spreading the practices of dialogue and deliberation widely (Buckley, 2010; Konieczka, 2010; Wolz, 2011). But even as budgets for public participation have grown, and as deeper forms of public engagement have been integrated into public, private, and non-profit organizations as a matter of course, the boundaries of "real" dialogue are increasingly fuzzy and the ability of deep democracy practitioners to gain a share of those budgets in their competition against other consultants and public relations firms is very much in doubt. While the D&D field in the United States is maturing, it nevertheless faces significant challenges. Chief among these challenges are concerns about the means and ends of participation: both ensuring access and equity in the professional field and in professionally run deliberations themselves, and securing the deeper social change that transformative public engagement promises in an era of stark inequalities.

Methods and Theoretical Approach

A number of researchers and field leaders[1] have focused on the professionalization and organizational infrastructures of public participation as subjects of study in their own right (Black, Thomas & Shaffer, 2014; Carson & Lewanski, 2008; Fischer, 2004; Fung, 2015; Gilmore & Holwerk, 2014; Glock-Grueneich & Ross, 2008; Hendriks & Carson, 2008; Jacobs, Cook & Delli Carpini, 2009; Leighninger, 2009; Levine, 2010; Levine, Fung & Gastil, 2005; Mathews, 2014a; Ryfe, 2002). These sources summarizing and providing expert commentary on deliberation organizations and their evolving relationships are extremely valuable for understanding changing practices and perspectives from diverse locations within the field.

This chapter is distinct from these analyses inasmuch as it draws on a five-year multi-method, multi-sited ethnography of the public participation field as a whole. An in-depth sociological field study was conducted by the author from 2006 through 2010 at sites in major cities in the US and Canada.[2] Extensive participant observation in various training and certification venues and professional conferences and over 50 informal interviews with diverse actors in the field provided perspective on the shared concerns and conflicts of deliberation practitioners regarding professional development and field advancement. Analysis of deliberation practitioners' listservs, organization and process websites, blogs, social networking sites, field handbooks, and unique data sources supplements the information gathered through participant observation (Small, 2011). Listserv postings were collected, coded by source, and stored in a full-text, searchable database containing over 8,400 documents representing four years of electronic conversations on the field. As a supplement to the fieldwork, informal interviews, and archival research, a non-random online survey of US dialogue and deliberation practitioners (N = 345), distributed through over 20 online listservs and web-based community networks in the field, was conducted in September and October 2009 in collaboration with Francesca Polletta of the University of California, Irvine, in order to solicit a broader perspective on the dominant tensions and shared beliefs surfacing in the qualitative research.[3]

By comparing data from a variety of settings, sources, and perspectives, this type of qualitative research across institutional domains and participant categories ensures theoretical saturation (Charmaz, 2006) and "looks to the logics of particular contexts as a way of illuminating complex interrelationships among political, legal, historical, social, economic, and cultural elements" (Scheppele, 2004, p. 390). As such, this research was conducted from the perspective of a comparative historical sociologist interested in the development of the field in the context of concurrent processes of US political and organizational development, rather than from the standpoint of advancing deliberation practice or theory (Mutz, 2008).

Contemporary scholarship on professional fields and elite movements provides valuable traction in terms of placing the struggles of public participation practitioners in their developing professional field in context (Fligstein & McAdam, 2011; Koller, 2010; Mizruchi & Fein, 1999; Powell & DiMaggio, 1991). Many of these struggles are by no means unique to dialogue and deliberation practitioners (Duffy, Binder & Skrentny, 2010; Medvetz, 2008), and identifying potential opportunities and challenges in the US public participation field in comparison to those in related settings should allow for a better sense of complex influences on the future of the field (Ryfe, 2007).

Field Organization and Scope

A number of trends in the US in the 1980s and 1990s drove demand for a field of skilled professionals who could facilitate intensive public participation among a broad cross-section of people. There was a sense that civic participation of ordinary folks was declining, and—not unrelatedly—that the participation processes that had been relied on for some time, such as environmental impact reviews and public hearings, were dominated by confrontational usual suspects and litigious interest group professionals who stymied any attempts at consensus-building. The "decide-announce-defend" model of administrative decision-making was not working. Today's collaborative and "deep" participation is often contrasted with the comparatively "thin" two-minutes-at-a-microphone model of gathering public input at hearings. The new public engagement's focus on reasoned discussion among putative equals has also coincided with a wave of enthusiasm in the academy for the idea of "deliberative" democracy, where participants might change their mind or find common ground by listening to others' viewpoints.

Thus, the field of professional public participation facilitation consulting developed in the late 1980s and early 1990s in response to demand for better methods of involvement, building on the alternative dispute resolution and community mediation movements of the 1970s and initial successes in the environmental planning field. These collaborative innovations were intended to reduce the litigation generated by an earlier phase of institutionalized participation enshrined in the National Environmental Policy Act (Layzer, 2008; Morrill & Owen-Smith, 2002; O'Leary & Bingham, 2003; Senger, 2003). Public deliberation, as a new civic form that brings together interest group representatives, activists, and laypersons as equal participants in decision-making sponsored by administrators, foundations, and businesses, also reflects the professionalization of activism, the reframing of corporate citizenship, and the increasing cross-sector collaborations that characterized organizational politics and strategy in the late 20th-century United States (Ansell & Gash, 2008; Lee, McQuarrie & Walker, 2015; Soule, 2009; Zald & McCarthy, 1980).

The outsourcing of public participation facilitation to trained practitioners from private consulting firms or non-profit organizations reflects the rearrangements of administrative power through devolution and privatization that characterized New Public Management and related management trends in the 1990s and 2000s (Handler, 1996; Kelleher & Yackee, 2009). This "veritable revolution . . . in the formation of organizations and a 'profession' devoted to the participation of ordinary citizens" has produced an extensive "organizational infrastructure for public deliberation" (Jacobs et al., 2009, p. 136). The major professional associations in the United States are IAP2 USA, an 845-member affiliate spun off in 2010 from the International Association for Public Participation (originally founded in 1990), and the National Coalition for Dialogue & Deliberation (NCDD), founded in 2002.[4] As of 2014, the NCDD had over 2,200 members and 34,000 subscribers to its monthly listserv (Heierbacher, 2015). Providers of products and services to facilitate deliberative engagement are now facing the prospect of expansive growth in and steep competition for the public participation facilitation market (Edelman, 2009; Martin, 2015).

Given this competition, it is useful to begin by better defining the field itself. "Professional public participation facilitation" is used in this chapter to refer to facilitation services aimed at engaging the public and relevant stakeholders with organizations in deeper, more interactive ways than traditional, one-way public outreach and information. The terms "public participation," "public engagement," and "public deliberation" are typically used interchangeably in the US context (consultation is used far less often than in other countries) to refer to the broad spectrum of reforms aimed at intensifying public participation and deliberation in governance, and this chapter uses all three terms in order to reflect their overlapping usage by US practitioners. Executive director of the Deliberative Democracy Consortium (DDC) Matt Leighninger notes that

> In common usage, "deliberation and democratic governance" = active citizenship = deliberative democracy = citizen involvement = citizen-centered work = public engagement = citizen participation = public dialogue = collaborative governance = public deliberation. Different people define these terms in different ways—and in most cases, the meanings are blurry and overlapping.
>
> *(Leighninger, 2009, p. 5)*

"Profession" is used to refer specifically to organizations and educational institutions offering training and degree programs, trained practitioners paid for their work in public participation facilitation, and their professional associations and occupational networks. "Field" refers to professionals, volunteer facilitators, facilitation clients, and process sponsors, but also more broadly to the academics, institutes, foundations, and other organizations that share a common language, set of practices, and interest in advancing public participation and deliberation.

Public participation professionals in the US may combine a variety of deliberative, dialogic, and participatory methods over the course of a particular project. They might convene a working group of major stakeholders for a series of meetings, produce an interactive website and host a series of online dialogues, or design and host a town hall meeting where participants share ideas in small groups and then vote on the options that have been developed. The responsibilities of the public participation consultant typically involve all aspects of process design and implementation, including production of informational and marketing materials, stakeholder outreach prior to the process, selection of methods, recruitment of participants and small group facilitators, facilitation of the overall process, continued communication with participants, presentation to the client of process outcomes, and evaluation of process efficacy. Some aspects of these tasks, such as recruitment of underrepresented groups, process branding, and software design, may also be outsourced to subcontractors like opinion research firms and marketing firms for large projects, but most contractors provide the complete range of process design and facilitation services from inception to evaluation, which may last from a few months, in the case of public participation on pandemic flu planning priorities, to 10 years or more in the case of stakeholder collaborations on contaminated sites remediation or natural resource management.

Field leaders often express frustration at the "microscopic" scale of deliberation activity compared to, for example, electoral advertising budgets (Levine, 2014b, p. 1), but the organizations served are some of the largest in the US and internationally, the lay participants involved in formal deliberation represent at least a quarter of the adult US population (Jacobs et al., 2009), and some of the decisions made—such as those over electoral reforms or health care—can affect state and national policymaking, even if they involve only a few hundred or a few thousand people directly in deliberation. Deliberation in the US is very much a "Fortune 500" phenomenon that has been embraced by elites and corporate executives. Those working in the field are oriented toward "scaling up" their practices to large groups, one of the reasons for their recurrent claims that they serve groups ranging from 10 people to 10,000 people. The fact that "thousands of well-moderated and well-organized deliberations may occur every year in a country like the United States" (Levine, 2014b, p. 1) is not insignificant, especially given that such engagement is far more intensive and demanding than viewing advertising.

Practitioners' Development and Demographics: Diverse Influences and Similar Backgrounds

Given that the field is relatively new, where did these professionals come from and how do their backgrounds influence public engagement? According to Leighninger, "[t]his is a field that emerged outside the boundaries of most professions or academic disciplines. You don't need a particular academic degree, professional license, or training certificate to be a practitioner or consultant on deliberative democracy" (Leighninger, 2009, p. 9). The 2009 practitioner survey found that practitioners, typically in their 50s, arrived at their public deliberation work from a variety of different pathways including community organizing, public relations, adult education, management consulting, and law. Practitioners draw on their experiences from all of these settings as they have constructed their products and services, borrowing techniques from participatory democracy, dispute resolution, and workplace participation and citing prior training experiences in corporate America and non-profits as relevant to their current practice. Many practitioners who are engaged in facilitation of public engagement on a regular basis nevertheless maintain footholds in other types of management consulting and coaching.

There is no typical public participation facilitation organization, as some practitioners work from within large departments of national and international environmental engineering and development firms (Colom, 2014), some are self-employed sole practitioners, some have developed their practice within for-profit partnerships, and others work for major national non-profits promoting a particular method. Half of US professionals in the practitioner survey described their organizational role as an independent consultant or sole practitioner, with another 30% selecting staff member (N = 222). While self-employment is the norm, many individuals with private practices belong to or have founded multiple organizations to support their research, coaching, and consulting work. On average, US professionals in the survey listed 1.7 organizational positions each. For this reason, the apparent diversity in the field of public participation organizations might be overstated by a focus on the organizations themselves. In understanding the multiplicity of individuals' affiliations, we can grasp both the usefulness for practitioners of distinguishing different types of work, and the heterogeneity of individual practitioners' workload and client base.

Demographically, the facilitator corps skews white, older, progressive, highly educated, and female. Among US respondents in our 2009 survey sample, whites are overrepresented as compared to the US population in the 2008 American Community Survey (88% versus 75%, N = 340). African-Americans and Asians were represented in our survey sample at about half the rate of the US population; those who selected Hispanic or Latino ethnicity were underrepresented by a factor of five as compared to the US population. As Matt Leighninger notes in describing conflicts between deliberation practitioners and community organizers, "most of these deliberative democracy advocates, at least at the national level, are white, whereas the leaders of community organizing and racial equity are a racially diverse group" (2010, p. 3). Civic studies scholar Peter Levine argues, "[w]e need more diverse leadership. I would roughly estimate that at least 90% of the top leaders of these 117 [civic renewal] organizations are white and have college degrees" (2010).

The demographics of our survey were similar to those noted at practitioner conferences. Keypad polling exercises to solicit demographic data of deliberation conference attendees often elicited commentary from the session facilitator of "well, the white folks showed up" or "the white folks are in the house" (Field notes). Seventy-one percent of US respondents in the survey held advanced degrees (beyond baccalaureate; N = 344). Sixty-two percent of US respondents were women (N = 344), a disproportion not likely due to gendered differences in response rates as the gender makeup of attendees at conferences is typically also 60/40 (Field notes). The median age of US D&D practitioners in the survey was 55 (N = 341). Among US practitioners, our 2009 survey found a ratio of conservative to liberal D&D practitioners of 1:32 (N = 337); this is, needless to say, far more liberal than the political perspectives of the US population generally as reported in the American National Election Study from 2004, but it is even more liberal than the 1:3 ratio of conservative to liberal college professors reported in the 2006 Politics of the American Professoriate Survey (Gross & Simmons, 2014).

Polletta and Chen claim that "the female gendered character of the contemporary field of organized public deliberation" has had positive impacts on women's participation in deliberations (2013, p. 291). Nevertheless, multiple forms of stratification and occupational segregation in the practitioner corps may threaten the success of future deliberation efforts if deliberation gets coded as "female" or as conducted *for* marginalized groups.[5] Scholarship on the feminization of professions (Menkel-Meadow, 1989; Reskin & Roos, 1990; Wright & Jacobs, 1994) and its impact on professional fields suggests that feminization in other occupations has sometimes resulted from male flight as occupations diversify and as status and pay decline.

Within the field, potential sources of exclusion and a concomitant inability to advance its professed ideals of equity are sources of continuing concern. Obstacles to entering the field for young people, and the possibility of young professionals possibly exiting the field for related digital campaigning, open source, or transparency initiatives worry field leaders, who organized a 2014 conference around the theme of "Democracy for the Next Generation," with scholarships for students and sessions devoted to discussing barriers to entry.

The seemingly homogeneous makeup of the facilitator corps was a matter of chagrin for some practitioners. One self-identified sociologist on the survey's public discussion website critiqued our presentation of results as "glossing over the insularity of the dialogue and deliberation crew. This community is largely a white, left leaning, highly educated, and (I am guessing) has an income generally greater than the median. . . . D&D is a field of privilege." Leighninger (2010) describes the racial and ethnic demographics of the public deliberation field as affecting relationships with activists and organizers. But interest in discussing equity issues is mixed, in part because of what McCoy describes as "concerns that our field will lose its credibility as an 'honest broker' with both liberals and conservatives and with governmental authorities" (2014, p. 3). Black et al. describe "the relationship between social justice and the processes we advocate, and the ways in which we do or do not adequately address diversity in our work" as "longstanding issues" for the field (2014, p. 3).

In a 2014 essay titled "The State of the Field in Light of the State of Our Democracy: My Democracy Anxiety Closet," field leader (and long-time executive director of Everyday Democracy, dedicated to inclusive local community dialogues) Martha McCoy laments the field's failure to address equity "head-on" and describes it as "reticent" "to incorporate analyses of structural racism and other inequities into their efforts." McCoy sees this reticence as directly lessening "our field's effectiveness in linking citizen voice to sustainable change. It also makes it less supportable to claim that deliberative democracy is about equitable voice and power sharing" (2014, p. 3). There are certainly many in the field who see "deliberation as a vehicle of political equality and social justice" (DDC, 2008), but diversity and justice concerns centered on ascriptive identity categories are also seen as a threat to productive deliberation in the short term and forward momentum with elites in the longer term.

Grasstops Mobilization and Field Advancement

The maturity of the public participation field can be seen by coordinated and collaborative mobilization efforts to advance the field itself. According to Button and Ryfe (2005, p. 21), "[i]t is fair to say that the deliberative movement around the globe is spearheaded by a relatively small cadre of experts." A number of opportunities to embed public participation nationally arose during the presidency of Barack Obama, whose administration sought to further formalize enhanced public engagement in government at the federal and international level (US Department of State, 2011). The administration's Open Government Initiative prompted a sustained effort on the part of professional deliberation associations to take advantage of this opportunity for integrating their services into government—typically called "grasstops" mobilization by scholars (Walker, 2014).

In February 2009, NCDD and IAP2 collaborated with member organizations to launch the Public Engagement Principles Project, an effort "to create clarity in our field about what we consider to be the fundamental components of quality public engagement, and to support President Obama's January 21, 2009 memorandum on open government" (Heierbacher, 2010). This participatory effort to synthesize and certify knowledge was not just internally focused, however. The lead organizations collaborated with members of related movements like the transparency movement, and won endorsements of the Principles from leading organizations in other fields, including the League of Women Voters, National League of Cities, and other established urban, community, and environmental organizations, further cementing the legitimacy of the public participation field as a leading civil society actor in national politics. Additionally, field elites dominated the online process to gain public input on the Open Government Directive, with AmericaSpeaks authoring six of the top ten ideas in the public brainstorming phase. Deliberative experts also won invitation-only roles as advisory experts to federal administrators and White House officials at meetings on the Open Government Partnership (OGP) and at conferences such as "Champions of Participation" 1, 2, and 3, and "Strengthening Our Nation's Democracy II." These efforts culminated in 2015 in the federal government's announcement of its own US Public Participation Playbook—a collaboratively developed document very similar to the Principles document and involving the participation of NCDD and others: "a team of 70 leaders across the government have worked side-by-side with civil society organizations and citizens in a collaborative effort to deliver this tool" (Zarek & Herman, 2015).

The elite character of deliberative mobilization at the national level is by no means unusual for contemporary social movements and reflects recent historical shifts in which institutional insiders play effective roles as movement actors (Armstrong & Bernstein, 2008; Duffy et al., 2010). In a special issue of the *Journal of Public Deliberation* on "The State of Our Field" in 2014, leaders argue for more of this kind of strategic action. Civic studies scholar Peter Levine urges more cross-sector collaborations with organizations in related fields, even if they are "adversarial," in order to marshal collective resources against moneyed interests: "we should look beyond the organizations that intentionally convene deliberations and also enlist organizations that preserve common resources, volunteer service groups, civics classes, grassroots public media efforts, and partisan, ideological, and faith-based movements that have some interest in discussion" (2014b, p. 1). Similarly, Levine's colleague Nancy Thomas, former director of the Democracy Imperative, suggests alliances "with reformers in different areas of democracy's ecological system. . . . justice and equal opportunity, knowledge and information development, and government integrity" (2014, p. 1).

AmericaSpeaks founder Carolyn Lukensmeyer argues that building national infrastructure will require further leveraging critical relationships not just with reformers, but with elites: The field should "focus its energy on . . . building a cadre of elected leaders and public officials . . . [and] engaging with the media so that it becomes an effective partner" (2014, p. 1). Nevertheless, to the extent that the strategic advancement of a field dedicated to lay participation may enhance organizational power at the expense of everyday people's capacity to organize, field leaders have expressed concerns, discussed further in the conclusion, regarding the costs of grasstops mobilization and further professionalization.

Managing Escalating Demand and Competition in the Market for Public Engagement Services

While many in the field refer to a "framing problem" or "branding problem" (McCoy, 2014) in scaling up deliberation, public participation consultants advertise their services to a wide variety of clients for different issues. Local organizations and government actors at the community level account for a substantial proportion of demand for deliberation services. In the 2009 practitioner survey, local and regional governments and community development corporations were most frequently selected as one of the top three sponsors for processes on which US professionals worked over the last two years, at 25% (N = 660). Local non-profit groups were next, at 22% of all selections.

The for-profit world is also a common client of deliberation practitioners. In the 2009 survey, businesses, chambers, and industry trade groups accounted for 17% of all client types selected. Jacobs et al. (2009) found that deliberative events were sponsored by businesses in 20% of cases. An internal IAP2 survey of member practitioners around the globe found that "private sector" actors were *primary* "customers, clients, and partners" for 16.2% of respondents; this does not include those who selected clients of multiple sectors (N = 167). The increasing trend in private investment to produce opportunities for deliberation reflects more general growth in private sponsorship of public participation across sectors and domains (Lee et al., 2015). While some deliberation theorists have critiqued private sponsorship as antithetical to democratic values, deliberation practitioners are highly conscious of the threat of commercialization and carefully resist commodification and co-optation in their work with clients and sponsors (Lee, McNulty & Shaffer, 2015).

It is important to note that "clients" with whom practitioners work directly to design processes may actually be separate from the "sponsors" who are underwriting deliberation. In describing non-public sponsors, Jacobs et al. assert that deliberation is funded "by third parties (government entities, foundations, and individuals) committed to the public-interest contributions of these forums and to reducing the costs to individuals of engaging in public talking" (2009, p. 147). In fact, a broader range of organizations in the US subsidize public deliberation, and these groups typically fit the profile of urban growth machine actors (Molotch, 1976). Foundations, community development corporations, and individual civic boosters play major roles, but newspapers, television networks, banks and mortgage lenders, utilities, health systems, universities, and residential and commercial developers also sponsor or underwrite public deliberation efforts on a regular basis. The involvement of community actors heavily involved in growth may result from the fact that growth management is often the subject of public deliberation. Forty-four percent of US practitioners in the 2009 survey had facilitated on the specific topic of comprehensive community planning over the last two years (N = 334).

What other common topics explain the rise in demand for public participation facilitation, and the choice to use it instead of other organizational strategies (Lee & Romano, 2013)? Most analyses of the expansive growth of public participation consulting in the US have focused on the proliferation and heterogeneity of deliberative methods, emphasizing the diversity of ways to recruit participants (from random selection of small, representative groups to massively inclusive invitations to whole communities), the variety of tools and technologies on offer, and the differing purposes of different processes (from dialogues aimed at conflict reduction to citizens' juries directed to produce judgments on policy proposals). This emphasis on producing typologies of deliberation methods is misleading, however, since it does not take into account the extent to which most methods share many similar characteristics and most processes focus on a few in-demand topics.

Despite the frequent categorization of "Appreciative Inquiry" as a unique method, for instance, other deliberative methods generally employ its explicitly positive and opportunity-focused philosophy. Not coincidentally, this strengths-based approach to assets (versus problems) is useful for sponsors and clients in settings related to financial crises. Lee and Romano find that "clients and sponsors typically seek deliberation as a strategy for management problems they face when existing or potential resistance to austerity policies arises from corporate reorganization, state retrenchment, and urban redevelopment" (2013, p. 743). Contention related to inequality was increasingly on the minds of organizational and political leaders in the US as the long-term dimensions of the economic crisis in Obama's second term became clear. The three most common topics on which US practitioners surveyed in 2009 had facilitated in the last two years shed light on similar framings of different economic problems. These were "education and youth" (167 practitioners), "comprehensive community planning and visioning" (147 practitioners), and "organizational development and human resources" (135 practitioners). Deliberations on these topics focus on the difficulty of confronting social problems (typically phrased as making "tough choices") in a challenging economic landscape of "tight times."

Deliberative processes about youth typically emphasize local efforts to curb at-risk youth's socially and economically destructive behavior, especially in cases where corporations have been targeted by activists and regulators, as in the case of childhood obesity (Lee & Romano, 2013). Consultants note that shrinking finances have compelled public clients to seek out deliberations on "comprehensive community planning" in order to manage protests over cuts. On a practitioner listserv, one director of a deliberation training organization in California marks the influence of budget pressures: "[f]or the municipalities we work with in California, we are finding a desperation on the part of many to involve the public quickly and cheaply in policy discussions from budgets to land use" (Database files). Similar pressures drive corporations to seek out deliberation for use with employees and organizational stakeholders in order to handle contention and dysfunction related to mergers and downsizing.

Obviously, managers have a number of tactics readily available for anticipated problems following corporate reorganization, but deliberation is generally employed in "tough" cases where prior remedies have not succeeded. As Martin argues in the case of state governments, "State officials concede new procedural rights of consultation—and create new opportunities for nongovernmental brokers of consultation—when their extractive demands provoke resistance" (2015, p. 110). This finding complements reports from practitioners that demand for deliberative "choicework" has surged during the financial crisis. While the research in this chapter focused on the US, scholars in Europe and Australasia have also found deliberation used in contexts of public hostility and conflicts over decision-making on economic development and private-sector growth (Atkinson, 1999; Barnes, Newman & Sullivan, 2007; Head, 2007; Talpin, 2011; Williams, 2004).

The fact that deliberation is used increasingly to manage contention creates distinct challenges for practitioners in the field. This is frequently confounded by the fact that organizations from outside the public participation field have resorted to deliberative tactics when other change management strategies have not worked. As community members, employees, and consumers have become more cynical about standard marketing and employee management techniques, firms without much experience in deliberation have changed their own tactics in what PR firm Edelman grandly calls "The Age of Engagement"—a new era of deeper involvement in customers' lives. The co-optation or corruption of deliberative techniques was a primary concern for respondents in the 2009 survey, who reported that one of five leading obstacles to deliberative processes was "participant experiences with bad processes" and "client experiences with bad public participation." Practitioners are at the front lines of these realities, since they are often called in to clean up the mess when clients have already conducted participation processes that failed.

An example of these concerns is in worries about the rapid explosion of software for online budget calculators that allow citizen "choicework." At the same time that there is excitement about the diffusion of participatory budgeting, a well-known and respected deliberative method, its potential contamination by deployment in rigged or non-deliberative settings has provoked online discussions among public engagement proponents, who anticipate that such efforts might be manipulated for sponsor gains but might also affect public enthusiasm for deliberative solutions. An expert on online budgeting software asked about a "budget challenge" run by the Los Angeles Mayor's Office: "[s]o is the Budget Puzzle in its current form deliberative? Hardly." Another public participation leader excited about local government adopting deliberative tools was nevertheless concerned:

> There are definite "Good", "Bad", and "Ugly" aspects to the initiative . . . Participants should quickly realize that not everything is on the table . . . because the Mayor says so. . . . The real "challenge" for all these projects will be to ensure participation is not biased nor wasted.
>
> *(Database files)*

The Kettering Foundation, a non-profit foundation that researches deliberative democracy, asked on their Facebook page: "What do you think: are budgeting exercises like these what we would call 'deliberative choice work'? If not, how are they related?"

Such concerns raise the issue of unintended consequences resulting from the diffusion of public participation technologies and standards across contexts. At the same time, public participation professionals discuss the relationship between what they do and privately administered public discussions that reach many millions of people, such as Oprah Winfrey's 2009 self-described "global conversation about consciousness" (a live interactive webinar series on New Age self-help writer Eckhart Tolle's book *A New Earth*) or Starbucks' 2015 "Race Together" Initiative. In an atmosphere of financial uncertainty and new sources of competition, new technologies and new markets for services are opening up extraordinary opportunities for public participation professionals to expand their practices to new audiences and markets.

Nevertheless, pursuing these opportunities entails risks to the perceived authenticity of public deliberation and potentially large downsides if everyday participants become cynical about public participation practices the way they have become cynical about public relations and ordinary politics. There is some evidence that participants can be "highly critical" of "the top-down power dynamics" in processes and skeptical of "broader societal or political impacts," suggesting that the field needs to go "beyond engagement exercises" (Powell, Delborne & Colin, 2011) or beyond the "field's strong emphasis on temporary public consultations" (Scully, 2014, p. 1). Leighninger goes so far as to describe a "harmful identity crisis" in the field in the lack of clarity around the democratic aims of practitioners' tools: "these aren't just props for conventional processes, but building blocks for new political systems" (2014, p. 1).

Growing Pains, Disruptions, and New Opportunities: Key Challenges Moving Forward

> There is a huge and troubling gap between what we in the "deliberative civic field" see on a regular basis and how most people experience public life. In the course of our work, we are fortunate to see empowered public voice and action and its effects on the lives of

individuals, families, and communities. And yet we also see the pre-dominant realities: people from different backgrounds and views are often disconnected from each other and from government; people with few economic means and people of color face significant barriers to advancement; government is gridlocked; and we face serious public problems that go largely unaddressed. . . . Even with growing successes in democratic innovation and practice, and with meaningful results from those practices, we haven't even come close to affecting the daily lives of most people. It's as though we have some knowledge about effective medicine for treating a rampant disease, but haven't figured out a way to mass produce and distribute it.

(McCoy, 2014)

The field of public participation in the United States has long been characterized as developing; by the mid-2010s, the field had advanced to the point that leading figures saw a moment for stocktaking regarding old problems and new challenges (Black et al., 2014; Gilmore & Holwerk, 2014). Sandy Heierbacher, president of NCDD, envisioned "extraordinary momentum and productivity in our field" at the same time that there was "a strong yearning in our field to break out of our current constraints, to find ways to collaborate more effectively with each other, to combine forces with those outside our field, and to scale up our efforts" (2014, p. 3). A plenary session at the October 2014 National Conference on Dialogue & Deliberation in Reston, VA, focused US practitioners on ways they could address "four barriers to the dialogue and deliberation community's success":

1. How might we overcome the lack of trust in our Democracy, our leaders, and in one another?
2. How might we make our D&D work more equitable, inclusive and empowering?
3. How might we more clearly delineate our field of practice for ourselves and those we seek to serve?
4. How might we eliminate structural barriers in our democratic systems?

(Breese, 2014)

The first two areas of concern demonstrate that field members are highly aware of the threats that contemporary political polarization, apathy, cynicism, and structural inequalities in the larger society might pose to achieving participation and empowerment in the projects they conduct. The third and fourth barriers relate to the challenges dialogue and deliberation practitioners see in their own field; on the one hand, how can they compete in a landscape where engagement is becoming a popular strategy among actors not seeking empowerment, and on the other hand, how can field actors institutionalize authentically deliberative decision-making in larger bureaucratic systems? The partial victories of the last decade, and the ongoing fallout from the financial crisis of 2008, have created a crossroads for public participation professionals.

Field champions and funders continue to express dismay at the challenges the field faces in addressing stark and increasing democratic deficits in the US, despite more than two decades of civic renewal initiatives. David Mathews, President and CEO of the Kettering Foundation, describes the state of the "emerging civic industry managed by professionals" as troubling given that "growth in organizations dedicated to strengthening the civic realm" may inhibit or work against grassroots efforts (2014b, pp. 5–6). Brad Rourke, a program officer at Kettering, describes this as: "a growing gap between the institutions meant to aid citizens in exerting control over their future and the citizens themselves," particularly as institutions attempt to respond to external pressures for accountability and professionalism (2014, p. 12).

On the one hand, the field is becoming stronger and thus better able to define its boundaries—but this consolidation of the field might prevent citizen empowerment by limiting access. Mathews warns against "the tendency of both government and nongovernmental organizations to colonize and unintentionally destroy the unique qualities of informal civic associations" (2014b, p. 5). Civic studies scholar Peter Levine argues of the larger civic renewal SAF,

> We need more organizations with grassroots constituencies. . . . I would say there is a rough inverse proportion between centrality in this [civic renewal] network and size of grassroots base. With a few exceptions . . . the organizations that have the most citizen members are peripheral to civic renewal, and the pure civic renewal groups are grant-supported professional organizations or foundations.
>
> *(2010)*

As one practitioner writes on a listserv, "All across the Net we see expert online communities of practice essentially involving professionals, but not everyday citizens" (Database files). Perhaps as a result, NCDD director Sandy Heierbacher noted in a 2014 essay "a strong swing back to a focus on the local level" from the national level—with even national-level efforts focusing on supporting local groups (p. 2).

While realizing "the full potential of democratic, empowered civic engagement" may involve "some hard choices" by field members (Scully, 2014, p. 1), practitioners and field leaders have expressed optimism about the potential of the field in advancing transformative change. Martha McCoy of Everyday Democracy writes that field-building exercises should be focused on "creating a vision, a strategy and an infrastructure that are powerful enough to transform our country" (2014, p. 3). Some leaders, like Joe Goldman in the introduction to this chapter, claim that further progress may require a rethinking of change tactics and beliefs in deliberation altogether—that to achieve the democratic aims public participation professionals want, they must begin thinking more like a movement and less like a professional field. Peter Levine argues that "rising signs of oligarchy in the United States" mean "It is time for us to begin to stir and organize—not for deliberation, but for democracy" (2014b, p. 3). Patrick Scully, a leading public participation consultant and researcher, puts this most starkly, seeing a need to resolve the "tension between reformism and more fundamental, even revolutionary changes to democratic politics." Even Scully, however, believes the field is capable of rising to the challenge: "[t]he theory and practice of deliberative democracy has achieved a sufficiently mature stage of development to allow it to push the boundaries of 'action' and 'activism'" (2014, p. 2).

Evidence from a multi-year ethnographic study indicates that US professional public participation is a field very self-consciously at a crossroads following 30-odd years of growth among a stable but aging and largely homogeneous facilitator corps. Public participation professionals have been successful at integrating episodic deliberative processes into public, private, and third-sector organizations, and have faced increasing demand for their services from organizations seeking to manage contention regarding cutbacks in the wake of the 2008 financial crisis. Field elites have collaborated with each other and across organizational fields to advance practices and standards, initiatives that have gained recognition and legitimacy in national politics. The potential for scaling up deliberative practices with new technologies has also meant competition from non-deliberative consultants, and field leaders worry that capacity growth among practitioners may come at the expense of laypersons. In Scully's opinion, "for a local civic infrastructure to thrive, it is essential that it be built and controlled not by deliberative practitioners alone, but in collaboration with ordinary citizens who have a strong stake in its success" (2014, p. 3). At the same time, national-level efforts to advance civic infrastructure will likely remain a grasstops affair (even if more and more diverse organizational collaborations are sought), due to the resources required. Given rising inequality and democratic deficits during the field's expansion, many field leaders hope for transformative change in not just the way they work, but in the world at large. As such, in the next 30 years, US public engagement leaders may seek to focus less on professionalization and more on democratizing access to the profession.

Notes

1 While invested in the field's advancement, field leaders are nevertheless often deeply critical and reflexive about their own efforts, in part because of their investments in and connections to academic research on public participation and accountability (for more on these overlaps, see David Kahane's work on "pracademics" in this volume).
2 See Lee (2015) for more detailed information on methodology and limitations. This chapter draws extensively on my book on the field and other publications from the project, particularly Lee (2011).
3 The survey, whose target population was volunteer and professional deliberation practitioners in the United States, yielded 433 completed responses, 345 of which were from respondents based in the United States. For a variety of reasons, we chose to focus

on surveying individual deliberation practitioners connected to the field through email listservs rather than conducting a random mail survey of deliberation organizations and consultancies. While the survey sample was non-random, we believe this is an important first step in understanding those areas of broad agreement and tension for a group of centrally located and deeply engaged actors within the field and a valuable supplement to the extensive field research and archival analysis described above. These data are described in the text as survey results and not cited parenthetically; the N given reflects the total number of valid responses. Percentage distributions of survey data given in the analysis are only intended to indicate percentage distributions in the particular group of survey respondents, a unique sample of US practitioners. More information on the survey, including demographic information and full results, is available at the public survey results website (http://sites.lafayette.edu/ddps).

4 As their names, relative size, and fee structures indicate, the NCDD includes a wider scope of deliberative democracy enthusiasts and non-professionals (typically more students, academics, and volunteer facilitators) than IAP2 USA. NCDD does not require membership dues and describes itself as a "big tent," with 300 members from 54 countries. IAP2 is dedicated to "serving the needs of P2 practitioners specific to the United States." Dues for individuals start at $50 per year.

5 In AmericaSpeaks' "Our Budget, Our Economy" deliberations, Esterling, Fung and Lee (2010) find slight underrepresentation of whites and overrepresentation of African-Americans compared to census data on the larger population in the six cities studied.

References

Ansell, C., & Gash, A. (2008). Collaborative governance in theory and practice. *Journal of Public Administration Research and Theory, 18*(4), 543–571.

Armstrong, E. A., & Bernstein, M. (2008). Culture, power, and institutions: A multi-institutional politics approach to social movements. *Sociological Theory, 26*, 74–99.

Atkinson, R. (1999). Discourses of partnership and empowerment in contemporary British urban regeneration. *Urban Studies, 36*(1), 59–72.

Barnes, M., Newman, J., & Sullivan, H. (2007). *Power, participation and political renewal: Case studies in public participation.* Bristol: Policy Press.

Black, L. W., Thomas, N. L., & Shaffer, T. J. (2014). The state of our field: Introduction to the special issue. *Journal of Public Deliberation, 10*(1). Retrieved from http://www.publicdeliberation.net/jpd/vol10/iss1/art1.

Bonnemann, T. (2010, November 16). Does the budget puzzle qualify as "deliberative choice work"? *Intellitics.* Retrieved from http://www.intellitics.com/blog/2010/11/16/does-the-budget-puzzle-qualify-as-deliberative-choice-work/.

Breese, C. (2014, December 17). Report: How should we tackle our field's biggest barriers to success? *The National Coalition for Dialogue & Deliberation Community Blog.* Retrieved from http://ncdd.org/16958.

Buckley, S. (2010, February 2). OpenGovRadio today (2/2/10): "Engagement-lite" and the OpenGov dashboard. *US Transparency.* Retrieved from http://ustransparency.blogspot.com/2010/02/opengovradio-today-2210-engagement-lite.html.

Button, M., & Ryfe, D. M. (2005). What can we learn from the practice of deliberative democracy? In J. Gastil & P. Levine (Eds.), *The deliberative democracy handbook: Strategies for effective civic engagement in the twenty-first century* (pp. 20–33). San Francisco, CA: Jossey-Bass.

Carson, L., & Lewanski, R. (2008). Fostering citizen participation top-down. *International Journal of Public Participation, 2*(1), 72–83.

Charmaz, K. (2006). *Constructing grounded theory: A practical guide through qualitative analysis.* London: Sage.

Colom, S. J. (2014). *Re-engineering democracy: The insertion of international engineering firms into the politics of representation.* Paper presented at the 2014 ASA Annual Meeting. Berkeley, CA. Retrieved from http://citation.allacademic.com/meta/p_mla_apa_research_citation/7/2/6/6/8/p726686_index.html.

Deliberative Democracy Consortium. (2008). *Where is democracy headed? Research and practice on public deliberation.* Washington, DC: Deliberative Democracy Consortium.

Duffy, M., Binder, A., & Skrentny, J. (2010). Elite status and social change: Using field analysis to explain policy formation and implementation. *Social Problems, 57*(1), 49–73.

Edelman. (2009). Public engagement in the conversation age: Vol 2. *Edelman.* Retrieved from http://fr.slideshare.net/EdelmanDigital/public-engagement-in-the-conversation-age-vol-2-2009.

Esterling, K., Fung, A., & Lee, T. (2010). *The difference deliberation makes: Evaluating the "our budget, our economy" public deliberation.* Washington, DC: AmericaSpeaks.

Fischer, F. (2004). Professional expertise in a deliberative democracy: Facilitating participatory inquiry. *The Good Society, 13*(1), 21–27.

Fligstein, N., & McAdam, D. (2011). Toward a general theory of strategic action fields. *Sociological Theory, 29*(1), 1–26.

Fung, A. (2015). Putting the public back into governance: The challenges of citizen participation and its future. *Public Administration Review, 75*(4), 513–522.

Gilmore, M., & Holwerk, D. (Eds.). (2014). *Connections: Taking stock of the civic arena.* Dayton, OH: Kettering Foundation.

Glock-Grueneich, N., & Ross, S. N. (2008). Growing the field: The institutional, theoretical, and conceptual maturation of "public participation". *International Journal of Public Participation, 2*(1), 1–32.

Goldman, J. (2014, January 2). A farewell to AmericaSpeaks. *The Democracy Fund.* Retrieved from http://www.democracyfund.org/blog/entry/farewell-to-americaspeaks.

Gross, N., & Simmons, S. (Eds.). (2014). *Professors and their politics.* Baltimore, MD: Johns Hopkins University Press.

Handler, J. F. (1996). *Down from bureaucracy: The ambiguity of privatization and empowerment.* Princeton, NJ: Princeton University Press.

Head, B. W. (2007). Community engagement: Participation on whose terms? *Australian Journal of Political Science, 42*(3), 441–454.

Heierbacher, S. (2010, August 1). Core principles for public engagement. *The National Coalition for Dialogue & Deliberation, Resource Center.* Retrieved from http://ncdd.org/rc/item/3643.

Heierbacher, S. (2014). The next generation of our work. *Journal of Public Deliberation, 10*(1). Retrieved from http://www.publicdeliberation.net/jpd/vol10/iss1/art23.

Heierbacher, S. (2015, January 5). NCDD's year in numbers infographic is out! *The National Coalition for Dialogue & Deliberation Community Blog.* Retrieved from http://ncdd.org/17127.

Hendriks, C. M., & Carson, L. (2008). Can the market help the forum? Negotiating the commercialization of deliberative democracy. *Policy Sciences, 41*(4), 293–313.

Jacobs, L. R., Cook, F. L., & Delli Carpini, M. X. (2009). *Talking together: Public deliberation and political participation in America.* Chicago: University of Chicago Press.

Kelleher, C. A., & Yackee, S. W. (2009). A political consequence of contracting: Organized interests and state agency decision making. *Journal of Public Administration Research and Theory, 19*(3), 579–602.

Koller, A. (2010). The public sphere and comparative historical research. *Social Science History*, *34*(3), 261–290.

Konieczka, S. P. (2010). Practicing a participatory presidency? An analysis of the Obama administration's open government dialogue. *International Journal of Public Participation*, *4*(1), 43–66.

Kuran, T. (1998). Insincere deliberation and democratic failure. *Critical Review*, *12*, 529–544.

Layzer, J. A. (2008). *Natural experiments: Ecosystem-based management and the environment*. Cambridge, MA: MIT Press.

Lee, C. W. (2015). *Do-it-yourself democracy: The rise of the public engagement industry*. Oxford: Oxford University Press.

Lee, C. W. (2011). Five assumptions academics make about deliberation, and why they deserve rethinking. *Journal of Public Deliberation*, 7(1), 1–48.

Lee, C. W., McQuarrie, M., & Walker, E. T. (Eds.). (2015). *Democratizing inequalities: Dilemmas of the new public participation*. New York: NYU Press.

Lee, C. W., McNulty, K., & Shaffer, S. (2015). Civic-izing markets: Selling social profits in public deliberation. In C. W. Lee, M. McQuarrie & E. T. Walker (Eds.), *Democratizing inequalities: Dilemmas of the new public participation* (pp. 27–45). New York: NYU Press.

Lee, C. W., & Romano, Z. (2013). Democracy's new discipline: Public deliberation as organizational strategy. *Organization Studies*, *34*(5–6), 733–753.

Leighninger, M. (2009). *Funding and fostering local democracy: What philanthropy should know about the emerging field of deliberation and democratic governance*. Denver, CO: Philanthropy for Active Civic Engagement.

Leighninger, M. (2010). *Creating spaces for change: Working toward a "story of now" in public engagement*. Battle Creek, MI: W.K. Kellogg Foundation.

Leighninger, M. (2014). What we're talking about when we talk about the "civic field" (and why we should clarify what we mean). *Journal of Public Deliberation*, *10*(1). Retrieved from http://www.publicdeliberation.net/jpd/vol10/iss1/art8/.

Levine, P. (2009, January 27). Collaborative problem-solving: The fake corporate version. *A Blog for Civic Renewal*. Retrieved from http://peterlevine.ws/?p=5615.

Levine, P. (2010, October 25). A map of the civic renewal field. *A Blog for Civic Renewal*. Retrieved from http://peterlevine.ws/?p=6024.

Levine, P. (2014a, January 3). Reflections on AmericaSpeaks on its last day. *A Blog for Civic Renewal*. Retrieved from http://peterlevine.ws/?p=13066.

Levine, P. (2014b). Beyond deliberation: A strategy for civic renewal. *Journal of Public Deliberation*, *10*(1). Retrieved from http://www.publicdeliberation.net/jpd/vol10/iss1/art19.

Levine, P., Fung, A., & Gastil, J. (2005). Future directions for public deliberation. *Journal of Public Deliberation*, *1*(1). Retrieved from http://www.publicdeliberation.net/jpd/vol1/iss1/art3/.

Lukensmeyer, C. (2014). Key challenges facing the field of deliberative democracy. *Journal of Public Deliberation*, *10*(1). Retrieved from http://www.publicdeliberation.net/jpd/vol10/iss1/art24.

McCoy, M. (2014). The state of the field in light of the state of our democracy: My democracy anxiety closet. *Journal of Public Deliberation*, *10*(1). Retrieved from http://www.publicdeliberation.net/jpd/vol10/iss1/art13.

Martin, I. W. (2015). The fiscal sociology of public consultation. In C. W. Lee, M. McQuarrie & E. T. Walker (Eds.), *Democratizing inequalities: Dilemmas of the new public participation* (pp. 102–124). New York: NYU Press.

Mathews, D. (2014a). *The ecology of democracy: Finding ways to have a stronger hand in shaping our future*. Dayton, OH: Kettering Foundation Press.

Mathews, D. (2014b). What's going on here? Taking stock of citizen-centered democracy. In M. Gilmore & D. Holwerk (Eds.), *Connections: Taking stock of the civic arena* (pp. 4–7). Dayton, OH: Kettering Foundation.

Medvetz, T. (2008). *Think tanks as an emergent field.* New York: Social Science Research Council.

Menkel-Meadow, C. (1989). Exploring a research agenda of the feminization of the legal profession: Theories of gender and social change. *Law & Social Inquiry, 14*(2), 289–319.

Mizruchi, M. S., & Fein, L. C. (1999). The social construction of organizational knowledge: A study of the uses of coercive, mimetic, and normative isomorphism. *Administrative Science Quarterly, 44,* 653–683.

Molotch, H. (1976). The city as a growth machine: Toward a political economy of place. *American Journal of Sociology, 82*(2), 309–332.

Morrill, C., & Owen-Smith, J. (2002). The emergence of environmental conflict resolution: Subversive stories and the construction of collective action frames and organizational fields. In A. J. Hoffman & M. J. Ventresca (Eds.), *Organizations, policy, and the natural environment: Institutional and strategic perspectives* (pp. 90–118). Stanford, CA: Stanford University Press.

Mutz, D. (2008). Is deliberative democracy a falsifiable theory? *Annual Review of Political Science, 11,* 521–538.

O'Leary, R., & Bingham, L. B. (Eds.). (2003). *The promise and performance of environmental conflict resolution.* Washington, DC: Resources for the Future Press.

Polletta, F., & Chen, P. C. B. (2013). Gender and public talk: Accounting for women's variable participation in the public sphere. *Sociological Theory, 31*(4), 291–317.

Powell, M., Delborne, J., & Colin, M. (2011). Beyond engagement exercises: Exploring the US National Citizens' Technology Forum from the bottom-up. *Journal of Public Deliberation, 7*(1). Retrieved from http://www.publicdeliberation.net/jpd/vol7/iss1/art4.

Powell, W. W., & DiMaggio, P. J. (1991). The iron cage revisited: Institutional isomorphism and collective rationality in organizational fields. In W. W. Powell & P. J. DiMaggio (Eds.), *The new institutionalism in organizational analysis* (pp. 63–82). Chicago: University of Chicago Press.

Reskin, B. F., & Roos, P. A. (1990). *Job queues, gender queues: Explaining women's inroads into male occupations.* Philadelphia, PA: Temple University Press.

Rourke, B. (2014). Philanthropy at a crossroads: Serving citizens and communities in an era of accountability and transparency. In M. Gilmore & D. Holwerk (Eds.), *Connections: Taking stock of the civic arena* (pp. 12–15). Dayton, OH: Kettering Foundation.

Ryfe, D. M. (2002). The practice of deliberative democracy: A study of 16 deliberative organizations. *Political Communication, 19*(3), 359–377.

Ryfe, D. M. (2007). Toward a sociology of deliberation. *Journal of Public Deliberation, 3*(1). Retrieved from http://www.publicdeliberation.net/jpd/vol3/iss1/art3/.

Scheppele, K. L. (2004). Constitutional ethnography: An introduction. *Law and Society Review, 38*(3), 389–406.

Scully, P. L. (2014). A path to the next form of (deliberative) democracy. *Journal of Public Deliberation, 10*(1). Retrieved from http://www.publicdeliberation.net/jpd/vol10/iss1/art12/.

Senger, J. M. (2003). *Federal dispute resolution: Using ADR with the United States government.* San Francisco, CA: Jossey-Bass.

Small, M. L. (2011). How to conduct a mixed methods study: Recent trends in a rapidly growing literature. *Annual Review of Sociology, 37,* 57–86.

Snider, J. H. (2010). Deterring fake public participation. *International Journal of Public Participation, 4,* 90–102.

Soule, S. A. (2009). *Contention and corporate social responsibility*. New York: Cambridge University Press.

Talpin, J. (2011). *Schools of democracy: How ordinary citizens (sometimes) become competent in participatory budgeting institutions*. Colchester, UK: ECPR Press.

Thomas, N. L. (2014). Democracy by design. *Journal of Public Deliberation, 10*(1). Retrieved from http://www.publicdeliberation.net/jpd/vol10/iss1/art17.

US Department of State. (2011, July 7). Secretary Clinton and Brazilian Foreign Minister to launch Open Government Partnership on July 12. *US DS*. Retrieved from http://www.state.gov/r/pa/prs/ps/2011/07/167745.htm.

Walker, E. T. (2014). *Grassroots for hire: Public affairs consultants in American democracy*. New York: Cambridge University Press.

Williams, M. (2004). Discursive democracy and New Labour: Five ways in which decision-makers manage citizen agendas in public participation initiatives. *Sociological Research Online, 9*(3). Retrieved from http://www.socresonline.org.uk/9/3/williams.html.

Wolz, C. (2011, March 16). Room for progress in online participation for open government. Retrieved from http://www.ictdev.org/pulse/20110316/influence/room-progress-online-participation-open-government-tim-bonnemann-sxswi.

Wright, R., & Jacobs, J. A. (1994). Male flight from computer work: A new look at occupational resegregation and ghettoization. *American Sociological Review, 59*(4), 511–536.

Zald, M. N., & McCarthy, J. D. (1980). Social movement industries: Competition and cooperation among movement organizations. *Research in Social Movements, Conflict, and Change, 3*, 1–20.

Zarek, C., & Herman, J. (2015, February 3). Announcing the US public participation playbook. *Office of Science and Technology Policy Blog*. Retrieved from https://www.whitehouse.gov/blog/2015/02/03/announcing-us-public-participation-playbook.

5

WHO'S THE CLIENT? THE SPONSOR, CITIZENS, OR THE PARTICIPATORY PROCESS?

Tensions in the Quebec (Canada) Public Participation Field[1]

Laurence Bherer, Mario Gauthier, and Louis Simard

Introduction

Public participation professionals (PPPs) are individuals who are paid to design and organize participatory processes. One of the important characteristics of this new profession is that PPPs are perceived to be impartial[2] actors dedicated to the service of the participatory process. Indeed, in academic texts (Moore, 2012) and in the eyes of some practitioners themselves (Lee, 2014), PPPs are seen as third-party actors positioned between the sponsor of a participatory process and citizens: in keeping with this ideal, their profession is said to be designed to foster dialogue and a better understanding of the differing viewpoints of the various actors (Moore, 2012). To achieve this, as the literature on this topic emphasizes, PPPs need to intervene in a balanced manner in order to appear impartial to both parties and to not reinforce power imbalances between the actors involved in a project (Spada & Vreeland, 2013). Attaining this ideal of impartiality may be difficult (Moore, 2012), but it would seem to imply at least two aspects. On the one hand, PPPs should not explicitly take either the sponsor's or the citizens' side: that is, they should not express their personal preferences in their discussions with the actors. On the other hand, they should avoid using practices that would bias the process in favour of a particular party or option. Leading and facilitating a participatory approach involves a number of actions that could in fact introduce bias and favour a certain actor or point of view (Moore, 2012). In other words, according to this ideal of impartiality, the success of a participatory process is based on the PPPs' ability to act in a disinterested fashion. But the context of commercialization in which public participation has been developing in recent years (Hendriks & Carson, 2008; Nonjon, 2012) raises the question of how to reconcile pressures toward commercialization with the application of the ideal of impartiality.

The heightened commercialization of public participation has stemmed from the fact that PPPs are largely hired by firms offering services in designing and implementing participatory arrangements. PPPs can also be found in public administrations and in universities (see Chapter 10, this volume). But they are involved in far greater numbers in private organizations or NGOs that sell their participatory services as private firms do, for the simple reason that sponsors[3] generally prefer to contract out the task of conducting participatory processes to third-party organizations. These firms in fact carry out these public participation mandates on behalf of a sponsor (the client) that needs this kind of services (Hendriks & Carson, 2008). They act as service providers specialized in public participation tools.

In this context, how are PPPs able to reconcile the interests of their clients, and of citizens, with their role as third-party actors? Can one work for both citizens and one's client? In other words, can one be impartial in a context of commercialization? This question, connected with one's professional autonomy, is a concern for all types of consultants. But the uncertainty and open-endedness of public participation complicates the role of the professional in this field of activity, as PPPs cannot guarantee a particular outcome for their client (Hendriks & Carson, 2008, p. 302). Managing the open-endedness and uncertainty of public participation (Simard, 2008) thus significantly influences the relationship between sponsors and PPPs.

On the one hand, there is a strong likelihood that the sponsor will want to lessen the uncertainty associated with participatory practices by putting pressure on the PPP to reduce the risks. This may mean that the PPP will be encouraged to opt for less transparency and a lower quality of information provided in the context of a participatory process, to narrow the categories of citizens that are asked to participate, to give citizens less time to speak during the PPPs' facilitation of the process, to synthesize citizens' opinions in such a way as to exclude certain discordant views, etc. And if sponsors are not very familiar with the participatory process, as is often the case (Cooper & Smith, 2012), the pressure that they put on PPPs to control the process is even harder to manage.

On the other hand, this uncertainty also affects the PPPs' abilities to resist sponsors' pressures. PPPs clearly need to respect the economic imperatives associated with their professional activity, which means offering enough of a guarantee so that the client will give them the contract, meeting the client's expectations during the carrying out of the mandate and maintaining a good reputation in the eyes of other potential clients: "It certainly takes a confident consultant to put herself/himself into a community, stir up issues and commit to a process with unknown consequences. Such confidence in the market of deliberative democracy appears to be rare" (Hendriks & Carson, 2008, p. 302). PPPs may therefore also be tempted to lessen the risks by placing more importance on their clients' demands than on the principles of transparency, inclusion, and empowerment when developing the participatory design. Overall, the pressures stemming from commercialization and the need to reduce the risks associated with participatory settings mean that it is difficult to sustain the ideal of impartiality. The context in which public participation service providers are evolving in fact favours listening to clients' needs rather than to what citizens want.

Using the case of the province of Quebec, Canada, the objective of this chapter is to examine the importance that the ideal of impartiality assumes in the practice of PPPs acting in a context of marked commercialization of their services. The work of Caroline W. Lee (2014) shows that PPPs are aware of the contradictions involved in their practice and of the risks associated with strong commercialization. To neutralize the negative effects of commercialization, PPPs in fact try to develop a reassuring discourse on the authenticity of their work. For example, they often feel the need to adopt an anti-commercial rhetoric and to mention unpaid activities that they have carried out to foster participation. This chapter takes this argument further and shows that PPPs are far from being a homogeneous community. Through their practices and the context in which they have developed their professional activities, they have gradually forged a professional identity that can take different forms. We will see that the niche that they occupy in the participation industry (that is, the type of participation mandate that they fulfill) and their understanding of the ideal of impartiality have led to the emergence of four distinct types of PPP personalities: the promoter, the reformer, the militant, and the facilitator. Their response to the pressure exerted by sponsors varies considerably according to the type of PPP that they represent. In other words, impartiality is not a norm shared by the profession as a whole. While it is an important value for some PPPs, who in fact use it to justify and sell their services, the ideal of impartiality is of far lesser concern to other members of the profession.

The analysis presented here is based on a study conducted between 2012 and 2015 on the public participation industry in Quebec. To develop a list of firms working in this sector, we used an approach focusing on the firm's reputation: this meant that in order to be selected, the firm had to be recognized by other members of the field as working in the public participation sector. By taking such a perspective, we were able to avoid selecting any given firm according to a more or less explicit ideal of public participation. This reputation-based approach was especially useful in planning the methodological strategy for the research. We in fact had to find a way of listing PPPs and the firms they worked for despite the rather limited visibility of these actors. They do not all use the same name for their profession, and the documentation on the various participatory processes rarely gives the name of the PPPs behind the process. So we concentrated on two strategies. The first was to prepare as complete a list as possible of public participation professionals working in Quebec. This involved listing professionals based on direct observation and participation in events (conferences, workshops), research on the Internet, and lists obtained from major public institutions in this sector, such as the Bureau d'audiences publiques sur l'environnement—BAPE (the Quebec environmental public hearings board, which we will come back to later on in the chapter). We were thus able to prepare a list of an initial group of individuals and organizations to interview. The second strategy was to ask the individuals and organizations in the interviews to identify firms working in the field of participation, as well as their competitors. This allowed us to complete our list of organizations and to plan a second series of interviews where the PPPs interviewed would in turn identify their competitors. A total of about 40 semi-structured interviews with PPPs were carried out between 2013 and 2015 by the three researchers involved in this project in order to learn more about the field, the PPPs' practices, and public participation in general in Quebec. With this inclusive approach, we were able to develop a list of about 60 firms offering public participation services.

In order to properly understand the context in which PPPs develop their professional identity, the first part of the chapter describes the field of public participation in Quebec, with particular emphasis on the history of public participation practices and professionalization, and provides a profile of the firms currently working in the public participation sector. We will see that whereas the requirements of the various laws and regulations in this field initially marked the development of an offer of participatory services, firms soon found new business opportunities, which have led to the rapid development and diversification of the participation industry over the last 15 years. The second part of the chapter shows how PPPs view their role and negotiate their services with their clients: that is, their understanding of the ideal of impartiality in a context of commercialization. In our conclusion, we will re-examine the context in which the public participation industry has developed in Quebec and look at the PPPs' different representations of their work. This will enable us to portray the various tensions operating in the field of public participation.

The Institutionalization of Public Participation in Quebec and the Question of Professionalization

The development of public participation in Quebec, as elsewhere, is closely linked to the history of the social demand for participation. Public authorities have in this respect been the source of the vast majority of participatory initiatives, through the adoption of laws and regulations that guide and sometimes mandate the creation of participatory bodies, as well as the holding of specific processes (Nabatchi & Leighninger, 2015). In Quebec, the Bureau d'audiences publiques sur l'environnement (BAPE), a public body created in 1978, strongly influenced the beginnings and development of the practice. The participatory impetus then gradually moved away from the BAPE model, especially due to the introduction of regulatory requirements and public participation practices in the sphere of land use planning and development. This proliferation of participatory initiatives encouraged the rapid development and diversification of the participation industry in fields other than the environment and land use planning and development. The objective of this section is to show how the new business opportunities created by this institutionalization and diversification of the demand for participation enabled PPPs to develop, over time, an offer of services specifically targeted to these new contexts of action. We then complete this history of public participation with a profile of the participation industry in Quebec today, which shows that this acceleration of professionalization has also been accompanied by a greater fragmentation of the public participation field. The analysis is based on interviews conducted with PPPs and on a systematic examination of the general profiles of the approximately 60 firms identified and the services they offer.[4]

A Short History of Public Participation in Quebec

In Quebec, the emergence of the occupation of PPP followed the setting up of a series of participatory procedures and institutions that made the use of public participation mandatory. The BAPE is the institution that has had the most influence on the development of a public participation market and on the professionalization of practices in this field. The BAPE is an independent body created in 1978 with the mandate to enquire into the environmental impacts of major infrastructure projects (Gauthier, Simard & Waaub, 2011; Simard, 2014). Its main tool of enquiry is the holding of public hearings where citizens are asked to give their opinions. When a project meets certain legal criteria, and if a citizen, municipality, or NGO makes a request to this effect, the environment minister mandates the BAPE to hold such public hearings. These hearings are overseen by a team of commissioners who are tasked to examine the rationale for such a project and to explore possible ways of improving the project with the help of the citizens and experts participating in the hearings. The public hearings process takes place over a period of no more than four months, and is divided into two parts. The first set of hearings is designed to provide citizens with information, for the holding of discussions, and for questions to be addressed to the proponent of the project. The second set of hearings allows citizens to express their opinions, mainly through the submission of testimony (verbally or in writing). After the hearings are finished, the commissioners submit a report to the government on the suitability of the project. The government then decides to authorize the project, to ask for changes to it, or to reject the project.

Because of its independence, the BAPE has become, over the years, a body of enquiry that is recognized by the public and a key government agency on the Quebec political scene. In a survey conducted in 2012, 66% of the citizens questioned said that they knew about the BAPE (BIP, 2013, p. 11). This finding is similar to that of another 2012 survey where 66% of the citizens responding stated that they were familiar with the BAPE and, among these, 93% felt that the BAPE was a credible organization (Montpetit & Lachapelle, 2013, p. 23). In its more than 35 years of existence, the BAPE has examined over 320 projects and a dozen major environmental policies.

The year of creation of the existing public participation firms would appear to confirm the hypothesis that the emergence of the public participation field was largely fostered by the BAPE's creation in 1978 (see Table 5.1). Indeed, as of the end of the 1980s, the number of firms had grown considerably (from 5% of firms created between 1976 and 1985 to 24% created between 1986 and 1995). This growth has continued and has been especially high in recent years, with 19% of firms having been launched between 1996 and 2005, and 34% between 2006 and 2015. We should, however, mention that a significant portion of these firms were already in existence before 1975 (17%), many of which are large corporations or law firms in which public participation represents a marginal activity.

The development of specialized public participation firms and services in the wake of the BAPE's creation is not surprising. As a result of the uncertainty surrounding the publication of the impacts of various projects and regarding the obtaining of government approval, proponents of projects began to adjust their practices in order to better control the risks created by media coverage of the BAPE public hearings. Proponents are generally apprehensive about citizens' reactions to their development projects and about how it may all be reported in the media. Because public hearings are open and public, they are also a stressful forum for proponents (Simard, 2003). Proponents quickly learned to adapt to this new environment by trying to develop different strategies, and in particular to provide more polished testimony at the public hearings, to promote their project (using a communications strategy), to negotiate agreements, and to use various tactics and strategies to counter opposition and impasses arising from acute controversies (Gariépy, 1991; Simard, 2003). The context created by the BAPE soon led to business opportunities for PPPs. A number of specialized firms were launched in the 1980s whose main role was to provide services to help sponsors during the public participation process: organizing meetings of various kinds with citizens and stakeholders, the writing of summary documents and popularization material, preparation for the public hearings, communications strategies, the

TABLE 5.1 Year of Creation of the Firms Examined

Year of creation		
	Number	%
Before 1975	10	17%
1976–1985	3	5%
1986 1995	14	24%
1996–2005	11	19%
2006–2015	20	34%
Unknown	1	2%
Total	59	101%*

*The percentage column adds up to 101% due to rounding.

forming of monitoring and follow-up committees, etc. These services were being offered by firms with expertise in environmental issues as well as by others specializing in public relations and communications, due, in the latter case, to the highly controversial nature of environmental conflicts (we will come back to this in the next section).

Over the years, and with the spreading of participatory practices outside the environmental sector, a second group of public participation firms quickly developed. The 1979 adoption of the *Act respecting land use planning and development* led to the gradual emergence of a culture of participation in Quebec municipalities. Since that time, municipalities have used a wide range of participatory mechanisms, in order to comply with the law, or voluntarily, to give the public the opportunity to participate in the process of developing various land use planning documents (Gauthier, Gariépy & Trépanier, 2008). These municipalities' openness to participation has represented another important element driving the professionalization of the practice, as municipalities have either hired PPPs within their public administrations or used specialized firms.

An analysis of the main areas of activity of the firms examined confirms the importance of the environmental and land use planning and development sectors (Table 5.2). The figures also show the importance that public relations firms assume in the public participation market, in a context where proponents want to control the message and the image that they convey at public hearings. We grouped the firms according to their main activity in order to identify the particular area in which they operate. It can be seen that some firms, especially the largest ones, have more than one main area of activity. Most of the firms fall into two main areas of activity within the 10 areas that we identified: that is, the *Environment* (including environmental impact assessment and strategic environmental assessment) and *Public and media relations*. When we group certain activities closely associated with these two areas together, we find an even clearer concentration of activities. Some 27% of the firms fall into the *Environment* + category (with the addition of the area *Land use planning and development and architecture*) and 30% into the *Public relations* + cluster (including *Market studies, marketing, and advertising*; *Public and media relations*; and *Public affairs and lobbying*). Public participation is a main area of activity in only 13% of the cases: that is, these firms have no important areas of activity other than public participation.

Table 5.2 clearly shows that most of the firms examined operate in one main area of activity, for which they offer public participation services as well. This finding is reinforced when we look at the selected firms' other sectors of activity, that is, what we can call their secondary areas of activity. Public participation is in fact the second most important area of activity for 27% of the firms (Table 5.3). Public participation is thus only one of several activities that they offer and is seen as an additional service within their main area of activity.

An even more detailed examination of the areas of specialization allows us to distinguish between three types of firms. It should be noted that Tables 5.2 and 5.3

TABLE 5.2 Main Areas of Activity of the Firms Examined[5]

Areas of activity	Number	%	% Total
Public relations +			
Public and media relations	14	17%	
Market studies, marketing, and advertising	6	7%	
Public affairs and lobbying	5	6%	
Total Public relations +	25		30%
Environment +			
Environment, EIA, and SEA	16	19%	
Land use planning and development and architecture	7	8%	
Total Environment +	23		27%
Public participation	11		13%
Consulting engineering and infrastructure project management	8		10%
Social, economic, and regional development	3		4%
Legal services	2		2%
Other	12		14%
Total	84		100%

TABLE 5.3 Firms' Secondary Areas of Activity

Areas of activity	Number	%
Public and media relations	3	3%
Market studies, marketing, and advertising	11	12%
Public affairs and lobbying	7	7%
Environment, EIA, and SEA	7	7%
Land use planning and development and architecture	7	7%
Public participation	25	27%
Consulting engineering and infrastructure project management	0	0%
Social, economic, and regional development	7	7%
Legal services	0	0%
Other	4	4%
No other areas	23	24%
Total	94	98%[*]

[*]The percentage column adds up to 98% due to rounding.

list the main and secondary areas of activity for all of the 59 firms identified. So the basic unit is the areas of activity and not the 59 firms (see Note 5). In Table 5.4, in order to distinguish between the three types of firms, we instead used the 59 firms as the basic unit and looked at the firms that mention their public participation activities on their website, either as a main area or as a secondary area, or that do not mention such activities. The figures show that only 19% of

TABLE 5.4 Number of Firms That Explicitly Mention Public Participation on the Firm's Website

Type of mention	Number	Percentage
Main area	11	19%
Secondary area	25	42%
No mention	23	39%
Total	59	100%

the organizations studied refer to public participation as their main area of activity; that is, they specialize in public participation. Most of the firms (42%) have an activity other than public participation as their main area and present participatory services as activities that are complementary to this main area. Finally—and rather surprisingly—whereas our research and interviews enabled us to identify these firms as offering public participation services, 39% of the organizations listed do not explicitly mention these services on their website.

Overall, these findings tend to show a strong division of labour between firms by sector, and it is their main area of activity that allows them to offer complementary participatory services. Firms that are specifically devoted to public participation only account for a small number of all the organizations involved in this field. Even more surprisingly, some firms would rather not publicize their offer of participatory services. This could mean that this is still a relatively recent activity for them, but it could also indicate that they do not wish to highlight this activity in their firm's positioning to avoid emphasizing the overly "participatory" stance of these activities, which could make them less attractive to potential clients. In the following section, we will take a more in-depth look at the firms identified.

What Kinds of Firms Provide Public Participation Services?

Our short history of the field of public participation in Quebec has shown the importance of participatory mechanisms in the areas of the environment, land use planning and development, and public relations, and how this has shaped the public participation industry. The objective of this section is to complete our profile of the Quebec participation industry by providing some data on the firms currently operating in the public participation field.

The figures on the year of creation of public participation firms (Table 5.1) show that the most important period for the launching of these firms was between 2006 and 2015, with nearly 34% of firms having been formed during this period. These figures thus reflect the fact that since the year 2000, there has been a rapid growth of professionalization in this field in Quebec due especially to the proliferation of participatory processes. But it is difficult to pinpoint the specific causes of this accelerated professionalization. Because Quebec society, like societies elsewhere in the world, has become increasingly divided and complex, the controversies that have emerged have been particularly acute and more and more diversified and numerous over the past 20 years. As the governments in power prioritized an intensified exploitation of Quebec's abundant natural resources, this also sparked a great deal of concern and controversy about the environmental impacts of these development projects. With the economic boom that it experienced in the 2000s, Quebec was able to plan and/or carry out many projects, in both urban areas and more remote regions of the province (Conseil du Patronat du Québec, 2015). In such a context, participatory approaches were developed in part in response to the need, on the part of project proponents, to manage or anticipate controversies.

This diversification of the demand for public participation has resulted, on the one hand, from the fact that public authorities are initiating participatory arrangements voluntarily, over and above any legal or regulatory requirements: this trend can be seen in municipalities, public hospitals, school boards, and universities, as well as in provincial government departments and agencies. On the other hand, the development of the participation industry has also benefited from a heightened interest in participation on the part of non-governmental actors (private enterprises and NGOs), as seen especially in the United States (Lee, 2015). An analysis of the clients of the firms that we have identified indeed confirms the diversification of the sponsors of public participation (Table 5.5). Whereas half (50%) of these sponsors are from the public sector, this also means that the other half (50%) of the sponsors of participation are not government actors. Private enterprises alone that are sponsoring participation processes are found in the same proportion as municipalities (21%), followed by NGOs (17%). The strategies

TABLE 5.5 Types of Clients Mentioned by the Firms Examined[6]

Types of clients	Number	%
Municipalities	51	21%
Private enterprises	50	21%
Public enterprises, crown corporations, government departments, or agencies	41	17%
NGOs and civil society organizations	41	17%
Public or para-public institutions (schools, universities, hospitals, etc.)	30	12%
Groups of private enterprises	6	2%
Trade unions	2	1%
Professional associations	0	0%
Other	20	8%
Total	241	99%*

*The percentage column adds up to 99% due to rounding.

developed in the 1990s by public and private proponents in the context of the BAPE's activities had already heralded this diversification of sponsors.

The firms active in the area of public participation are generally quite small, or even very small, in size (Table 5.6). Indeed, the number of employees shows that most of the firms working in the participation field in Quebec have from 1 to 20 employees (66%), with more than half (42%) having only 10 or fewer employees. A significant number of firms (24%), nonetheless, have more than 41 employees.

When we cross the variables relating to the types of mentioning of public participation activities on the firms' websites with the number of employees (Table 5.7), we obtain an even clearer profile of these firms. Of the firms specializing in PP (PP1), almost all have fewer than 20 employees, with most (73%) having fewer than 10. The distribution of firms with PP as a secondary area of activity (PP2) is more varied, in that 28% have more than 41 employees. Thus, of

TABLE 5.6 Number of Employees of the Firms Examined

Number of employees	Number of firms	%
1 to 10	25	42%
11 to 20	14	24%
21 to 30	1	2%
31 to 40	1	2%
41 +	14	24%
Unknown	4	7%
Total	59	101%*

*The percentage column adds up to 101% due to rounding.

TABLE 5.7 Number of Employees by Type of Mentioning of Public Participation Activities on the Firms' Websites

Number of employees	Number of firms	PP mentioned			PP not mentioned
		PP1	PP2	PP1 + PP2 (%)	
1 to 10	25	8 (73%)	7 (28%)	15 (42%)	10 (43%)
11 to 20	14	3 (27%)	8 (32%)	11 (31%)	3 (13%)
21 to 30	1	0 (0%)	1 (4%)	1 (3%)	0 (0%)
31 to 40	1	0 (0%)	0 (0%)	0 (0%)	1 (4%)
41 +	14	0 (0%)	7 (28%)	7 (19%)	7 (30%)
Unknown	4	0 (0%)	2 (8%)	2 (6%)	2 (9%)
Total	59	11 (100%)	25 (100%)	36 (101%)	23 (99%)

The last two percentage columns add up to 101% and 99% respectively due to rounding.
PP1 = Public participation as a main area of activity.
PP2 = Public participation as a secondary area of activity.

TABLE 5.8 Status of the Firms

Status	Number	Percentage
Private enterprise	52	88%
NGO or third-sector organization	7	12%
Total	59	100%

all the firms mentioning public participation activities (PP1 + PP2 = PP3), most are quite small (with 42% having 1 to 10 employees and 31%, 11 to 20), whereas another group is much larger (with 19% having 41+ employees). For firms that do not mention their participatory services, there is one group of very small firms (43%) and another cluster of very large firms (30%).

Moreover, the vast majority of the firms identified are for-profit organizations (88%). Only 12% are third-sector organizations.

Public Participation as Part of an Array of Services Offered; or, a Dilution of the Ideal?

The relative invisibility of public participation services (the fact that only 19% of the organizations examined specialize in public participation, see Table 5.4) should be considered alongside the fact that there are a wide range of definitions of public participation, as shown by an analysis of the participation services offered by the firms operating in this field.[7] This is seen in the fact that the services listed go beyond those that can strictly be described as public participation and include lobbying, negotiation, or communication activities: that is, services that directly or indirectly involve "stakeholders" other than the sponsors. This is due to the fact that some PP firms have a more flexible definition of public participation and associate it with services existing on the boundaries between participation and other areas of activity, such as public relations. It also means that some firms offer turnkey services that combine lobbying, public relations, and public participation activities. Overall, although the wording and vocabulary vary a great deal from one firm to another and the websites differ considerably in the amount of detail given in describing these services, a systematic analysis enables us to identify a half dozen types of services identified as participation services by these firms.

The first type of services involves activities related to *representation and lobbying*. This may mean representing or assisting sponsors appearing before provincial regulatory bodies and tribunals, proposing strategies to influential people, setting up coalitions, finding public spaces in which to promote their views, obtaining partners and allies, and managing social media. It is a matter of representing and/or defending clients' interests. These services may be offered on a short-, medium-, or long-term basis.

The second type of services is more specifically targeted in that it involves *crisis management, mediation, or negotiation* services. These services may consist of coordinating stakeholders and citizens, drafting agreements, or developing community engagement plans.

Consulting, communications, and information are a third type of services. These are client-oriented activities designed to inform the client about the context, to identify the stakeholders and for largely one-way communication from the sponsor to the stakeholders. They include press reviews, media monitoring, social media analysis, strategic planning, stakeholder mapping, conflict analyses, acceptability studies, legal services, surveys and questionnaires, focus groups, or the development of a storytelling approach. Also included in this category are activities to manage the client's reputation and image, awareness-raising campaigns, media relations, the writing of various types of documents, website creation, communication plans, the designing of digital tools and social media management.

As can be seen, these first three types of services are, on the one hand, strongly influenced by the regulatory requirements specific to the environmental field and, on the other hand, centered on needs associated with managing controversy. The goal is to offer sponsors services to help them prepare for the BAPE public hearings and deal with the outcomes of these hearings, or to provide a complete range of services including lobbying, media management, various kinds of representation, and the organizing of participatory processes. The other three types of services represent more "purely" public participation services.

Dialogue and collaborative services focus on reciprocal interaction and more two-way discussion with stakeholders and citizens. On the one hand, this category includes services aimed at an initial level of interaction: that is, first consulting citizens and stakeholders through various mechanisms without necessarily wishing for collaboration and the joint development of projects and solutions. This may involve facilitating various forms of public meetings, pre-consultation or formal or institutionalized consultations, social acceptability processes, and online participation platforms. On the other hand, this category also includes other types of services offered with the aim of a second level of interaction with stakeholders. These services are designed for collaboration in developing projects and mechanisms with stakeholders in order to reach a higher level of consensus. They may, for example, involve developing a vision, a participatory process, collaboration and social innovation or being driven by the principle of "the largest possible number of participants," a "stakeholder engagement program," or social project management. Specific examples of some of the mechanisms included in this fourth type of services are shown in Table 5.9.

The fifth type of services offered is *training and capacity building*. More specifically, this may include training on relations with stakeholders and citizens, on media relations, or on acting as a spokesperson. It may involve training or presentations on various participatory mechanisms, on how they work and the possibilities they offer.

TABLE 5.9 Examples of Participation, Dialogue, and Collaboration Mechanisms

Participatory budget
"Art of Hosting"
Learning circles and practices
Collective intelligence methods
Living Laboratory
Open Space Technology
World Café
Appreciative Inquiry
Visual facilitation

The aim of the last type of services is the *setting up, development, and maintaining of long-term relations between stakeholders, citizens, and the sponsor.* This type of services involves the creation and facilitating of advisory and follow-up committees in order to develop corporate social responsibility plans or to monitor development projects. They may also be aimed at helping to arrange long-term cooperation between the sponsor, stakeholders, and citizens on community activities or emphasizing the positive impacts associated with a project. This type of services is increasingly in demand, especially because government decrees authorizing projects in the context of environmental impact assessments encourage proponents to set up follow-up committees.

Overall, this profile of Quebec public participation firms highlights a number of characteristic features. In general, most of these firms are private enterprises and are small, or very small, in size. They mainly operate in three specific areas of activity: the environment, land use planning and development, and public relations. Although a significant number of them specialize in public participation, few of the firms working in public participation do so in a large number of areas. They prefer to create niches for themselves by combining specialization in a particular sector of activities and public participation. They are also specialized in their offer of participation services: the typology of public participation services in fact shows that firms provide several types of participatory services, without offering all of them, which enables them to set themselves apart and strengthen their niche. However, a significant proportion (39%) of the firms do not mention their public participation services. These are often firms for which public participation is only one service within a wide range of services that they offer in a variety of activity sectors. Finally, it should be noted that, whereas the number of public participation firms has been growing since the early 2000s, this type of firm began to emerge in larger numbers in the late 1980s. Although 50% of their clientele is in the public sector, most firms took advantage of the diversification of the demand for public participation and have attracted a growing number of non-governmental clients. Along a spectrum representing the various types of public participation firms, we would thus find large engineering or law firms at one end that offer participation services among other types of services, with, in the middle, medium-sized or small firms specializing in public relations that include public participation services as part of their communication services, and, at the other end, very small firms that offer public participation services exclusively and that may be either private enterprises or third-sector organizations. In other words, the participation industry is quite diverse. It is made up of large firms active in a number of sectors and with considerable resources, firms for which public participation services are closely linked to their public relations work, and very small organizations that offer participation services exclusively and often in specific activity sectors. In the following section, we will see how these contrasting organizational profiles are combined with very different visions of their role in public participation and very different views on impartiality.

The Ideal of Impartiality in Practice; or, How to Deal with the Commercialization of Public Participation

How do PPPs see their role as third-party actors? How does this influence their practices and their relations with sponsors and the public? In other words, how do they reconcile the ideal of impartiality with the context of commercialization associated with their profession? Our portrait of Quebec PP firms shows that the public participation industry is made up of firms with different profiles which do not necessarily offer the same participatory services and for which public participation is either a main activity or a rather secondary activity among the range of services that they provide. In this section, we will see that the niche in which these firms work (their area of specialization) combined with their understanding of the ideal of impartiality allow us to distinguish between four types of PPP personalities. So, even although they all work in a context of strong commercialization, they clearly do not react to the ambiguity that characterizes their relations with their clients and the public in the same way: their particular activity sectors and vision of public participation shape their professional identity and, ultimately, whether or not they believe in the ideal of impartiality.

More specifically, two types of differences or divisions influence the position that PPPs take. The first difference has to do with the political salience of the projects that they are involved in (Kollman, 1998). A project is said to be politically salient if it is particularly large and controversial compared with other projects and for the communities directly affected by the project or for public opinion in general. A controversial project means that the public pays attention to it. There is indeed a difference between PPPs working in the area of megaprojects that are subject to a formal environmental impact assessment procedure (such as the procedure involving the BAPE's intervention) and PPPs that offer participatory services associated with less politically salient or less controversial projects, which are often smaller. Megaprojects are the focus of vigorous controversies stemming from the differing viewpoints on their environmental and social impacts. This

	Politically salient projects	Less politically salient projects
Strong support for the project from PPPs	The promoter	The militant
Less support for the project from PPPs	The reformer	The facilitator

FIGURE 5.1   The Four Types of PPP Personalities in Regard to Impartiality

creates a flourishing market for public participation, as environmental controversies often arise in Quebec due to the province's intensive exploitation of natural resources and the importance of hydro power generation in its economy.

The second difference or division is connected with the PPPs' vision of impartiality: do they explicitly support the project promoted by their clients? Is it important for PPPs to agree with the project in order to accept the mandate? Do their clients ask them to promote the project? Impartiality here is tied to the question of whether to agree or to refuse to support the project, that is, to make a judgment on the quality of the project before accepting the mandate. We will see that the PPPs do not all interpret this idea of supporting or not supporting a project in the same way. Whereas some PPPs think very carefully about how well their personal values correspond with the intrinsic quality of a given project, others devote far less thought to this aspect.

Overall, when we combine these two kinds of differences, the result is four types of PPP personalities in regard to impartiality: the promoter, the reformer, the militant, and the facilitator (see Figure 5.1). We do not find these four types of professionals exactly as such in reality, but they effectively illustrate the strong divisions that exist within the field of public participation.[8]

The Promoter

The *promoter* does not see himself/herself as an impartial actor, but as serving the client first and foremost and thus seeking to have the project approved:

> Clients call on us to develop communication plans associated with the launching and implementation of projects. Our role is to assess the situation,

to properly map the stakeholders' positions and expectations, and to see how we can get everyone to support the project. So we evaluate the risk factors and make recommendations on the activities that the client should focus on to be able to carry out the project.

(Interview 1)

This professional values the relationship established with the client and sees himself/ herself as the client's agent in a context that is often marked by controversy. The promoter's objective is to help the client to carry out the project by using a series of tools to reduce the uncertainty created by public protests or by the government approval procedure associated with the BAPE. So appearing impartial in the eyes of the public is not a concern.

This type of PPP generally works in a large engineering firm that has been mandated to help the client throughout the entire environmental impact assessment procedure, including the consultation phase. In this case, these firms are asked to provide not only public participation services but a whole range of other services as well to get the client through the BAPE procedure and obtain government approval to carry out the project. This type of PPP may also work in a communications and public relations firm. PPPs in these firms see their work in terms of crisis management and as responding to the need to revamp the project's, and the client's, image:

Our expertise lies in combining community relations, media management and management of political and governmental concerns. So we offer a complete range of services, including facilitating large meetings with the public. Talk, talk, gab, gab for six months to arrive at a decision together isn't really our way of doing things.

(Interview 2)

"Promoter" PPPs sometimes refer to what they do as "creating social acceptability," in the sense of gaining public support and acceptance for a project, and this expression is increasingly being used in Quebec by governmental and other actors. Promoters include under this term services that were formerly called "environmental communication" to designate a series of communication and participation tools targeted to the communities directly concerned by a potentially controversial project.

Their involvement in other sectors of activity as well as the public participation field means that promoters are less comfortable with being called PPPs. They work in firms that advertise participatory services and/or respond to calls for tender that explicitly require skills in public participation, but often see themselves as working on the fringes of the public participation field, especially in the case of those who are also active in the area of public relations:

The question is how much room to manoeuvre we have in the participation process: is our role more to promote the project or to assess the situation and make recommendations that will alter the parameters of the project? It's a little of both, a little of both.

(Interview 1)

This uncertainty as to whether the promoter belongs to the public participation field is further intensified by the fact that these professionals are employed by engineering or communications firms where participation services generally represent only a small portion of their contracts. But even though public participation mandates comprise only a small part of their revenues, these firms are interested in developing skills in this area, since demand for these services has clearly been increasing in the past 15 years, as we saw in the previous section. It is also a way for them to obtain more contracts to provide turnkey solutions, which allow clients to take advantage of a range of services, in which participatory mechanisms are combined with other services. Engineering firms may thus combine participatory mechanisms, legal services, and the conducting of environmental impact studies, while organizations specializing in communications and public relations may link participatory services with crisis management or communication plans. These firms sometimes contract out some complementary services, such as lobbying, training, and even services associated with follow-up committees.

The Reformer

The *reformer* sees the promoter as an unwanted competitor working in the same market of controversial projects. In contrast to the promoter, who is more inclined to promote a project, the reformer wishes to appear impartial in the eyes of the public:

> There is a considerable difference between helping citizens (i.e. being socially useful) or promoting a project and helping the proponent to make money out of the project. We are not the client's spokesperson, or the defender of a project. If I ever feel that I've helped the project too much, I'll change my occupation.
>
> *(Interview 3)*

In concrete terms, this means that the reformer does not agree to organize press conferences, to focus on media relations, or to having his or her name on materials distributed by the sponsor. In other words, the reformer does not want to act as the client's spokesperson, but rather to perform the role of an actor at the service of the participatory process who remains faithful to a participatory ethics.

The reformer thus sees himself/herself as an agent of change working with the sponsor and citizens to change their views on an issue. It is this strong belief in their capacity to change other actors' attitudes and opinions that makes this type of professional a reformer. In keeping with this ideal, the contribution that PPPs make is seen as helping to improve a project and, more generally, to transform the views of sponsors and citizens. For reformers, a project is not intrinsically good; there is always room for improvement and collaboration. In order to achieve this, it is obviously very important to design appropriate participatory mechanisms, as studies on participatory innovations suggest. But this also implies investing considerable time and energy in discussions with the project's sponsor during private meetings to prepare and define the mandate. As one of the PPPs interviewed states: "We need to influence the organizations that hire us" (Interview 4). These working meetings are especially important to help sponsors understand the role and principles of public participation and for PPPs to gain the necessary room to manoeuvre to make participatory exercises useful for everyone.

Transforming sponsors' attitudes is not always an easy task, as many of them have an instrumental or minimalist view of public participation. They very often call on PPPs to act as spokespersons for their project or to simply facilitate public meetings, two roles that reformers reject. That is why, when negotiating a contract, reformers try to gauge the client's attitude toward participation: "In order to maintain our neutrality in the eyes of the public, we don't choose the types of projects we take on, but the client's openness: is the client open to a rigorous and honest approach?" (Interview 5). To do this, these PPPs have to reconcile their choice of clients with their choice of projects:

> Do we want to be associated with this type of project? Is it the project that's important or the openness of the client (who, if he has a project that's not consistent with our ethics, is nonetheless willing to adapt it)? This is an important discussion to have, especially for younger PPPs, who see respecting values as important.
>
> *(Interview 5)*

The fear of working with bad clients is quite palpable among reformers, who are very concerned about their firm's reputation:

> Because there aren't many firms that do what we do, how we position ourselves isn't always easy. It means that we have to ask questions about our impartiality on a regular basis. Our firm's leadership does that every week. They have to, because we don't have a lot of models to help us define who we are.
>
> *(Interview 6)*

Some of these PPPs say that they refuse to accept contracts from a closed-minded client, as this would doom the process to failure and affect the professional's legitimacy in the eyes of the public and other potential clients. If the sponsor is open to participation, reformers feel that it is better for them to take on the contract rather than seeing it given to a "promoter" type of PPP: "Poor public participation designed by public relations or engineering firms is lethal for the practice because it's often just for show and undermines the practice's legitimacy. Public participation's clientele is the public" (Interview 7).

But defending the public's place in the process is not a persuasive argument for obtaining contracts. And refusing too many contracts is not a viable long-term economic strategy. So reformers, like other professionals, have to reconcile their economic imperatives with their professional values. This is a rather tricky endeavour that is not without its contradictions. Reformers in fact use a vocabulary and a discourse that is similar to that of "promoter" PPPs to achieve this feat. This is because, even if they do not want to promote a particular project, they need to show how their approach will foster the carrying out of the project. Their main strategy is to discuss the risks of the project being aborted, by using well-known cases where citizens' protests led to such an outcome. Reformers thus try to show how communications and public relations strategies do not work, and can even enflame conflicts with citizens. What they recommend, on the contrary, is a more bottom-up approach tied to the setting up of relations of dialogue and transparency with the communities concerned. They clearly favour services that involve collaboration, training, and long-term relations with the communities affected by a development project.

Reformers, more than other types of PPPs, thus feel a strong relationship of interdependence between themselves and their client. Their ability to convince the client of the validity of altering the project affects the amount of credibility that they have with the public. This credibility is particularly important if they are to continue to develop the field of public participation and to compete with promoters. The sense of competition is even greater in that reformers have a very different approach to public participation, and one that is harder to sell. The participatory services that they provide are not part of a broader service offering, as is often the case with promoters. For reformers, public participation is a separate and distinct activity within the process of developing the project and is associated with a particular ethics. They feel that, in order to maintain their integrity, it is important that participatory mechanisms not be designed by the same individuals as those involved in project development and communications. In other words, reformers are thereby promoting the idea of an impartial process. This position is reflected in the organizational profile of reformers, who are often self-employed or work in small firms that only offer public participation services.

The Militant

The attitude taken by the *militant* may at first glance seem similar to that of the promoter, since, like the promoter, the militant supports the project in which he/she is involved. But, unlike promoters, militants choose the projects that they work for, as they would rather not develop participatory settings for projects that are not in line with their political values. So the militant does not act as a spokesperson for the project, like the promoter, but primarily as a sympathizer with the general principle underlying the project. Thus, unlike the reformer who may accept a mandate even though the project does not correspond to the reformer's own personal values, as long as the sponsor has an open attitude to participation, the militant prefers mandates from equally open-minded clients but who are developing projects that the militant sees as politically acceptable:

> One suburban municipality approached us for a contract involving farmland that had already been rezoned for residential development. We had extensive discussions with the board of our organization to see whether we wanted to bid for the contract and, in the end, we opted out because it was urban sprawl [an issue that our organization is against]. We have an agenda that you won't find in a neutral firm.
>
> *(Interview 8)*

Militants find it important to choose the projects that they work on for two reasons. First, they are very concerned about the effect a participatory process can have in legitimizing a project. Because a participatory process more often leads to the project being altered than to it being scrapped, militants prefer to make their choice ahead of time in order to concentrate on the projects that they believe are worth improving. Militants thus share the reformers' view that the main objective of participation is to transform a project, but they do not believe that a politically unacceptable project can be improved.

Second, militants want to choose which projects they work on because they do not believe in the impartiality of their position as professionals. They feel that their intervention in a participatory process, whether it be at the time of designing the mechanism, preparing the information, or facilitating the event, will affect the way that the project is presented to the public: "We cannot, we should not, be neutral. Planning is political, one can't be neutral. Participation tools aren't neutral. How you ask the questions isn't neutral. I have a bit of a problem with neutrality" (Interview 8). Militants feel that their support for the project is vital so that they can do a good job, properly present the project, and be fair to both the sponsor and citizens.

Like the reformers' stance, the militants' position means that there are long discussions on the appropriateness of the mandate. Militants are thus trying to evaluate both the sponsor's willingness to be influenced by participatory processes and whether the project is consistent with the militant's political values. It is not only a matter of reconciling the professional's personal values with the project, as is the case for the reformer. It is also a question of considering the political values that the organization is seeking to defend and promote as a provider of participatory services. These values may have to do with both the content of projects that are worth becoming the focus of a participatory process and the public interest of a project:

> Potential clients often ask us: "Why should we give the mandate to you?" We reply: "Because you'll get an accurate assessment of what the public is saying, and you may not like what you hear. . . ." And then we tell them

outright: "I'm not working for you; you're paying me but I'm working for the public, I'm working for the progress of our society. You have a role to play in this society, and it's to your advantage that this participatory process exists, but you'll learn that the process doesn't mean managing your image."

(Interview 9)

This concern with the values that are being defended is much less important for the reformer, whose primary focus is on working to transform the project: "[Organization 'X'] has a certain agenda. We don't have an agenda. Our agenda is in fact to try not to have an agenda," says one reformer (Interview 3).

Militants work in organizations providing participatory services that more or less explicitly indicate their political preferences. This position is, however, easier to maintain for non-governmental organizations (NGOs) that offer participatory services. NGOs are more easily associated with a militant stance, so that potential sponsors aren't offended by this. Clients may even try to be seen as a member of civil society in order to give credibility to the participatory process or simply because they believe in the same values. Sponsors can thus demonstrate their goodwill by hiring an organization that claims to be close to the public and supportive of the general interest, or that advocates a particular cause, such as sustainable development. These organizations in fact use this sales pitch in affirming their position as militant but non-partisan NGOs. This stance is relatively easier to maintain in that the projects that militants work on are generally small (contracts under $100,000 CAD) and not very controversial. Militants see these projects as having strong political dimensions, but this is not necessarily how citizens or sponsors see them. In such a context, the militant's objective is to help citizens to better assess the potential impacts of a project.

The Facilitator

Facilitators define themselves as impartial actors, but unlike reformers, they do not operate in a competitive market of large, controversial projects. Like the militant, they handle smaller, less politically salient contracts. The facilitator is less involved in aspects that take place before and after the participatory forum, unlike the reformer and to a lesser extent the militant. Most of the services provided by the facilitator are closer to the actual task of facilitation.

This situation influences the facilitator's professional stance. Impartiality is less of a key issue for the facilitator than it is for the reformer, who feels threatened by "promoter" PPPs. Facilitators are not so strongly concerned about such competition. Rather, impartiality is part and parcel of their professional identity in providing services that essentially focus on facilitating long or short participatory processes:

I had been speaking for less than three minutes at the start of the meeting when someone stood up and said: "So you're going to tell me here, and I've been involved in the environmental sector for 25 years, and you come here and they introduce you as an expert; I've never heard about your organization, I don't know you. . . . are you sure you're someone that's credible in this area, because I've never heard of you?" So I answer him: "I'm very glad that you asked the question, sir, and yes, you're absolutely right, I'm not an expert, I'm not at all, at all credible in all these issues of environmental management; my expertise is not in that area, my expertise is in processes, participatory processes where people like you who are interested in the same issue come together to work toward a solution that will satisfy the most people possible, of the people here: that's where the expertise of my organization lies. And you're absolutely right: I know nothing at all about environmental issues."

(Interview 10)

In other words, the facilitator is primarily a specialist in processes, but his or her positioning in the provision of facilitation services means that facilitators see themselves as impartial actors that help participants to arrive at a solution together. The issues may be strategic ones, issues that spark discussion, but they are not as conflictual in scope as in the major development projects that promoters and reformers work on. The fact that most of the facilitators' mandates concern the phase of project conception, often in a context of collaboration and sharing of ideas, is what reinforces the consensual dynamics of their mandates. The services that facilitators provide fall within the sphere of organizational learning, social innovation, and co-design, and are targeted to public or private clients involved in a process of organizational change or in carrying out very small local development projects or dialogue processes with stakeholders. Ordinary citizens can attend these participatory forums, but many of the facilitators' approaches focus mainly on the stakeholders.

Moreover, unlike militants, facilitators do not feel the need to position themselves politically. Facilitators are, however, concerned about the transformative capacity of the process that they are engaged in. In this case, the scope of this change is less social than organizational. Facilitators tend to refuse mandates to simply lead meetings, as this kind of intervention is too specific and does not allow them to design a process to support transformation of the internal dynamic of the organization. They prefer longer processes where they can help the transformation to occur. And this requires a great deal of investment in participatory initiatives and meetings. This is also a major challenge for reformers, but, as we have seen, a large part of their time is devoted to changing their clients' views. This is less of a concern for facilitators, as their clients are often already open to participation and understand what this means and do not have to deal with highly controversial situations. In other words, the consensual nature of the mandates that facilitators are engaged in and their less politicized analysis of projects allow them to take a consensual approach. Facilitators are generally found in very small private firms specializing in innovative and collaborative strategies. The success of their approach lies in their ability to work within innovative, open-lab processes.

Discussion and Conclusion

The starting point for this chapter was the question of how public participation professionals reconcile the ideal of impartiality that is very often associated with the occupation of PPP, with the context of the strong commercialization of participatory services. This is an important issue, as it raises the question of who or what PPPs are working for: for their client, for citizens, or for the participatory process? The fact that PPPs are most often hired by firms mandated to conduct participatory processes on behalf of their clients means that most participatory settings today are marked by this ambiguous relationship that PPPs have with their client and the public. Can PPPs resist the pressures exerted by their clients to reduce the uncertainty characteristic of participatory processes (and especially regarding the effects of these processes on whether or not a project is approved by the government)? Do they all want to resist these pressures and to strive towards the ideal of impartiality? How do PPPs reconcile the need to obtain mandates, and thus to satisfy their clients, with the need to maintain their reputation in the eyes of the public and to set up participatory processes that are seen as legitimate and fair to all parties? Despite the difficulty of answering these questions clearly and explicitly, our research does allow us to suggest some answers. More specifically, we looked at the professional identities that PPPs have developed in connection with their role as third-party actors and in terms of whether or not they respect the principle of impartiality that is often discussed both within the profession and in the literature on participatory democracy. We were thus able to show how, in the case of Quebec, the four types of PPPs envision their actions in a context of commercialization.

First, for the promoter, the effects of the commercialization of participatory services are of little concern. The promoter fully endorses his or her role as the client's representative and attempts to create conditions that will help the project in question to be authorized by the government and to gain a certain level of public acceptance. As the promoters' actions often involve dealing with controversial issues, they see themselves as specialists in crisis management. Because promoters generally work in large firms where public participation is a secondary activity within a wide range of other services, the ideal of impartiality associated with public participation is in competition with other activities of the firm where this notion is not as central.

For the reformer, on the other hand, the principle of impartiality is a major concern. This is especially because this PPP has very often worked in close collaboration with the BAPE, an independent state agency in charge of public hearings on environmental issues, which is presented as a neutral third party. For the reformer, the idea of impartiality is thus closely associated with the model conveyed by this experience (Gauthier & Simard, 2011). In such a context, the reformer has a very high regard for his or her role and integrity: the reformer profoundly believes in public participation's capacity to change the client's, and the public's, attitudes, and, ultimately, to improve the content of the project. This strong belief in his or her role and in the benefits of public participation is seen by the reformer as the best defence against the effects of commercialization.

The militant also believes in the transformative effects of public participation but takes a very critical view of its use. The militant is aware that the conducting of a participatory process strongly increases the likelihood that a project will be implemented. That is why this professional chooses projects that are in keeping with his or her personal values and does not hesitate to emphasize these values to clients. The militant feels that this strong conviction is what enables him or her to resist pressure from the sponsors of participation.

Finally, the facilitator is attached to the idea of impartiality but does not see a possible contradiction between working for a client and serving the interests of the public. What could be interpreted as nonchalance stems from the fact that the mandates in which this professional is involved tend to generate little controversy, and the politically salient character of the public participation process is less evident. So this PPP's role is more easily that of a facilitator with participants that consider themselves as equals and favour innovation.

The case of Quebec thus shows that the greater popularity of participatory mechanisms among sponsors has made this activity sector more attractive and has offered business opportunities to firms with very different visions of the objectives of public participation and especially of the ideal of impartiality. The division between firms that are not public participation specialists (mainly public relations and engineering firms) and firms that offer participation services almost exclusively is quite revealing in this regard. Even though reformers are the ones most apt to notice the rising market share of promoters, all types of PPPs are affected by the competition coming from the public relations and communications sector. The small size of certain public participation firms makes them especially vulnerable to this competition from larger organizations with more resources. But the PPPs' responses to this challenge vary: professionals in smaller firms are themselves divided in their conceptions of their impartiality and in their approaches to public participation. In other words, if the firms specializing in public participation feel threatened by firms that are not public participation specialists, they still do not agree on their understanding of public participation. This division explains the very great fragmentation of the field of public participation and the diversity of participatory experiences.

Ultimately, we may ask what effect the ever-growing influence of "promoter" PPPs will have on the practice of participation in the coming years. With the arrival of new players for whom public participation is only one corporate service among a range of other services, there is a considerable risk that the practice of participatory democracy will be shaped by sponsors', and not citizens', needs. Participatory democracy could thus turn into a public communications exercise or become diluted within a panoply of corporate services centered on the technical realization of development projects. In such a context, participatory processes could become increasingly associated with strategies to manage public protest, rather than with achieving the objectives of equality among the parties involved, the sharing of information, and reciprocal discussion. The danger is that this could create confusion in the minds of the public about the objectives of participatory forums, which could engender a mistrust of participatory exercises and further increase political cynicism in our society.

List of interviews

Interview 1 conducted in October 2013

Interview 2 conducted in March 2014

Interview 3 conducted in July 2013

Interview 4 conducted in November 2014

Interview 5 conducted in October 2013

Interview 6 conducted in October 2013

Interview 7 conducted in October 2013

Interview 8 conducted in June 2015

Interview 9 conducted in March 2014

Interview 10 conducted in September 2015

Notes

1 This chapter was written in the context of the project entitled "Expertise, champ et diffusion des pratiques de participation publique" (The expertise, field and dissemination of public participation practices) funded by the Social Sciences and Humanities Research Council of Canada (Grant No. 435–2012–1024). We would like to thank our colleagues Alice Mazeaud, Magali Nonjon, Anne Mévellec, and Martin Papillon for their comments on an earlier version of this text. We would also like to thank Magali Nonjon and Alice Mazeaud for their sustained input throughout the course of this project, which greatly influenced our own thinking. Finally, we would like also to thank Geneviève Nadeau (Ph.D., Public Administration, University of Ottawa), Benoit Morissette (Ph.D. candidate, Political Science, Université de Montréal), and David Deault-Picard (MA candidate, Political Science, Université de Montréal) for their research and contribution for the quantitative section of this chapter.

2 Whereas some of the PPPs that we interviewed use the term "neutrality," we prefer here to employ the term "impartiality," which means unbiased and fair to all parties equally. Neutrality usually means not taking sides with conflicting parties and is often associated with passivity and inaction. Whereas both concepts are often used interchangeably in common, everyday language, without any difference in meaning, there is an extensive literature, specifically in peacekeeping and mediation, on their different meanings (see for example Weiss, 1999).

3 In this text, the terms "clients" and "sponsors" are employed to designate organizations that use participatory services provided by PPPs.
4 This profile of the participation industry today is based on an analysis of the websites of 59 firms, using a detailed analytical framework. Each piece of information and its interpretation was verified by two different researchers and discussed in a wider team context when the interpretations differed (this approach was inspired by the work of Edward T. Walker (2014) on public affairs consultants). This analysis led to the creation of two data banks: a qualitative data bank in the form of descriptive files on each of the firms and a quantitative data bank that allowed us to make certain generalizations about the field in question by aggregating the data.
5 In Tables 5.2 and 5.3, the totals of the main and secondary areas of activity (84 and 94 respectively) are greater than the number of firms examined (59) because some firms have developed more than one main or secondary area of activity.
6 These figures come from firms that explicitly mention their public participation activities (see Table 5.4) and identify the types of clients for which they have provided such services. Of course, the firms generally mention more than one type of client.
7 To be quite clear, in this section, we have only selected here so-called "participation" services offered by firms that mention such activities (PP1 + PP2).
8 This section is based on approximately 40 semi-structured interviews conducted with Quebec PPPs.

References

Bureau d'intervieweurs professionnels (BIP). (2013). *Sondage web sur la démocratie et la participation citoyenne*. Sondage réalisé pour le compte de l'Institut du Nouveau Monde.

Conseil du Patronat du Québec. (2015). *Les ressources naturelles au Québec: une source naturelle de prospérité. Étude sur la prospérité n° 2*. Conseil du Patronat du Québec. https://www.cpq.qc.ca/wp-content/uploads/2015/06/etude2prosperite080615.pdf.

Cooper, E., & Smith, G. (2012). Organizing deliberation: The perspectives of professional participation practitioners in Britain and Germany. *Journal of Public Deliberation, 8*(1). Retrieved from http://www.publicdeliberation.net/jpd/vol8/iss1/art3/.

Gariépy, M. (1991). Toward a dual-influence system: Assessing the effects of public participation in environmental impact assessment for Hydro-Quebec projects. *Environmental Impact Assessment Review, 11*(4), 353–374.

Gauthier, M., Gariépy, M., & Trépanier, M. O. (Eds.). (2008). *Renouveler l'aménagement et l'urbanisme: planification territoriale, débat public et développement durable*. Montréal: Les Presses de l'Université de Montréal.

Gauthier, M., & Simard, L. (2011). Le Bureau d'audiences publiques sur l'environnement du Québec: Genèse et développement d'un instrument voué à la participation publique. *Téléscope, 17*(1), 39–67.

Gauthier, M., Simard, L., & Waaub, J. P. (2011). Public participation in strategic environmental assessment (SEA): Critical review and the Quebec (Canada) approach. *Environmental Impact Assessment Review, 31*(1), 48–60.

Hendriks, C. M., & Carson, L. (2008). Can the market help the forum? Negotiating the commercialization of deliberative democracy. *Policy Sciences, 41*(4), 293–313.

Kollman, K. (1998). *Outside lobbying: Public opinion and interest group strategies*. Princeton, NJ: Princeton University Press.

Lee, C. W. (2015). *Do-it-yourself democracy: The rise of the public engagement industry*. Oxford: Oxford University Press.

Lee, C. W. (2014). Walking the talk: The performance of authenticity in public engagement work. *The Sociological Quarterly, 55*(3), 493–513.

Montpetit, É., & Lachapelle, É. (2013). *L'opinion des Québécois sur les gaz de schiste: une comparaison avec la Pennsylvanie et le Michigan.* Montréal: Centre de recherche sur les politiques et le développement social, Université de Montréal.

Moore, A. (2012). Following from the front: Theorizing deliberative facilitation. *Critical Policy Studies, 6*(2), 146–162.

Nabatchi, T., & Leighninger, M. (2015). *Public participation for 21st century democracy.* Hoboken, NJ: Jossey-Bass.

Nonjon, M. (2012). De la "militance" à la "consultance": les bureaux d'études urbaines, acteurs et reflets de la "procéduralisation" de la participation. *Politiques et management public, 29*(1), 79–98.

Simard, L. (2003). *Conflits d'environnement et concertation: le cas du Québec et de la France autour des lignes THT.* Doctoral thesis in sociology, Institut d'Études Politiques, Paris.

Simard, L. (2008). Conducting projects in uncertain times: The case of electric power lines. *Public Works Management & Policy, 12*(4), 578–589.

Simard, L. (2014). Environmental governance, public action tools, and public participation: The Bureau d'audiences publiques sur l'environnement and the Régie de l'énergie (Québec). In C. Roberge & C. Conteh (Eds.), *Canadian public administration in the twenty-first century* (pp. 117–140). Boca Raton, FL: CRC Press.

Spada, P., & Vreeland, J. R. (2013). Who moderates the moderators? The effect of non-neutral moderators in deliberative decision making. *Journal of Public Deliberation, 9*(2). Retrieved from http://www.publicdeliberation.net/jpd/vol9/iss2/art3/.

Walker, E. T. (2014). *Grassroots for hire: Public affairs consultants in American democracy.* Cambridge: Cambridge University Press.

Weiss, T. G. (1999). Principles, politics, and humanitarian action. *Ethics & International Affairs, 13*(1), 1–22.

6

EXPERTISE, PROFESSIONALIZATION, AND REFLEXIVITY IN MEDIATING PUBLIC PARTICIPATION

Perspectives from STS and British Science and Democracy

Jason Chilvers

Introduction

The rise of formal attempts to build ever more participatory and inclusive forms of democracy in most parts of the world over the past half century is often widely celebrated, but also comes with a distinct set of ironies that can be particularly troubling. In many respects, citizens are nowadays more informed, consulted, and engaged in science and political decision-making than ever before, yet feel increasingly distant from centres of power and calculation under prevailing conditions of globalization, modernity, and economic and science-led progress (Leach, Scoones & Wynne, 2005; Stirling, 2008). A further paradox is evident closer to the immediate concerns of this book. Whereas underlying motivations for deepening participation and empowerment have sought to challenge overly centralized, elitist, and technocratic ways of governing democratic societies, moves to build more participatory alternatives have brought about their own sets of specialisms, technologies, professions, and expertise—raising the spectre of a "technocracy of participation" (Chilvers, 2008a, 2008b; Voß & Amelung, 2016).

It is in the context of these paradoxical conditions that this chapter critically analyzes the emergence of expertise on, and the professionalization of, public participation in Western democracies, with specific reference to developments in the United Kingdom. It draws on two in-depth qualitative studies[1] into the emergence of public participation experts (or, as termed in this volume, public participation professionals or PPPs) and associated participatory practices around science, technology, and environmental issues in the UK over the past decade and a half. The initial study represents one of the first systematic social science analyses of PPPs and was undertaken in 2001–2003 (Chilvers, 2004, 2008a). It involved engaging 26 participatory practitioners from industry, academia, government, and civil society in in-depth interviews, along with documentary analysis, to explore emerging of networks of public participation experts, their roles and relations, and interventions in mediating deliberative public engagement practices. The second study, undertaken almost a decade later in 2009 after a period of institutionalization and professionalization of the public participation field (Chilvers, 2010), involved a similarly diverse range of 21 participatory practitioners in professional networks relating a UK Government–sponsored expert centre on a particular form of deliberative public engagement called "public dialogue."[2]

At one level, then, this chapter can be viewed as providing a view into how the public participation field in the UK has grown and become professionalized and institutionalized over the past two decades, with particular reference to the domains of science and the environment. This partial overview of the UK participation landscape, which offers potential for cross-national comparisons with other country studies included in this volume, forms the focus of the second section of the chapter. Particular emphasis is placed on how networks of public participation professionals—and the roles of and relations between actors, organizations, and institutions within them—have evolved over time around practices of deliberative participatory processes and public dialogue on science and technology.

The overall aim of the chapter seeks to be more ambitious than this in drawing out deeper theoretical and analytical insights from across the two empirical studies. These themes, developed in the three further sections of the chapter, offer more widely applicable explanations about the nature of public participation expertise, the processes through which participation becomes technicalized and professionalized, and the effects that result from this. In developing these interpretive insights, the chapter draws on work from the field of Science and Technology Studies (STS), which offers valuable resources for understanding the construction and performance of participatory expertise. STS is an interdisciplinary field, formed at the intersection of sociology, history, anthropology, and philosophy, that has become established since the late 1960s. STS views science as an inherently social activity and is thus interested in how scientific knowledge, expertise, and technologies are constructed, how they become established and gain authority across different times, places, and cultures, and the effects they have on nature and society (Jasanoff, Markle, Petersen & Pinch, 1995). STS is therefore excellently placed to study emerging practices, expertise, technologies, and institutions of public participation attended to in this volume.

Yet, the field of STS has taken up this challenge only in the last few years. This is partly because the types of participatory experts and professions explored in this volume have themselves recently become formalized. It is also because such a move can place some STS scholars in a tricky position. For those within the field who have spent years promoting the "democratization of science" and democracy and intervening in developing new participatory practices, turning to critically and reflexively analyze these very same practices can be uncomfortable and disorientating (cf. Irwin, 2006). Despite this, over the past decade a strong body of STS scholarship has developed new social studies of participation, turning constructivist STS approaches to understanding the co-production of science and society on to participatory democratic innovations, practices, and expertise (Chilvers, 2008a; Chilvers & Kearnes, 2016a; Felt & Fochler, 2010; Irwin, 2006; Jasanoff, 2011; Laurent, 2011; Lezaun & Soneryd, 2007; Marres, 2012).

This work takes issue with dominant modes of participatory research and practice to date, which has centered on developing and institutionalizing new participatory processes and evaluating their effectiveness (e.g. Gastil & Levine, 2005; Rowe & Frewer, 2000). The emphasis has been on methodological refinement of participatory techniques and expertise to more accurately represent an externally pre-existing public. Dominant perspectives on participation are avowedly normative in making highly specific, often unstated, assumptions about what participation is, what better democracy might mean, and who should be involved. A constructivist STS approach, on the other hand, views participation in all its forms as thoroughly constructed. In this sense, the forms (models), publics (subjects), and issues (objects) of participation do not exist a priori, but are actively constructed through the performance of participatory practices (Chilvers & Longhurst, 2016). All dimensions of participation are not objective and neutral. Rather they are constructed, through human interventions, political power plays, and enrolling human and non-human actors in particular configurations.

In this perspective, rather than simply being an input to participatory policymaking processes and existing in a natural state waiting to be discovered, "the public," public opinion, and "social concerns" can be more accurately viewed as the outcome of heavily mediated participatory experiments (Irwin, 2006). This highlights public participation as a phenomenon in itself, which has effects, in producing publics, expertise, citizenship, and democracy. STS work in this vein has taken different emphases and entry points (see Chilvers & Kearnes, 2016b for an overview), including:

- studying how *participatory experiments and practices* are constructed and mediated through performative work in assembling heterogeneous collectives of participants, procedures, social science theories, methodologies, and other artefacts, and how this co-produces objects (issues), subjects (participants), and models (procedures/philosophies) of participation (Callon, Lascoumes & Barthe, 2009; Irwin & Michael, 2003; Lezaun, 2007);
- the construction, standardization and circulation of *expertise and technologies of participation* across time, place, and cultural-political settings, including the rise of mediators and facilitators as a new category of expert, their roles and interventions in assembling "technologies of participation," and how these instruments and related forms of expertise become more or less stabilized and effects as they move and travel around the world (Chilvers, 2008a; Elam, Reynolds, Soneryd, Sundqvist & Szerszynski, 2007; Laurent, 2011; Soneryd, 2016);
- how both practices and technologies of participation form *part of, shape, and are shaped by wider systems* of institutions (Brown, 2009), controversies and issue spaces (Marres, 2007), and political cultures and constitutions (Jasanoff, 2011).

The deeper interpretive themes developed in this chapter do not map directly on to these three areas but draw on them in developing empirically grounded insights from the perspective of participatory practitioners involved in the two empirical studies. After providing an overview of UK developments in public participation expertise in the next section, the three further sections each develop new understandings that go right to the heart of public participation expertise and its paradoxical nature. The third section develops insights into the nature and qualities of public participation expertise as seen through the eyes of participatory practitioners. In the fourth section, processes by which participation becomes professionalized and institutionalized are explored through the case of public dialogue in Britain. The fifth section then explores the effects of professionalization processes, particularly the ways in which they can "close down" potentials for reflective learning about participation, publics, and public issues, as well as the ability to recognize and value diverse or distributed forms of public involvement and vernacular forms of participation expertise.

Inherent tensions and paradoxes are exposed in each of the three themes. For example, the analysis reveals conflicting demands on facilitators of participatory processes to remain neutral and independent while at the same time powerfully intervening to make participation work. It shows that professionalization imperatives to grow, "scale up," and standardize participation serve to strip it of its contextual meanings, politics, and narrow down around dominant democratic innovations. In addition, hopes for learning, reflection, and the appreciation of otherness—core principles of many philosophies of participation—appear oxymoronic at the level of institutions and wider deliberative systems. In conclusion, I consider what these participatory paradoxes might mean for public participation in science and democracy in the future. I argue that while the professionalization of participation can have damaging effects under current regimes, these are not inevitable. Overcoming this requires moving beyond current obsessions with "effective practice" and its critique, in order to build more reflexive and responsible approaches that can better account for the exclusions, uncertainties, diversities, and politics of participation.

The rise of British Public Participation Experts and Public Dialogue

Public participation professionals belong to a new category of expert and expertise associated with the rise of post-industrial knowledge societies—that of the mediator. For Osborne (2004), a mediator resembles an "enabler," "catalyst," and "broker" of knowledge, always "in the middle of things." Mediation is thus "integrally public, collective and interactive" (p. 443). Facilitators and mediators of public participation processes represent a specific type of what Rose (1999) has called "experts of community," who invent, operate, and market "technologies of community"—citizens' juries, consensus conferences, focus groups, and the like.

This chapter's focus is on expertise and innovations in deliberative public engagement, specifically public dialogue in the domains of science, technology, and the environment.

This focus is set within broader developments in the public participation field in the UK, which date back until at least the late 1960s. Deliberate attempts to consult citizens in political decision-making was formally introduced in the UK planning system following the findings of the Skeffington Report of 1969. The 1970s saw a mushrooming of citizen participation activities often in local level planning decisions and associated with movements such as advocacy planning, community development, and forms of public protest (Warburton, 1998). Some practitioners involved in the most recent study drawn on in this chapter noted that these moves towards participation took a downturn through the 1980s under the Conservative government of Margaret Thatcher. The 1990s saw rapid growth in institutional commitments to public participation. The policy and practical imperatives for this were diverse but included sustainable development agendas in the early 1990s (Macnaghten & Jacobs, 1997), the modernizing and inclusionary agendas associated with the Third Way ideology of the New Labour government from 1997 onwards, and advocacy through think tanks and civil society organizations (Thorpe, 2010). The 1990s saw the onset of moves towards a recognizable field of public participation professionals emerging.

Against this backdrop, developments in public dialogue on science, technology, and environmental issues can be traced back to at least the late 1990s, when constitutional relations between British science and democracy were being shaken to the core in the wake of the BSE (or "mad cow disease") crisis and high-level controversies over GM crops and radioactive waste management. Due to waning public confidence in science advice, science-public relations in Britain were undergoing a well-documented shift (at least rhetorically) from an emphasis on public understanding of science (PUS) and one-way science communication before the late 1990s to public engagement and two-way/multi-way forms of dialogue since then. This new mood was famously and influentially heralded by the House of Lords Select Committee on Science and Technology's landmark *Science and Society* report in 2000, which made explicit use of the term "public dialogue" with reference to approaches of deliberative public engagement and consultation (including the techniques of consensus conferences, citizens' juries, and stakeholder dialogues). The report also warned, however, that "the need for more and better dialogue between the public and science in the United Kingdom requires us to go beyond [such] event-based initiatives" (House of Lords, 2000, para. 5.18).

The half decade immediately following the House of Lords report saw a growth in public dialogue practice. A key feature of this early period was the rise of deliberative public engagement processes, which were mainly framed in terms of environmental risk issues such as high-profile national processes on GM crops and radioactive waste, as well as controversies over waste management at regional and local scales. An "epistemic community" of deliberative public engagement experts began to emerge around this early public dialogue practice—comprising participatory practitioners (based in consultancies and charities) and academic social scientists—who were being commissioned by key decision-making institutions in government and industry to provide advice and mediate participatory experiments on their behalf (Chilvers, 2008a). This also marked the beginnings of a deliberative public engagement industry that, although embryonic and highly fragmented at the time, had begun to form into distinct communities of practice centered on competing participatory approaches. This division was most apparent between mediators interested in "stakeholder dialogue" versus those advocating "public deliberation," each promoting different constructions of the models and subjects of participation (see Chilvers, 2008a). In terms of the former, most prominent was the stakeholder dialogue approach championed by The Environment Council (TEC), a charity supported by a network of independent facilitators and consultancies. The latter public deliberation model centered on citizen panel–type approaches organized by consultancy companies, civil society organizations, as well as academic social scientists. (For further details on the nature and character of these nascent public participation expert networks, see Chilvers, 2008a).

Since 2005 onwards, UK public dialogue activity underwent intensifying processes of institutionalization and professionalization, which coincided with official calls and commitments by UK science and policy institutions to move public engagement further "upstream" in processes of scientific and technological development (e.g. HM Treasury, 2004; Wilsdon & Willis, 2004). Central to this drive to both upstream and institutionalize public dialogue was the UK government's move to set up a new organization called Sciencewise in 2004, following the demise of the Committee on Public Understanding of Science (CoPUS) and in response to the Council for Science and Technology's (Council for Science and Technology, 2005) recommendation that government should develop a "corporate memory" about how to "do dialogue well." Relaunched as the Sciencewise Expert Resource Centre for Public Dialogue in Science and Innovation in 2007, Sciencewise instigated a program of capacity building, learning, and embedding good practice in public dialogue across government and beyond. Over the period 2005–2011, Sciencewise co-funded and guided 17 flagship public dialogue experiments on issues ranging from nanotechnology and stem cell research to synthetic biology and geoengineering of climate change (see Macnaghten & Chilvers, 2014). These dialogues were co-sponsored by UK Government departments and other institutions, such as UK Research Councils, and informed their decision-making processes around emerging areas of science and technology. Sciencewise provided good practice guidance, resources, and support services aimed at those commissioning and organizing dialogues, delivered by a network of "Dialogue and Engagement Specialists" (DES).

The most recent study drawn in this paper provides insights into the professionalization of the wider public participation field in the UK by 2010 (for further details see Chilvers, 2010). By this time, the field had matured and become more institutionalized. Key developments can be summarized in relation to four main roles taken up by public participation professionals as identified by Chilvers (2013) (a typology that has informed the framing of this volume—see Chapter 1):

- *Coordinating*: participation institutions had formed and developed taking on roles of networking, overseeing, and developing good practice within the participation field, including Sciencewise itself, and organizations like Involve, a UK-based think (and do) tank set up in 2003 to advocate and build capacity in public participation, alongside international professional associations like IAP2;
- *Practicing*: the design, facilitation, and reporting of public dialogue processes was still largely outsourced to external consultants, and had become dominated by large specialist consultancies and market research companies;
- *Orchestrating*: roles of commissioning, funding, and sponsoring of public dialogue processes remained with science and policy institutions mainly in the public sector;
- *Studying*: roles of researching, theorizing, evaluating, and reflecting on public dialogue processes were predominantly adopted by academic social scientists who had become more removed from practicing dialogue and had taken up more critical and reflexive positions in relation to the professionalization agenda.

In the following three sections, the interpretive themes drawn from the two empirical studies are now developed, each in turn considering the nature and construction of public participation expertise, processes of technicalization and professionalization of public dialogue, and the effects of professionalization processes.

Public Participation Expertise

Given that scholars in STS and cognate social science disciplines have been central to both understanding forms of scientific expertise and prompting new modes of public engagement with science, it is perhaps surprising that the notion of public participation expertise has scarcely been directly considered. Whereas much has been done to analyze the performance of expertise and citizen-specialist interactions that form part of deliberative processes (e.g. Davies & Burgess, 2004), and the interactional expertise inherent to relations between scientific and contributory expertise in spaces of engagement (Collins & Evans, 2002), such insights only partially touch upon a fuller understanding of expertise associated with the mediation of participatory experiments. The basis for such understanding is developed in this section through a grounded analysis of practitioners' talk, both in terms of their reflections on the roles and interventions of facilitators in mediating UK experiments in public dialogue and on the nature and character of public participation expertise relating to this. Interviews across both empirical studies drawn on in this chapter are included in the analysis to establish significant themes. In both instances, respondents mainly referred to the mediation of group-based deliberative processes.

Experiential and Contextual Expertise

A key characteristic of public participation expertise repeatedly expressed by interviewees in both studies was that, while informed by social science theories, training, and methods, it is fundamentally grounded in personal experience, learning by doing, and an ethical commitment to empowerment. Mediators involved early on in the development of UK public dialogue continually emphasized how it takes time to learn from experience and become viewed as an expert in participation. This perspective has continued in the more professionalized context of Sciencewise and its formal learning infrastructure, as this practitioner closely involved in delivering Sciencewise dialogues put it:

> [D]on't expect to know it in five minutes by reading a book and going to a Sciencewise meeting. If you want to get to grips with the complexities and then do it well, it takes a lot of time, a lot of thinking and a lot of experience.
> *(Participatory practitioner, market research company, interviewed February 2009)*

In this respect, facilitation as a form of expertise was viewed to be more like a learned art, craft, or skill. Related to this highly experiential nature of participation expertise, many practitioners revealed how professionally mediated public participation processes are most often bespoke and designed to be appropriate to local circumstances, or established techniques are tweaked, hybridized, and made to be locally "fit for purpose." While particular participatory formats, such as the Citizens' Jury, have undoubtedly become standardized techniques that move and travel around the world, in-depth reflections of mediators brought into question the notion of highly stabilized "technologies of participation" as purely rational techniques. As this practitioner involved in Sciencewise public dialogue experiments on issues of climate change and emerging biotechnologies noted:

> It's difficult to generalize because every single project that we do is bespoke, it is tailor made and there is no such thing as off the shelf expertise, like "if you've done ABC, you can do XYZ."
> *(Public engagement practitioner, science institution, interviewed March 2009)*

Embodied Expertise

In addition to this experiential emphasis, a further theme central to practitioners' talk in both studies highlighted the embodied nature of public participation expertise. One social scientist able to reflect across the roles of facilitators in mediating earlier citizen and stakeholder-based dialogues on GM crops and waste management captured the sense of this very well:

> That makes them very stressful processes to actually develop and in my experience of the individuals that I have worked with . . . they have to be somewhat special people to be able to run these types of processes.
>
> *(Academic social scientist, interviewed September 2001)*

Interviewees taking up different roles across the Sciencewise network in the most recent study similarly referred to the need for mediators of public dialogue to be an "extraordinary amazing person" (Participatory practitioner, civil society organization) and possess the "right personality" (Participatory practitioner, government agency) to successfully mediate upstream public dialogues. The "right person" being imagined here most often had the ability to reconcile multiple perspectives and embody the inherent tension of simultaneously intervening in and remaining "neutral" in dialogue processes.

Independence versus Intervention

In many respects, this represents a defining feature of public participation expertise and a dynamic written through all interviews—i.e. the constant tension between the irreconcilable demands of independence and neutrality versus intervention and artificiality in attempting to achieve "good" public dialogue. This is what Lezaun (2007) has called the "chameleon-like qualities" and "kaleidoscopic identity" of those that mediate deliberative processes. Many respondents emphasized the need to create a "neutral space" (Participatory practitioner, civil society organization) in dialogue processes, stating that "it's the facilitator's job to be neutral and independent" (Participatory practitioner, government agency). This was held in constant tension with the need to intervene in framing or anchoring the issue in question, ensuring fair deliberation, producing the products of participation, and so on. Central to practitioners' reflections in both the current study and earlier interviews, then, was frequent reference to the boundary work (Gieryn, 1995) that goes into maintaining a distinction between a facilitator's process expertise and procedures from: (i) the science and technology-related issue forming the focus of public dialogue; (ii) process participants and other competing participatory collectives; and (iii) decision-making and the wider policy world (cf. Laurent, 2011). These three aspects are now explored in turn for the remainder of this section.

Relations to the Issue in Question

First, with regard to the science-related issue forming the object of participation, when reflecting on public participation expertise, practitioners often spoke about technical participatory procedures irrespective of the actual issues involved, as if technologies of participation could be unproblematically applied to *any* issue. This perspective was illustrated by this participatory practitioner, from a government agency that has supported the delivery of governmental public dialogue:

> It doesn't particularly matter to us as a facilitator whether you're talking with the public, business, or within government. We don't even have to know about the subject particularly, just to ask the right questions and design a process that gets people out at the other end.
>
> *(Participatory practitioner, government agency, interviewed February 2009)*

Yet at the same time this operated in tension with the requirement for experts of participation to have at least some ability to grasp the issues involved in order to effectively mediate public dialogue while not being a substantive expert in the area, as this social scientist stated when reflecting more broadly on recent developments in the UK public dialogue field:

> It's better to be independent . . . you know in terms of the process. But that having been said, [facilitators] need to have the professional competence to grasp the scientific issues.
>
> *(Academic social scientist, interviewed February 2009)*

Insulating the Process and Disciplining Participants

Second, in a similar way to these relationships between participatory procedures and the science-related issue in question, tensions were evident in the way mediators of public dialogue discussed boundaries between their own procedural techniques and the subjects of participation (i.e. participants themselves) and/ or alternative expressions of public issues in wider society. A revealing insight into this dynamic was offered in the earlier interviews, with reference to invited small group deliberative processes such as citizens panels and community advisory committees (CACs) applied to issues of waste management (including radioactive waste). These reflections from two practitioners closely involved in the development of early UK public dialogue practice illustrate very well the simultaneous burden and tensions involved in balancing between naturalness (whereby participants go on their own self-determined personal journey, mediators allow participants to speak through them, and the products of participation to emerge "naturally") and intervention (where participants' behaviour and reflexivity is controlled to make it fit with the design blueprints of a particular technique or to ensure discursive ethics relating to equality of access to the deliberation):

> [T]he common thing is that people have to go on a journey. They have to define for themselves what are the issues, they have to find out what is the

history to date, why is there an issue, and then they have to come to their own conclusions after listening to experts.

(Participatory practitioner, private consultancy, interviewed August 2001)

[T]hey're literally sort of off the shelf . . . And the people have to squeeze into the process, and the issue and the people and everything needs to squeeze into the process.

(Participatory practitioner, civil society organization, interviewed August 2001)

Furthermore, efforts in mediation often involved insulating invited deliberative processes (such as citizens' panels and CACs) from competing participatory processes and uninvited spaces of engagement occurring "outside" as part of wider ecologies of participation in particular controversy contexts. This also involved making deliberative processes more responsive to external contexts as this interviewee noted:

All the counter debate going on tends to make the process itself that you're in the middle of have to be highly reactive and responsive to what's going on outside. . . . They have all suffered this sort of challenge from outside when this sort of participation is going on, particularly in the dioxin area.

(Academic social scientist, interviewed September 2001)

Managing Social Science–Policy Relations

The third dimension of boundary work evident in practitioners' talk concerned connections with decision-making and the policy world. In this regard, an important component of public participation expertise expressed by respondents was the ability and skill of mediators to make connections and maintain distinctions between participatory experiments on the one hand and policy and policymaking on the other. This point was repeated by a number of actors central to Sciencewise and its wider network, including this practitioner when reflecting upon upstream public dialogue practice across the Sciencewise portfolio, including the areas of nanotechnology, emerging biotechnologies, and energy futures:

[T]here are other people who are really good facilitators, who will really run a group well but don't have the experience of the whole policy-influencing process. So they'll do their little bit or they're quite good at bringing stakeholders together and analyzing who should be in the room and so on, but less good at seeing that as part of the whole process of actually changing policy.

(Participatory practitioner, private consultancy, interviewed February 2009)

Interfacing with policy in this way was seen to involve "negotiation and persuasive skills" (Academic scientist) beyond the immediate participatory setting in order to enhance the value and productivity of public dialogue. These dynamics were reflected more broadly in structural relations in UK public dialogue networks, where the outsourcing of dialogue and reliance on external mediators maintains their distance from policy while allowing decision institutions and participation experts to influence the "optimal" framing of public debate.

The analysis in this section thus reveals an inherent paradox lying at the heart of participatory expertise. Facilitators and mediators remain largely invisible, or are otherwise seen as "neutral," in both the products of participatory processes and writings on deliberative democratic theory and practice (cf. Moore, 2012). Yet, deliberative processes would not happen without continual work and interventions by facilitators who are adopting increasingly powerful roles in mediating relations at the science–policy–society interface.

The ability of PPPs to negotiate these tensions and boundaries is a defining feature of participatory expertise and crucial to the successful generation of participatory experiments and their products. Furthermore, the embodied nature of participatory expertise, coupled with careful boundary work in relation to science, politics, and society, has allowed mediators of public dialogue to mobilize both themselves as experts and associated technologies of participation. This was certainly the case in the years immediately following House of Lords report in 2000, when certain mediators of public dialogue were able to move, often with great ease, between mediating participatory experiments in distinct environmental risk issue domains, such as switching between areas of radioactive waste management and GMOs and beyond (see Chilvers, 2008a). Practitioner reflections in the current study illustrate how deliberative technologies of participation have been "copied cross" from these "downstream" domains into areas of anticipatory governance of emerging technologies, although not unproblematically (Chilvers, 2010). In a detailed study of the making of consensus conferences on the subject of nanotechnology in the US and France, Laurent (2009) has also shown how solidifying a boundary between the issue and the procedure is central to stabilizing and standardizing participatory devices, which "allows some actors (and notably private companies) to make the procedure travel and replicate it across various technological issues" (p. 30).

Technicalization, Professionalization, and Innovation Pathways in Public Dialogue

Public participation expertise, of the sort just outlined, has become a key feature of a globally connected public engagement industry involved in the transnational circulation of people, knowledge, skills, and technologies of participation, reaching beyond European settings to encompass deliberative goods and services in Australasia (Hendriks & Carson, 2008) and the US (Lee, 2015), through to participatory development in the "global South" (Kothari, 2005). The rapid growth in institutionally commissioned public dialogue on science and technology in the UK means that processes of institutionalization, technicalization, and professionalization have been particularly apparent in this national context. In-depth interviews with mediators of public dialogue in the later study drawn on in this chapter provide insights into these dynamics. More specifically, these interviews offer reflections on the processes and inscriptions that codify forms of mediation, mechanisms of enrollment, and definitions of participation into more or less persistent forms (Latour, 1988; Rose & Miller, 1992), and set particular trajectories of innovation in public dialogue. This second analytical theme is explored in this section through the cases of two key developments in the Sciencewise network, namely: (i) drives to institutionalize and professionalize public dialogue and (ii) mechanisms of resource allocation related to the emergence of a public dialogue market.

As outlined above, quite distinct networks of public participation experts had emerged around competing stakeholder and public models of invited public dialogue in the early years immediately after 2000. In reflecting back on the development of UK public dialogue since this initial period, almost all interview respondents emphasized increasing institutionalization, professionalization, and growth of a dialogue industry in the second half of the decade and with this the production of a more coherent and to some extent stabilized model of public dialogue. The dominant meaning of public dialogue in this post-2005 period was seen to be an invited-micro public deliberation model with an emphasis on enrolling small groups of public participants reflective of key demographic characteristics and constructing the public as "innocent citizens" (i.e. prioritizing participants with limited a priori interest or knowledge in the issues under discussion). This vision of participation and the public, which had dominated policy discourses surrounding the emblematic *GM Nation?* public debate in 2003 (Irwin, 2006; Lezaun & Soneryd, 2007), had become further entrenched in later moves to upstream engagement under the auspices of Sciencewise. While linguistically this more avowedly public model of "public dialogue" represented a hybridization of the two previously distinct models of *public* deliberation and stakeholder *dialogue*, in practice it reflected the waning importance of the stakeholder dialogue model in UK participatory politics, as this practitioner summarized:

> The [stakeholder] dialogue community, we've been quite reactionary to that I think and quite protective of what we do . . . but we've not been very good at expressing what that particular stuff that we do is and the most extreme example of that is The Environment Council not capturing the convening type of role. They didn't do that and then at the same time the language of dialogue got taken on by Sciencewise in a non-dialogue kind of way and you've got Opinion Leader Research coming in and branding things, you've got citizen summits and deliberative this and that.
>
> *(Participatory practitioner, independent consultant, interviewed February 2009)*

In addition to strong evidence from interviews, this shift was clearly evident in documentary evidence of actual public dialogue experiments. The majority of public dialogues co-sponsored by Sciencewise, in the period from 2005 up until the time of interviews in 2009, were based on invited-micro public deliberation centered on a citizen panel–type model. Of the 13 Sciencewise co-sponsored dialogues that were active during this period, 10 enrolled public participants (who were often paid an incentive, had no strong prior interest in the issue, and reflected key socio-demographic characteristics of a specific locality) into small group deliberative events held at multiple sites in different regions across the UK that were then reconvened, often involving participants from different sites being brought together in a final workshop at a central location (for overviews see Chilvers, 2010; Macnaghten & Chilvers, 2014; Warburton, 2010). These 10 experiments all involved publics interacting with specialists and expert witnesses. They were centrally orchestrated and mediated by professional facilitators contracted by host science and policy institutions.

Five of these dialogues exclusively employed this multi-sited reconvened citizen panel model including the *Industrial Biotechnology* dialogue, the *Forensic use of DNA* dialogue, the *Nanodialogues*, the *Big Energy Shift*, and the *Trustguide* dialogue. The other five dialogues took this same general citizens panel model as the central component used in conjunction with other assistive or "scaling up" techniques, including an online consultation (*Drugsfutures* dialogue); a national opinion poll (*Synthetic Biology* dialogue, *Hybrids and Chimeras* dialogue); stakeholder interviews (*Stem Cells* dialogue); and outreach to wider interested public groups (*Sciencehorizons* dialogue). This dominant approach was replicated in dialogues commissioned by other UK science policy organizations over the same time period, including UK Research Council processes on nanotechnology for healthcare and energy futures (e.g. Bhattachary, Stockley & Hunter, 2008; Ipsos-MORI, 2007). The central place and consistency of this multi-sited reconvened citizen panel model is really quite striking given that all 10 dialogue processes had different contractors, steering groups, commissioning bodies, decision makers and addressed different science and technology-related issues.

There are a number of possible explanations for this shift and greater coherence around a particular meaning of UK public dialogue on science and technology. Here, two key developments deemed particularly important in interviews are considered, as stated at the beginning of this section. First, the establishment of Sciencewise as a formal participation organization, and through this attempts to promote and improve the practice of public dialogue and professionalize the field, began to inscribe and codify a particular definition of public dialogue and the formats, configurations, and skills for enrolling heterogeneous collectives that make up public dialogue experiments (Rose & Miller, 1992). A steering group comprising representatives from government, industry, participatory practice, and academic social science was formed early on in the establishment of Sciencewise which agreed on a particular definition of public dialogue, stated in published guidance as a two-way conversation with members of the public, to inform . . . decision-making on science and technology issues. . . . [It] is a process during which members of the public interact with scientists, stakeholders and policy makers to deliberate on issues likely to be important in future policies.

(Sciencewise-ERC, 2009)

Evident within this vision is the centrality of public participants, with interested stakeholders being positioned in a more peripheral, supportive, or assistive role. Alongside scientists and policy-makers, stakeholders are actors who publics are in dialogue with rather than being actual subjects of the dialogue themselves. A key ambition of Sciencewise within government and beyond was to "grow the number of possible people who can do [public dialogue] well" (Academic scientist) and "begin to mainstream all this a bit more effectively" (Participatory practitioner, social research company). This drive to grow and promote "best practice" through a learning infrastructure and networking activities further codified and inscribed the Sciencewise vision of proper public talk through training courses and mentoring schemes, knowledge exchange mechanisms including a web-based knowledge hub, and associated systems of evaluating the effectiveness of public dialogue processes (see Chilvers, 2013). As part of this support network, Sciencewise assembled a team of Dialogue and Engagement Specialists (DES) to mentor and advise commissioners of public dialogue processes (Warburton, 2010). This included a number of participation experts from the stakeholder dialogue community who were deemed by some to have "got a stranglehold on Sciencewise" (Participatory practitioner, independent consultant) but had in fact become enrolled into an "innocent citizen" problematization of participation (Latour, 1988), although not without some degree of resistance and much ambivalence (as the practitioner quote earlier in this section testifies).

A second key development expressed in interviews, which helps explain the production of a more stabilized vision of public dialogue and the prioritization of certain technologies of participation over others, was structures of resource allocation and the related growth and commercialization of a public dialogue market. For all interviewees, one of the most striking developments from the mid-decade (2005) onwards was the growth of a public engagement industry driven by government funding, which meant that the resourcing and control of public dialogue became centralized around UK science and policy institutions. This was highlighted by the following two statements from interviewees closely involved in Sciencewise dialogues:

[T]he combination of wider government funds and things like Sciencewise, has meant that money is there much more now and it's attracted . . . professional agencies basically moving in, more traditional market research agencies.

(Participatory practitioner, consultancy company, interviewed February 2009)

> [W]hen our projects were initially funded, Sciencewise was providing grants to run projects whereas it's obviously changed its focus significantly and now a project is commissioned by a policy maker.... [O]bviously many people would perceive government therefore taking a much firmer grip on what a process may look like and therefore potentially steering the process.
>
> *(Science and society manager, science institution, interviewed March 2009)*

From a situation where independent facilitators and smaller groups (including charities and academic social scientists) took on mediator roles early on in the development of UK public dialogue, almost all interviewees noted that—in step with the growth of a dialogue market—the field had become increasingly captured by larger consultancy companies that had "taken over" (Participatory practitioner, participation organization) and "obliterated all the rest of the range of different approaches" (Participatory practitioner, independent consultant). This was particularly the case with large market research companies—such as the British Market Research Bureau (BMRB), Ipsos-MORI, and Opinion Leader Research (OLR)—that had developed capabilities in deliberative processes and were able to draw on close ties and long track records in providing evidence of public opinion to government departments based on statistically representative national surveys of the "general public" (Osborne & Rose, 1999). For most interview respondents, the introduction of formal mechanisms for resource allocation, called framework contracts, played a crucial role in this transformation of UK public dialogue networks. These instruments had been introduced by organizations commissioning public dialogue processes, including government departments and agencies, in order to identify and maintain recognized lists of participatory experts deemed sufficiently qualified to provide advice and support. There was a sense that such mechanisms served to privilege the so-called "big players" and thus further stabilize networks around particular visions of participation, public dialogue and expertise associated with them:

> [Y]ou've got all the big players in there like Ipsos-MORI and OLR and that just keeps getting reinforced by things like these framework contracts so it's not impossible to envisage that soon you can't do any central government work unless you do it through the back door, unless you're on one of those framework contracts, and to get on a framework contract you have to have all the things that big organizations are required to have which many of us independents don't have.
>
> *(Participatory practitioner, independent facilitator, interviewed February 2009)*

In further extending the idea of technologies of participation, democratic innovations in the UK field of public dialogue on science and technology can thus be seen to have followed a particular innovation pathway and exhibit some of the classic features of "lock in" (Arthur, 1989) so often seen in other areas of scientific and technological development. Over the post-2005 period considered in this section, highly centralized forms of resourcing and control around science and policy institutions, structures and processes for allocating resources (such as framework contracts), processes of professionalization and commercialization, and other discursive and infrastructural attachments, served to close down and to some extent lock in commitments to invited-micro forms of public dialogue, centered on innocent citizens. This emphasises a further paradox of participation in that the very processes that allow expertise and practices of participation to be mobilized, scaled up, and travel around the world can also serve to strip them of their contextual meanings, diversity, politics, and purposes.

Professionalization Effects and Participatory Closures

As these insights into the professionalization and technicalization of public dialogue show, an important effect of these processes is to close down the dimensions of participation that STS perspectives emphasize as being constructed through the performance of participatory practice. This includes closures in relation to: the meanings of participation itself (around a model of public dialogue as invited mini-publics), subjects of participation (around a construction of the public as innocent citizens), and to some extent of the science and policy-related issues at stake. Some practitioners involved in the most recent study drawn on in this chapter held serious concerns over trends towards the professionalization and commercialization of public participation, including the potential for it to compromise the ethical integrity of participation. Other interviewees, mainly participatory practitioners working in consultancies and policymakers in government, emphasized more positive effects, maintaining that professionalization is essential to ensure the quality and enhance the "scale" of public dialogue. Yet, deeper analysis of interview discourses emphasizes the closing role of professionalization and institutionalization processes. This section considers effects in terms of closures relating to learning, reflection and the appreciation of otherness, which are key virtues and rationales underpinning many participatory philosophies and approaches (e.g. Petts, 2007; Webler, Kastenholz & Renn, 1995).

Some of the developments to professionalize and institutionalize public dialogue through Sciencewise noted in the previous section were deliberately aimed at enhancing learning, through knowledge hubs, guidelines, training courses, capacity building, formal systems for monitoring and evaluating the effectiveness of public dialogue processes, and so on. In one sense this enhanced learning, but mainly learning of a particular type. Institutional learning about and from public dialogue was predominantly instrumental only—i.e. instrumental acquisition of new knowledge and understandings to optimize existing strategies or goals. This centered on capacity building (growing practice) and best practice (ensuring better practice) around a relatively narrow definition of what public dialogue is and can be. It was about learning "more of the same," rather than challenging underlying assumptions about the models (formats), subjects (publics) and objects (issues) of participation at play. A good example of this is how evaluation procedures associated with moves to standardize and judge the quality of public dialogue led to set evaluation criteria based on the Sciencewise principles being applied to judge different public dialogue processes in evaluations which were required report very soon after a dialogue project had ended. As some interviewees noted, this served more to legitimate and defend the credibility of specific dialogue processes rather than enhance learning and reflection in relation to them.

This closed down potentials for more reflexive and relational forms of learning—i.e. processes of critically evaluating our own assumptions which frame participatory knowledge-commitments, and those of others (cf. Wynne, 1993). In terms of learning *from* public dialogue, science and policy institutions were not seen to be effectively listening and responding to public values and concerns in potentially changing the ways that they frame and think about key governance issues. Furthermore, a similar lack of reflexivity was highlighted by some respondents when considering learning *about* participation within the network, in terms of the potential for mediators to learn about their underlying assumptions, commitments and possible effects relating to the forms of public dialogue they orchestrate or are exposed to (see Chilvers, 2013). Such closures were not only brought about through professionalization processes, however, but were also due to the "unreflexive institutional culture of science and policy itself" (Wynne, 2006, p. 213), a finding confirmed in a later study of key British science policy organizations and their (lack of) responsiveness to public concerns (see Macnaghten & Chilvers, 2014).

A further effect of professionalization and institutionalization of participation, closely related to these points on learning, is the way in which it can close down recognition and acknowledgement of other forms of public engagement, publics and participatory expertise. This was an important insight of the most recent study drawn on in this chapter. While most respondents from government and industry emphasized the view of public dialogue that had become established in and around Sciencewise (as discussed in the previous section) a smaller group of respondents (mainly academics and representatives of civil society organizations) pointed to more diverse meanings of participation and the public. This included for example public dialogue occurring in the macro public sphere (cf. Hendriks, 2006), forms of do-it-yourself public dialogue, such as the DIY citizens juries (e.g. PEALS, 2003), and bottom-up or "uninvited" public dialogues (cf. Wynne, 2007) which are led by citizens themselves as opposed to host institutions. In terms of the last category this opens up to alternative models of public dialogue initiated and organized by citizens and groups in society themselves, such as forms of protest, activism, social movements, special interest groups, instances of citizen science, and sites of distributed or grassroots innovation (cf. Chilvers & Longhurst, 2016). Not only does this bring forward alternative models of participation and the public. As one interviewee implied, it also represents other distributed forms of mediation and vernacular, lay or grassroots participation expertise:

> I think to some extent the CSOs didn't realize that we already use a lot of these kind of techniques within our own meetings, to reach decisions and yeah, so there is a kind of experience of participatory decision making that hasn't been really labelled as such, if you like. But then that would be within the people that actually join in a network or come to a climate camp or whatever it is.
>
> *(Civil society organization representative, interviewed February 2009)*

From the perspective of this civil society organization (CSO) representative—who had direct experience of participatory collectives in CSO networks and activist expressions of climate change issues—public participation expertise is not limited to the professional forms of mediation (as explored under the first analytical theme, above) but also exists in more informal, tacit, less codified ways, and often not recognized as such. Despite these few references to alternative forms of public dialogue and public participation expertise, they were not being acknowledged or accounted for by incumbent institutions at the time of interviews in 2009. As these statements from a government representative and academic respectively illustrate, the dominant institutional response to public issues emerging from citizen-led and uninvited spaces of engagement was often one of denial (cf. Welsh & Wynne, 2013), while localized, distributed, or "wild" forms of public participation expertise were being delegitimized in the Sciencewise network:

> Citizen-led, citizen framed discussions are great but . . . if we're spending public money, we can't have something that goes on for too long or costs too much in a way, it's got to be about balance and fit for purpose.
>
> *(Policymaker, government agency, interviewed March 2009)*

> We have this failure to engage even with people who are doing community engagement work out in communities. Continuously if you say something about anything that's done at a local level it gets [thrown out] as not being relevant to a discussion of upstream public engagement. . . . So we've got this privileging of experience and knowledge, not overtly, it's almost happening subconsciously I think . . . people trying to protect their particular skill areas.
>
> *(Academic social scientist, interviewed February 2009)*

Experience in the years since has seen instances where meanings of public dialogue in the Sciencewise network have shifted somewhat—for example in the case of a biofuels dialogue process which has experimented with a more distributed model of dialogue—and some evidence of instances of reflexive learning in informal or "shadow spaces" (Pallett, 2014; Pallett & Chilvers, 2013). Yet, forces of closure when it comes to learning about and from public dialogue remain. This penultimate section, then, has raised a further paradox of participation: that hopes for learning, reflection, and the appreciation of otherness—core principles of many philosophies of participation—can appear oxymoronic at the level of institutions and wider systems and cultures of participation.

Towards Reflexive Participation?

Through developing new understandings of the expertise and professionalization of public participation in British science and democracy, this chapter has exposed inherent paradoxes and tensions lying at the heart of participation expertise and attempts to institutionalize it. There is no doubt from this analysis that the professionalization and institutionalization of participation can have damaging effects, especially when compared to the more radical normative aspirations of movements seeking to build more participatory forms of democracy in late-modern societies. But professionalization and the development of expertise and technologies of participation is not necessarily bad or damaging in itself. If left unchecked it can tend towards closing down and depoliticizing participation in some of the ways outlined in this chapter, but this is not inevitable.

Taking a co-productionist STS perspective on participation allows one to move beyond the sterile dichotomy that has defined the participation field over the years—between a positive and affirmative perspective that seeks to grow and ensure better participation practice through methodological revisionism versus a more critical tradition that focuses on the apolitical and oppressive potential of participation to disempower and exclude (e.g. Cooke & Kothari, 2001). Both positions gain their power of critique through judging participatory practices and institutions against (often very partial) pre-given normative assumptions about what "good" participation means. As I have argued from the two studies drawn on in this chapter and other works, in order to deal with the inherent paradoxes and dilemmas of participation (including those outlined in this chapter), diverse practices of participation need to move beyond simplistic positions of promoting "effective practice" and its critique to one of *reflexive participation* (see Chilvers, 2013; Chilvers & Kearnes, 2016c).

Reflexive participation actively takes account of how the subjects (publics), objects (issues), and models (formats) of participation are *actively constructed and co-produced* through the performance of participatory practices, interventions by mediators, powers lodged in expertise and technologies of participation, and conditions established in wider institutions, systems, and political cultures. A reflexive approach seeks to open up, anticipate, and be continually responsive to the exclusions, underlying purposes, politics, framing effects, uncertainties, unintended consequences, social implications, and effects of public participation. This calls for more responsible and reflective forms of participation in theory and practice, especially under conditions where participatory expertise becomes professionalized and technicalized.

Strategies for doing so are many and need to be creatively explored in future work (for a more comprehensive elaboration of future possibilities, see Chilvers & Kearnes, 2016c). In relation to the three analytical themes developed in this paper, for example, interventions could involve the following moves. First would be commitments by mediators and facilitators to build more deliberately reflexive participatory practices that open up and reflect on framing effects and exclusions in relation to the subjects (publics), objects (issues), and models (formats) of participation, rather than simply referring to the objectivity and neutrality of participatory expertise (Chilvers & Longhurst, 2016). A second practical possibility would be to engage public participation professionals of diverse types in processes of collective experimentation to build anticipatory reflection over the social and ethical implications, effects, and alternative pathways of emerging forms of expertise and technologies of participation, which can in turn modulate and shape processes of professionalization and democratic innovation in "real time" and in more responsible ways (see Chilvers, 2013). A third set of possibilities relates to catalyzing more reflexive and relational learning that can overcome instrumental imperatives not only at the level of individual actors but in institutions and wider distributed systems (Pallett & Chilvers, 2015). Moves like these can play important roles in dealing with the ironies of participatory expertise and rendering the democratization of science and democracy—including that of public participation itself—more reflexive, socially responsible, and accountable in the longer term.

Notes

1 The earlier study partially drawn on in this chapter was funded by the UK Economic and Social Research Council. The more recent research project was supported by a grant from the UK Department for Business, Innovation and Skills (BIS) and the Sciencewise Expert Resource Centre. I am very grateful to all those who gave up their time to participate in both studies.
2 In both studies, in-depth interviews lasted for between one and two hours and were audio recorded, fully transcribed, and coded in Atlas.ti qualitative analysis software (along with documentary evidence) to identify key analytical themes. Full details of the methodologies employed in the first and second studies are provided in Chilvers (2008a) and Chilvers (2010, 2013) respectively.

References

Arthur, W. B. (1989). Competing technologies, increasing returns, and lock-in by historical events. *The Economic Journal*, *99*(394), 116–131.
Bhattachary, D., Stockley, R., & Hunter, A. (2008). *Nanotechnology for healthcare*. Prepared for the Engineering and Physical Sciences Research Council. British Market Research Bureau. Retrieved from https://www.epsrc.ac.uk/newsevents/pubs/nanotechnology-for-healthcare/.

Brown, M. (2009). *Science in democracy: Expertise, institutions, and representation.* Cambridge: MIT Press.

Callon, M., Lascoumes, P., & Barthe, Y. (2009). *Acting in an uncertain world: An essay on technical democracy.* Cambridge: MIT Press.

Chilvers, J. (2004). *Participatory environmental risk policymaking in an age of uncertainty: UK actor-networks, social learning and effective practice.* Unpublished PhD thesis, University College London, London.

Chilvers, J. (2008a). Environmental risk, uncertainty, and participation: Mapping an emergent epistemic community. *Environment and Planning A, 40*(12), 2990–3008.

Chilvers, J. (2008b). Deliberating competence: Theoretical and practitioner perspectives on effective participatory appraisal practice. *Science, Technology, & Human Values, 33*(2), 155–185.

Chilvers, J. (2010). *Sustainable participation? Mapping out and reflecting on the field of public dialogue on science and technology.* Harwell: Sciencewise Expert Resource Centre.

Chilvers, J. (2013). Reflexive engagement? Actors, learning, and reflexivity in public dialogue on science and technology. *Science Communication, 35*(3), 283–310.

Chilvers, J., & Kearnes, M. (Eds.). (2016a). *Remaking participation: Science, environment and emergent publics.* Abingdon: Routledge.

Chilvers, J., & Kearnes, M. (2016b). Participation in-the-making: Rethinking public engagement in co-productionist terms. In J. Chilvers & M. Kearnes (Eds.), *Remaking participation: Science, environment and emergent publics* (pp. 31–63). Abingdon: Routledge.

Chilvers, J., & Kearnes, M. (2016c). Remaking participation: Towards reflexive engagement. In J. Chilvers & M. Kearnes (Eds.), *Remaking participation: Science, environment and emergent publics* (pp. 261–288). Abingdon: Routledge.

Chilvers, J., & Longhurst, N. (2016). Participation in transition(s): Reconceiving public engagements in energy transitions as co-produced, emergent and diverse. *Journal of Environmental Policy & Planning, 18*(5), 585–607.

Collins, H. M., & Evans, R. (2002). The third wave of science studies: Studies of expertise and experience. *Social Studies of Science, 32*(2), 235–296.

Cooke, B., & Kothari, U. (Eds.). (2001). *Participation: The new tyranny?* London: Zed Books.

Council for Science and Technology. (2005). *Policy through dialogue: Informing policies based on science and technology.* London: Council for Science and Technology.

Davies, G., & Burgess, J. (2004). Challenging the "view from nowhere": Citizen reflections on specialist expertise in a deliberative process. *Health and Place, 10,* 349–361.

Elam, M., Reynolds, L., Soneryd, L., Sundqvist, G., & Szerszynski, B. (2007). *Mediators of issues and mediators of process—A theoretical framework.* ARGONA FP6 Project Report, Göteborg: Göteborg University.

Felt, U., & Fochler, M. (2010). Machineries for making publics: Inscribing and describing publics in public engagement. *Minerva, 48*(3), 219–138.

Gastil, J., & Levine, P. (Eds.). (2005). *The deliberative democracy handbook: Strategies for effective civic engagement in the twenty-first century.* San Francisco, CA: Jossey-Bass.

Gieryn, T. F. (1995). Boundaries of science. In S. Jasanoff, G. E. Markle, J. C. Petersen & T. Pinch (Eds.), *The handbook of science and technology studies* (pp. 393–443). London: Sage.

Hendriks, C. M. (2006). Integrated deliberation: Reconciling civil society's dual role in deliberative democracy. *Political Studies, 54*(3), 486–508.

Hendriks, C. M., & Carson, L. (2008). Can the market help the forum? Negotiating the commercialization of deliberative democracy. *Policy Sciences, 41*(4), 293–313.

HM Treasury. (2004). *Science and innovation investment framework 2004–2014.* London: The Stationery Office.

House of Lords. (2000). *Science and Society*. London: The Stationary Office.

Ipsos-MORI. (2007). *Energy research dialogue: A public dialogue on UK energy research priorities.* Retrieved from https://www.epsrc.ac.uk/newsevents/pubs/energy-research-dialogue-a-public-dialogue-on-uk-energy-research-priorities-final-report/.

Irwin, A. (2006). The politics of talk: Coming to terms with the "new" scientific governance. *Social Studies of Science, 36*(2), 299–320.

Irwin, A., & Michael, M. (2003). *Science, social theory and public knowledge*. Maidenhead: Open University Press.

Jasanoff, S. (2011). Constitutional moments in governing science and technology. *Science and Engineering Ethics, 17*(4), 621–638.

Jasanoff, S., Markle, G. E., Petersen, J. C., & Pinch, T. (Eds.). (1995). *The handbook of science and technology studies*. London: Sage.

Kothari, U. (2005). Authority and expertise: The professionalisation of international development and the ordering of dissent. *Antipode, 37*(3), 425–446.

Latour, B. (1988). *Science in action: How to follow scientists and engineers through society*. Cambridge: Harvard University Press.

Laurent, B. (2009). Replicating participatory devices: The consensus conference confronts nanotechnology. *CSI Working Paper* (18). Retrieved from http://www.csi.mines-paristech.fr/working-papers/WP/WP_CSI_018.pdf.

Laurent, B. (2011). Technologies of democracy: Experiments and demonstrations. *Science and Engineering Ethics, 17*(4), 649–666.

Leach, M., Scoones, I., & Wynne, B. (Eds.). (2005). *Science and citizens: Globalization and the challenge of engagement*. London: Zed Books.

Lee, C. W. (2015). *Do-it-yourself democracy: The rise of the public engagement industry*. New York: Oxford University Press.

Lezaun, J. (2007). A market of opinions: The political epistemology of focus groups. In M. Callon, Y. Millo & F. Muniesa (Eds.), *Market devices* (pp. 130–151). Oxford: Wiley-Blackwell.

Lezaun, J., & Soneryd, L. (2007). Consulting citizens: Technologies of elicitation and the mobility of publics. *Public Understanding of Science, 16*(3), 279–297.

Macnaghten, P., & Chilvers, J. (2014). The future of science governance: Publics, policies, practices. *Environment and Planning C: Government and Policy, 32*(3), 530–548.

Macnaghten, P., & Jacobs, M. (1997). Public identification with sustainable development: Investigating cultural barriers to participation. *Global Environmental Change, 7*(1), 5–24.

Marres, N. (2007). The issues deserve more credit: Pragmatist contributions to the study of public involvement in controversy. *Social Studies of Science, 37*(5), 759–780.

Marres, N. (2012). *Material participation: Technology, the environment and everyday publics*. Basingstoke: Palgrave Macmillan.

Moore, A. (2012). Following from the front: Theorizing deliberative facilitation. *Critical Policy Studies, 6*(2), 146–162.

Osborne, T. (2004). On mediators: Intellectuals and the ideas trade in the knowledge society. *Economy and Society, 33*(4), 430–447.

Osborne, T., & Rose, N. (1999). Do the social sciences create phenomena? The example of public opinion research. *British Journal of Sociology, 50*(3), 367–396.

Pallett, H. (2014). *Organising science policy: Participation, learning and experimentation in British democracy*. Unpublished PhD thesis, University of East Anglia, Norwich.

Pallett, H., & Chilvers, J. (2013). A decade of learning about publics, participation and climate change: Institutionalising reflexivity? *Environment and Planning A, 45*(5), 1162–1183.

Pallett, H., & Chilvers, J. (2015). Organizations in the making: Learning and intervening at the science-policy interface. *Progress in Human Geography, 39*(2), 146–166.

PEALS (2003). *Do-it-yourself citizens jury—Jury verdict.* Newcastle upon Tyne: Newcastle University.

Petts, J. (2007). Learning about learning: Lessons from public engagement and deliberation on urban river restoration. *Geographical Journal, 173*(4), 300–311.

Rose, N. (1999). *Powers of freedom: Reframing political thought.* Cambridge: Cambridge University Press.

Rose, N., & Miller, P. (1992). Political power beyond the state: Problematics of government. *The British Journal of Sociology, 43*(2), 173–205.

Rowe, G., & Frewer, L. J. (2000). Public participation methods: A framework for evaluation. *Science Technology, & Human Values, 25*(1), 3–29.

Sciencewise-ERC (2009). *The government's approach to public dialogue on science and technology.* London: Department for Innovation, Universities and Skills. Retrieved from http://www.sciencewise-erc.org.uk/cms/assets/Uploads/Project-files/Sciencewise-ERC-Guiding-Principles.pdf.

Soneryd, L. (2016). Technologies of participation and the making of technologized futures. In J. Chilvers & M. Kearnes (Eds.), *Remaking participation: Science, environment* (pp. 144–161). Abingdon: Routledge.

Stirling, A. (2008). "Opening up" and "Closing down": Power, participation, and pluralism in the social appraisal of technology. *Science Technology, & Human Values, 33*(2), 262–294.

Thorpe, C. (2010). Participation as post-Fordist politics: Demos, new labour, and science policy. *Minerva, 48*(4), 389–411.

Voß, J. P., & Amelung, N. (2016). Innovating public participation methods: Technoscientization and reflexive engagement. *Social Studies of Science, 46*(5), 749–772.

Warburton, D. (Ed.). (1998). *Community and sustainable development: Participation in the future.* London: Earthscan.

Warburton, D. (2010). *Evaluation of Sciencewise-ERC: Final report.* Harwell: Sciencewise Expert Resource Centre.

Webler, T., Kastenholz, H., & Renn, O. (1995). Public participation in impact assessment: A social learning perspective. *Environmental Impact Assessment Review, 15*(5), 443–463.

Welsh, I., & Wynne, B. (2013). Science, scientism and imaginaries of publics in the UK: Passive objects, incipient threats. *Science as Culture, 22*(4), 540–566.

Wilsdon, J., & Willis, R. (2004). *See-through science: Why public engagement needs to move upstream.* London: Demos.

Wynne, B. (1993). Public uptake of science: A case for institutional reflexivity. *Public Understanding of Science, 2*(4), 321–337.

Wynne, B. (2006). Public engagement as a means of restoring public trust in science: Hitting the notes, but missing the music? *Community Genetics, 9*(3), 211–220.

Wynne, B. (2007). Public participation in science and technology: Performing and obscuring a political-conceptual category mistake. *East Asian Science, Technology and Society: An International Journal, 1,* 99–110.

SECTION II
Actors and Networks

7

MAKING IT OFFICIAL

Participation Professionals and the Challenge of Institutionalizing Deliberative Democracy

Oliver Escobar

Why Research into *Official* Participation Professionals?

Public institutions in the United Kingdom (UK) are building capacity to engage "publics," "communities," "citizens," and "stakeholders" in policy- and decision-making and co-production of public services (Barnes, Newman & Sullivan, 2007; Newman, 2012). A growing cadre of *official* public participation professionals (PPPs) are responsible for organizing public engagement processes. These official PPPs are distinct from their counterparts in the private and non-profit sectors. They have the status and working conditions of public servants, their operational context is public administration, and they must navigate the institutional politics of policymaking.

US scholars have investigated the "role of agents in creating and facilitating opportunities for deliberative democracy" (Feldman, Khademian, Ingram & Schneider, 2006, p. 89), thus unpacking the world of civic engagement practitioners (e.g. Forester, 1999; Lee, 2015). However, much research focuses on professionals working on participatory experiments rather than everyday democratic processes. In turn, UK scholars have studied "community engagement professionals" (Mayo, Hoggett & Miller, 2007; Taylor, 1995), organizational "boundary spanners" (Williams, 2012), and "civic entrepreneurs" (Durose, 2011), as well as practitioners in science public engagement (Chilvers, 2008; Pieczka & Escobar, 2013). Internationally, research illustrates their "increasingly influential and powerful role in policy-making processes," and "wider problems of instrumentalism and industrialization" related to the commercialization of participation by external consultants spearheading the "emergent deliberative industry" (Amelung, 2012, pp. 13–14; Cooper & Smith, 2012; Hendriks & Carson, 2008; Lee, 2015).

The chapter contributes to this literature by investigating the opaque world of official PPPs working permanently within public administration (rather than as external consultants), operating across policy domains, and constrained and enabled by evolving institutional arrangements. The professionals studied here are distinct because they organize official participatory processes embedded in institutional policy contexts—in contrast to processes outside public administration organized by civil society organizations. The second contribution of this chapter is to offer an account that goes beyond the visible role that PPPs play as facilitators in public forums. If we think of participatory processes as spaces for performance, borrowing Goffman's (1971) theatrical metaphor, studies tend to focus on frontstage phenomena and disregard the backstage.

If PPPs are increasingly powerful, what does this actually entail? This chapter analyzes their backstage political work, for they are "public stewards, not just apolitical neutrals. They are organizers of public debate and deliberation, not just convenors who serve water and ask everyone to be polite" (Forester, 1999, p. 168). I therefore follow Geertz's (1973, p. 5) advice: to understand participatory and deliberative democracy you "should look in the first instance not at its theories or . . . what its apologists say about it; you should look at what the practitioners of it do." I thus examine their work as agents entangled in evolving policymaking cultures and their struggles to embed engagement work in public administration. I am less concerned here with what participation *is* or *generates* than with the changing professional practice that brings it into being.

Learning with PPPs: Methodological Notes

The research design entailed a multi-method approach because studying the complexity of practice requires a "toolkit logic" (Nicolini, 2009, p. 1403). My ethnographic toolkit included six data sources (Escobar, 2014). This chapter draws on three: participant observation, interviews, and focus groups. Participant observation entailed two years of fieldwork shadowing official PPPs, attending 117 meetings, and 15 weeks of work placements. The first year focused on frontstage work, exploring the terrain and building relationships. Then, I negotiated placements, accessed new processes, and focused on both backstage and frontstage work.

I adopted the modality of participant observation known as "shadowing," suitable to study agents across diverse settings (Czarniawska, 2008). The premise is to follow the agent to make sense of unfolding relationships: "how things hang together in a web of mutual influence or support or interdependence" (Becker, 1996, p. 56). I spent 817 hours[1] shadowing PPPs, distributed over 131 days, and generating 969 pages of transcribed field notes.

I conducted semi-structured interviews to understand the web of actors around PPPs, explore meaning-making processes, and collect stories of practice (Forester, 1999). This resulted in 44 in-depth interviews using snowball sampling: PPPs (13), elected representatives (8), local government officials (12), National

Health Service officials (4), and community activists and non-profit sector representatives (7). Finally, I conducted three focus groups to explore engagement work via group interaction and "joint construction of meaning" (Bryman, 2008, p. 474). The focus groups included seven citizens, five PPPs from the National Health Service, and four PPPs shadowed during placements.

The PPPs I shadowed worked in local government, which in Scotland takes the form of 32 "Local Authority Areas" (LAAs), with an average of 162,000 people each. I sought to study the institutional world of official PPPs to develop a grounded theory of public participation work (see Escobar, 2014). Consequently, I selected one LAA reflective of national socio-demographic and institutional characteristics in Scotland, and with a team of PPPs willing to give me access. I named the LAA Wyndland to preserve anonymity. Anyhow, shadowing this team and their community of practice often took me to other LAAs.

Following nodal agents is a productive option to generate rich data in multi-sited ethnography. This qualifies the deceptive appearance of single-n cases, as they often entail "multiple observational areas within their geographic, organizational, or political settings; multiple interviews and chats; multiple events observed" (Yanow, 2009, p. 294). I have come to see Wyndland as a microcosm of Scottish participatory and deliberative democracy, and these official PPPs as exemplars of a broader community of practice that shares many of their trials and tribulations.[2] However, this research is not intended to be amenable to generalization in a conventional sense. The challenge in political ethnography is to "select small sites that open windows onto larger processes of political transformation" (Shore & Wright, 2011, p. 12). Therefore, I don't present Wyndland as a local manifestation of a global phenomenon, but as one of many sites in which that phenomenon is constituted. The next research step is using this ethnographic groundwork to elaborate a survey of PPPs across the country.[3]

PPPs in Institutional Context: Community Planning Partnerships in Scotland

Although "community workers" have been integral to the UK welfare state since the 1960s (Craig, Mayo, Popple, Shaw & Taylor, 2011), recent local governance developments (Stoker, 2004) have ushered a new generation of official public participation professionals. On the one hand, there has been a proliferation of "partnership" arrangements between local government, public agencies, and non-profit organizations, which has extended "the range of institutional actors with responsibilities and powers for delivering public policy" (Barnes & Prior, 2009, p. 5). On the other hand, this has been accompanied by increased opportunities for public participation through "new spaces within which citizens and officials meet together to deliberate, make and review policy" (Barnes, 2009, p. 33; Barnes et al., 2007). Despite the challenges of combining both partnership governance and public participation (Sullivan & Lowndes, 2004), variations of such arrangements remain central to the project of constructing "a new set of relationships between government, communities and citizens" in the UK (Barnes & Prior, 2009, p. 5). Official PPPs, working at the nodes of such relationships, are thus becoming more prominent as participatory processes multiply.

In Scotland, the pursuit of that double feat—governance via partnerships + public participation—started with the Local Government in Scotland Act 2003 and is called Community Planning (CP). Over the last 20 years, molded through a series of policy statements, developments, and evaluations, CP has become integral to how successive governments have envisioned the future of local governance (Audit Scotland, 2013). There are 32 CP Partnerships, one per Local Authority Area. Each Partnership has a Board and various policy-themed strategic forums, which bring together representatives from the government (Councils are tasked with leading and thus employ PPPs), the National Health Service, the non-profit sector, police, emergency services, and business, education, and community associations. At the local level, there are also Neighborhood Partnerships or Local Area Forums for stakeholder deliberation and community participation. This is the institutional architecture that the PPPs I shadowed traverse, and research participants described them as "the life and blood of Community Planning." Their jobs didn't exist before CP, and CP did not exist before them—they brought each other into being.

The purpose of this chapter is to study what Dewey might have called Wyndland's "practical ecology" of participation (Wagenaar & Cook, 2003, p. 167), thus providing an account of participatory policymaking as a "continuous process of contestation across a political space" (Wright & Reinhold, 2011, p. 86). First, I will explore tensions elicited by PPPs' work. Second, I will argue that those tensions are constitutive of a contested "culture change" project front-lined by official PPPs. Third, I will illustrate how they negotiate those tensions and how that affects them. Finally, I will offer reflections on the professionalization and institutionalization of public engagement work in Scottish local governance. In sum, the chapter analyzes the relational ecology of official PPPs; that is, the milieu of practices and networks that shapes, and is shaped by, their actions and interactions—thus offering insight into emerging professional practices within public administration.

Being Wanted and Unwanted: Collusions and Conversions

During fieldwork, a PPP confided that she often felt "unwanted." I used this as a heuristic and, inspired by Becker's (1993) ethnographic way of unravelling a single word, I sought to learn about PPPs by investigating their "unwanted-ness." Initially this was puzzling, since the team was constantly receiving demands to organize participatory processes. Indeed, their expertise seemed in good currency.

Wanted

Some officials appreciate the PPPs help to comply with mandatory public engagement, and value their expertise and networks. Many praised their ability to work across organizational boundaries—"they are not siloed and see the bigger picture"—and noted that they "are getting well known in the communities." One explained: "they are actually doers and enablers.... I am more of a policy person, not the kind of getting my hands dirty."

A second group seeking their assistance includes elected representatives trying to make participation work for their electoral agendas. As a senior official explained, PPPs "can get pulled in several directions and because they . . . are engaging lots and lots of people . . . many councillors want a slice of that."

Finally, there are citizens and community representatives who welcome them as mediators. A non-profit organization executive noted their increasing value since the financial crisis: "we have been challenged by the global economic situation.... so the change from 2008 has also meant that we have to get around tables and have proper conversations that actually involve partnership." Some citizens argued that official PPPs made "a huge difference" to their participation experience:

> They move you forward, look after the group and make sure that egos don't get in the way. They also have a direct link to councillors and the Council.... that can be very advantageous.... You can't do away with the professionals.... community groups can be problematic, there are factions, it can be very messy. And I am happy to give time, but I still want the support.

The high demand made these PPPs feel "overwhelmed" and "stretched," or "dragged into meaningless processes" (i.e. "traditional consultations") instead of focusing on their preferred deliberative forums. Their institutional context favoured quantity over quality. Therefore, somewhat paradoxically, as PPPs become popular, their interventions can become self-defeating.

Unwanted

A PPP had previously worked as a welfare officer: "Everyone wanted you there, and here is so frustrating because you're being attacked and belittled." Research participants often mentioned widespread "hostility" against PPPs—Councillor Sullivan: "the really sad thing is the amount of people that come up against [them] for just doing their job, the abuse that they have had from certain quarters." PPPs often spoke about "resistance" by officials who feel overburdened by participatory processes. A non-profit organizer explained: "every other department within the Local Authority fights Community Planning, and does not believe in it. They do it because the [national] government has told them, [the PPP] does it because she believes in it." That commitment, however, elicits strong reactions and officials often complained about being "nagged." Some felt uncomfortable with participatory processes that challenged their authority and expertise, and deployed a repertoire of micro-resistances (De Certeau, 1988)—i.e. not reporting, overlooking emails, missing deadlines, abandoning meetings, or ignoring forum requests.

Regarding elected representatives, some saw PPPs as tampering with their influence. A Cabinet member explained that some colleagues "still find it difficult to accept that they are not the only show in town." An extreme case was a Cabinet member who was "really abusive," and tried to prevent deliberative forums by admonishing official PPPs: "I don't want any of this in my turf!" Opposition politicians were also often unsupportive, and sometimes accused PPPs of being political instruments of the current administration.

The team also felt unwanted by some non-profit sector and community representatives, who saw them as interloping in their community engagement and leadership. PPPs often described such community groups as "defensive," "unwilling to participate," and "protectionist." A community activist argued against citizen forums: "you cannae give power when there is decision-making to people who, no disrespect, who are ignorants." Accordingly, some community groups saw them as "invaders rather than supporters," and PPPs endured situations "where these people could come and rip up your professional practice and you'd basically just had to sit and take it" in order to "try and sort of negotiate or allay some fears with these groups."

In sum, PPPs are wanted because of their expertise on participation, and unwanted because not everyone likes how deliberative forums invite new participants and redefine established roles and relationships.

Making Converts

Despite challenges, some PPPs seemed optimistic: "We are making converts." Over time, they could turn critics into allies—e.g. Health Forum citizen: "I wondered if it was just lip-service to democratic participation, but more recently I am persuaded that it is a genuine effort to involve the public in the work of the Health Service." Conversions highlighted the possibilities of forums as transformative "contact zones" (Newman & Clarke, 2009, p. 62). Unforeseen collaboration sometimes emerged from the ashes of animosity. Interviewees repeatedly placed emphasis on "mindsets," "personalities," and "relationships." Yet, institutional reforms typically concerned "structures." From strategic to local forums, participatory arrangements were constantly reformed.

Structures, unlike "personalities" or "culture," can be designed and reassembled. They offer a visible target when compared to the milieu of mindsets and interaction patterns that make up the practical ecology of participation. Of course, structures do shape processes, but it is through processes that forum participants render structures meaningful. Therefore, participatory assemblages represent cultural crucibles—understanding culture as "a set of material practices that constitute the meanings, values, and identities of a social order" (Fischer, 2000, p. 120).

While making sense of the wanted/unwanted spectrum, I began to understand PPPs not only as deliberative practitioners but also as culture change agents, and used this to learn about their institutional landscape.

The "Culture Change" Project

Often characterized as a "congested and confused policy space" (Durose & Lowndes, 2010, p. 342), the local crossroads of partnership and participation assembled through Community Planning Partnerships has been nurtured by successive Scottish governments "adding to but not wholly displacing pre-existing governing arrangements—thus creating further complexity" (Cowell, 2004, p. 497). As Lowndes (2005, p. 297) observes:

> local authorities have been encouraged and then required, to change their arrangements for political leadership and decision-making. But they have for the most part insisted on driving the new vehicle down the old path— whatever the discomfort involved!

PPPs work at the vortices where that discomfort unfolds. These difficulties have been recurrent since Community Planning started in Scotland. Abram and Cowell (2004, p. 213) have noted ongoing "fundamental disputes" about its purpose and "the beliefs and power relations that could hold it together." The dominance by the largest partners (i.e. Council and NHS), the ambiguous possibilities for the non-profit and community sectors, and the new roles for elected representatives, officials, and citizens, made these governance partnerships spaces where "different operational cultures are held in suspension" (Abram & Cowell, 2004, p. 216). Although such spaces can open roles and relationships to renegotiation, they also present considerable challenges:

> existing arrangements of local governance . . . are deeply embedded through informal norms and conventions. When reformers attempt to introduce new institutional frameworks . . . they are faced with the equally important, but rarely recognised, task of de-institutionalising old ways of working. . . . Those who benefit from existing arrangements are likely to defend the status quo; when formal change becomes inevitable, they may seek to incorporate old ways of working into new partnership structures.
>
> *(Sullivan & Lowndes, 2004, p. 67)*

What Culture? What Change?

PPPs often talked about "the political culture" and argued that "a lot of people in public service are very cynical, they don't really believe that Community Planning and engagement can work or is worth the effort, especially when it affects their patch." In contrast, other officials had a more optimistic outlook: "you need to change your processes and procedures and the culture gradually spreads."

In this context, "culture" represents an empty signifier capable of encapsulating diverse concerns and aspirations. Understanding the wanted/unwanted quality of PPPs' work offers insight into the institutional culture that enfolds, and evolves with, participatory forums. Here, institutions are not the same as organizations, but "stable, valued and recurring patterns of behaviour" that constitute "the rules of the game" (Huntington, 1968). Informal rules can be as influential "as official codes of conduct and written constitutions in determining opportunities and constraints for participation" (Lowndes, Pratchett & Stoker, 2006, p. 546). Ostrom (1999, pp. 37–38) argued that the most powerful institutions are "invisible," and coined the concept "rules-in-use" to understand them. Following Lowndes et al. (2006, p. 542), rules-in-use here refer to the combination of "formal and informal institutions that influences participation in a locality, through shaping the behaviour of politicians, public managers, community leaders and citizens themselves."

PPPs described their "culture change" role as "reshaping ways of working"— that is, reshaping institutional rules-in-use. In this, they were supported by those, like Councillor Wilson, who criticized "the old days when the politicians and the officers knew best," and insisted that "you've got to throw old protocols out of the window." The next sections explore those two key domains in the policy world of official PPPs—i.e. their relationships with fellow officials and politicians. This addresses an important gap. Research often pays attention to "citizens, users, and publics who are to be engaged, coerced, empowered and made responsible through participatory initiatives" but often overlooks how "public officials negotiate their roles and identities" (Barnes, 2009, p. 34). In other words, whereas much research focuses on what participatory arrangements do to citizens, here I focus on what they do to institutions that host them.

Official PPPs and Public Servants: Changing Public Sector Governance

For the past two decades, the UK public sector has undergone various "modernization" agendas often framed as management improvements (Clarke & Newman, 1997). In parallel, particularly since the 1997 New Labour UK government and the first devolved Scottish government in 1999, partnership and participation have become prominent (Mayo et al., 2007; Orr & McAteer, 2004). To be sure, the emphasis on efficiency and performance remains, but "overlaid on it" are "new demands that public services should empower citizens and communities, develop partnerships, collaborate with 'civil society' groups, and foster 'co-production' arrangements with service users" (Newman & Clarke, 2009, p. 6). In this context, PPPs find themselves—as one explained—"trying to encourage and cajole staff to be able to engage well with the public." Public sector officials faced by new roles and dilemmas (Goss, 2001) sometimes "refuse to 'know their place'" in these new arrangements (Newman & Clarke, 2009, p. 60), which means that the "joining-up" can be "strongly resisted" (Newman, 2012, loc. 3215). Official PPPs interpreted that "resistance" in terms of "control" and "expertise."

A PPP argued that some public servants fear deliberative forums because they "worry that if we evidence too much need things will have to change, so there is that tension that they'd lose control." Another argued that the Partnership Board is used by key actors for "rubberstamping" decisions made offstage, rather than as a frontstage for inclusive policymaking. A non-profit sector representative explained: "it's not in their interest to make it diverse because that dilutes their power and their ability to make decisions, certain decisions are always made outside of the room, in secret, in the areas with largest budgets." This referred to Council and National Health Service senior officials. When I interviewed them, it seemed apparent that these were accepted rules-in-use—e.g. NHS executive: "it's the same for any decision-making process, consensus-building goes on outside the meeting and . . . it's really important that it is aired at the meeting but you would obviously want to talk to people before." In this way, the inner workings at the Partnership's strategic level were often negotiated offstage, beyond the backstages and frontstages where PPPs have room to manoeuvre.

Consequently, much of the PPPs' work entailed a politics of exposure: trying to "drag" actors and issues into more visible spaces with the hope of eliciting deliberative discipline and the sharing of policymaking jurisdiction. This materialized in myriad ongoing backstage negotiations.

Fischer (2000, p. 259) argues that certain governance discourses have given way to an "increasingly technocratic form of public decision making." Renegotiating the existing politics of expertise constitutes a key dimension in public engagement practice. Claiming expertise is a way of asserting professional jurisdiction over a social domain (Abbott, 1988). In representative democracy, politicians and expert officials have traditionally claimed jurisdiction over policymaking. PPPs' allies often noted that opening participation processes depended on officials "not feeling threatened" by new configurations of knowledge/power (Foucault, 1980), and emphasized the difficulty of changing rules-in-use—e.g. NHS official: "I sit around some of my colleagues . . . and I find myself in that position as well going: it's easier just to do it ourselves, we know best."

Consequently, the allocation of roles implicit in how PPPs script (see Escobar, 2014) and facilitate participatory processes is sometimes unwelcomed by officials who see them as encroaching on their expertise and domain. This seems typical in transitions from technocratic to participatory policymaking (Fischer, 2000). Officials are being asked to relinquish power afforded by their authority and expertise and to develop new kinds of contact with citizens and stakeholders. Engagement work pushes new forms of evidence and knowledge (local, experiential) into decision-making processes. As noted earlier, some PPPs believe that, insofar these officials are "around the table," they can "make converts" by exposing them to various others (ideas, people) and entangle them into collaboration. In this process, previously unquestioned technocratic expertise may be exposed to new deliberative scrutiny.

Official PPPs and Politicians: The Interplay of Democratic Practices

PPPs and politicians sometimes need each other, but their relationship embodies the very frictions between the distinct practices of democracy that they embody and enact. Although these frictions have been noted previously in Scotland (e.g. Orr & McAteer, 2004; Sinclair, 2008), we still know little about how they are negotiated. This section, therefore, addresses the role of politicians, their relationship with PPPs, and the impact of electoral dynamics on participatory processes.

Participatory and deliberative democracy can be seen as "supplementary to electoral democracy, shoring up its functional weaknesses" to generate legitimacy locally, "issue by issue, policy by policy, and constituency by constituency" (Warren, 2009, p. 8). Participatory arrangements are often ambiguously appended to representative mechanisms, and elected representatives may struggle to "develop different, more interactive ways of governing with, rather than on behalf of, the public" (Sullivan, 2009, p. 52).

While shadowing PPPs, I met elected enthusiasts of participation who saw themselves as "a new breed of politician" whose job is "to put into action what local communities want to achieve." Others had a more critical stand: "we'll listen to what people say, but they don't know anything about the budgets, they don't know the issues in other areas, they're not in a position to make a judgment." Many feared "ignorant" and self-serving publics, saw public forums as secondary, and only made appearances when nudged by PPPs. These varied attitudes cut across, and within, party-political divides, and support for public participation depended on individual "political champions." Councillor Wilson, the proverbial "facilitative leader" celebrated in the literature (Bussu & Bartels, 2013), describes his Cabinet struggles:

> Some politicians find it difficult to let go, some politicians don't trust local people, and there was lots of debate about how we could do it, how we could fund it. . . . So a lot of my time was spent persuading my colleagues.

This was problematic for PPPs as new forums were initially dominated by traditional party politics. A councillor illustrated this:

> local councillors were dominating . . . and local people are thinking: we are wasting our time, if that lot are just gonna be talking amongst themselves and deciding. And [official PPPs] through me and through their own persuaded other councillors . . . to [take] a step back . . . not just carrying on as if they are running the show.

PPPs were instrumental in renegotiating the role of elected representatives. Initially, it was a matter of preventing forums from becoming party-political "stumping grounds" or "shouting matches." Once certain councillors relaxed the premise that "I've got to stamp my authority on this place," they focused more on policy deliberation. Nonetheless, some councillors regarded public participation—a Cabinet officer explained—as a way of "abdicating their responsibility to make decisions." Interestingly, as PPPs noted, the diffusion of responsibility also entails a diffusion of "credit." When public forums achieved outcomes (e.g. capital investment, new services), ruling councillors had to share credit with other participants and politicians. Accordingly, some councillors kept distance from the forums—they questioned their purpose or struggled to find ways of doing, and speaking about, participatory politics.

Building relationships with elected representatives is critical for official PPPs. Although sometimes they struck cross-party alliances, they worked most closely with Cabinet members who were instrumental to the forums' influence on decision-making. PPPs often spoke about the "double-edged sword of working with councillors": "we're pulled off in all sorts of directions, but on the flipside, we also have their ear." Indeed, this was not a unidirectional relationship—"we use them and they use us," explained a PPP. In that trade, PPPs risked losing relational capital ("trust," "face," "reputation"), as councillors could use participatory processes to advance electoral agendas (e.g. being seen to channel resources to their ward). In turn, PPPs used elected representatives for strategic purposes:

> there is the legitimacy stuff. . . . We write all the briefing stuff that they stand up and say at the beginning [of public forums], we frame everything to fit the way we want it to be, we use them to get access to information, to get things onto an agenda, we use them when other departments are not playing ball.

Often, after public forums, PPPs and ally councillors would find a quiet corridor to "plot" moves—e.g. how to reframe forum issues to tap into existing budgets, how to mobilize departmental resources to service a forum, or how to bring in officials who weren't "playing ball." Accordingly, PPPs did considerable backstage work to get support—or at least acquiescence—from councillors. One PPP found this "kind of entertaining, it's what makes it interesting, and it's about working up people and playing people, and working out who I can work with and who I can ignore." PPPs typically devised three roles for the councillors: completely engaged, engaged at some stage, or kept "at arms-length." The three entail risks and opportunities that PPPs must calibrate. For instance, having Cabinet councillors completely engaged can "give clout" to a participatory process—a clear link to the administration and departmental resources. The downside is that when those councillors lose elections, entire processes can be in jeopardy.

In the wake of the 2012 local government elections in Scotland, a PPP explained: "election time is just exhausting, the amount of councillors I've spoken to in the last 2 weeks is unbelievable, they just want to see if some things can get done." It was not unusual that ruling councillors would announce large budgets for some participatory forums just before an election. The opposition leader was furious: "things are being manufactured at this late stage . . . to manipulate the electorate." Recurrent stories amongst Wyndland's official PPPs concerned the impact of the 2007 elections on previous public forums. The new administration shut them down and opened new ones elsewhere. "They just abolished them, the community was shattered," said the then opposition leader. In contrast, a Cabinet councillor argued that "what the opposition mean by that is that we took the ability for them to control a budget away," and criticized them for seizing participatory forums "as an opportunity to gain some of the power" that they had lost electorally.

A new change of administration in May 2012 turned the world of Wyndland's PPPs upside down. It was particularly difficult for those who experienced the 2007 "fiascos." Tears, uncertainty, and frantic office days ensued. Suddenly, meticulously "scripted" processes (see Escobar, 2015), carefully facilitated forums, and painstakingly built relational capital were in jeopardy. Some officials ignored phone calls, and PPPs no longer had full access to the forums' backstages that had been their turf. After a week, they received provisional answers from the new administration: some forums were suspended, others could continue but without commitments. This infuriated the PPPs: "they are asking us to waste our time in a process that may go nowhere"; "this forum is now a complete farce." Unable to script, without backstage leeway, frontstage performances risked becoming farces (Escobar, 2015).

PPPs agonized: "we have involved officials from the outset, the Leader of the Council, the councillors, we had the political support of both sides, everything to make sure that we were not putting ourselves in this position." And they kept trying to anticipate what may be next—as this office conversation illustrates:

PPP 1: Maybe they will actually respect the practice and the community engagement that went into it. . . . [and] that these processes are quite robust. This shows you how vulnerable these things are.

PPP 2: [The new administration] will likely . . . pull out of the areas where we are working now, and take it back to where it was initially. I was working there, it was all closed down so badly, so I don't have credibility there. . . . I might as well just quit.

TRAINEE PPP: So many people have worked so hard for years, brought so many groups together, got people passionate and now . . . that meeting is cancelled, this meeting is cancelled, no idea what's going on here.

PPP 2: In this job, you work closer to policy and politicians that you would do in a traditional CDO [Community Development Officer] position.

CDO: Your job sucks [everyone laughs].

Indeed, participatory processes that had engaged hundreds of citizens and stake-holders, but were connected to outgoing councillors, became "under review." As the outgoing Cabinet had stopped forums in 2007, PPPs expected a repeat of this retaliatory approach. Arguably, Wyndland offers a prime exemplar of the vicious circle in which partisan and electoral dynamics trump participatory politics and deliberative processes.

To salvage some forums, official PPPs tried to regain leeway in the (new) backstage. First, they investigated who would lead their department—"we used to have a champion in Cabinet, we need someone like that." Then, they convened forums that still had "momentum" and where participants could question new ruling councillors about intentions and budgets. Indeed, citizens and new opposition councillors kept pressing on. PPPs often spoke tactically at the forums—e.g. "hearing [new councillors] saying that this is going ahead is heartening for everyone here." Limited in backstage room for manoeuvre, PPPs made the most of the frontstage—using it to influence inaccessible backstage domains. The "frustration" of not being privy to spaces where things were being worked out eventually turned into a renewed sense of possibility.

They began to mobilize relational capital and strike new alliances—sometimes unexpectedly. Like the evening when a new Cabinet councillor confided bitter disagreements within his party: "I've been taking drugs to cope with this shit since the election.... I shouldn't probably say this, but fuck it!" The official PPP replied: "with time you'll know me and you'll find that I'm a very discreet person." One forum was in this councillor's town, and he assured the PPP that "this will fucking happen, or they will be in for a rough ride." He insisted that "the town comes before the party" and that he will become independent if necessary. This was unexpected insight for the PPP: "I shouldn't be hearing this, I'm a Council officer." The Councillor laughed: "that's what your manager always says." Such sensitive information was extremely valuable, as PPPs built new foundations for their work. Potential new allies emerged; new windows of opportunity opened. The PPPs' political nose tracked new trails, carving up a new backstage from where to try and salvage previous forums. For example, in participation processes at risk of becoming "farces," they casted senior public servants giving public assurance, so that they would have a face-saving interest in negotiating backstage with the new administration.

As for how to shield participatory processes from electoral politics, the PPPs experience suggests some options: keeping forums away from councillors—but risk losing influence and legitimacy; forging cross-party alliances—a considerable challenge; or keeping forum lifecycles within the legislature's timeline—which requires impeccable scripting. When I concluded fieldwork in September 2013, some forums were still ongoing, albeit delayed and pending Cabinet decisions. In Wyndland, deliberative democracy remains subservient to electoral competition and representative institutions.

Burning Out: PPPs and Internal Activism

The official "job description" of the PPPs studied here was to engage citizens and stakeholders in deliberative forums, but it didn't mention anything about fostering "culture change." This explains the bewilderment some PPPs felt about the political nature of their role. A basic distinction helped me to interpret their diverse approaches to engagement work—namely, that between the administrative and the activist PPP.

The former adopts a fairly bureaucratic role, working within parameters set by others, while the latter carries out political work to reshape policy worlds. The administrative PPP accepts existing cultures, whereas the activist becomes a culture change agent. The former adapts to existing rules-in-use, whereas the latter seeks to foster new ones. While the administrative PPP closes the office for the day, the activist strikes a tactical conversation in the car park. To be sure, I am not describing specific PPPs, but two ways of being a PPP. Indeed, the ones I met fluctuated between these ideal types depending on various dimensions—including the nature of the participatory process at hand, their experiences and feelings about the job, and their broader web of interactions. In some cases, time and challenges forged the activist PPP, yet in others, they made way for more administrative approaches.

Internal Activism

I have illustrated the PPPs internal activism through their backstage struggles to develop participatory processes. That activism doesn't focus necessarily on substantial issues, but on the form that policy processes take to deal with them (i.e. participatory and/or deliberative). Thinking about official PPPs as internal activists challenges the "stereotypical distinctions between activist outsides and incorporated insides" (Newman, 2012, loc. 4551). It seems "too simplistic to associate subversion solely with action outside the official sphere of participation" (Barnes & Prior, 2009, p. 10). As Goss (2001, p. 5) argues:

> working in the space between bureaucratic, market and network cultures, creates space for innovation. . . . The constant collision of different assumptions and traditions offers scope to challenge on all sides. The very messiness begins to break down old systems and procedures. . . . New [entrepreneurial] skills and capabilities are needed.

Official PPPs can be understood as institutional entrepreneurs (DiMaggio, 1988), policy entrepreneurs (Roberts & King, 1991), or "civic entrepreneurs" (Durose, 2011). As activist insiders, PPPs can deploy relational capital and micro-political know-how seeking "to balance multiple competing constituencies" and "induce co-operation" thus "forging new coalitions" (Freeman & Peck, 2007, p. 925).

A PPP argued that taking an internal activist approach "depends on your personal politics": "some are quite happy to let things take their own course," but "this is far too important" to let it become an "administrative task" with no scope for "reshaping governance." PPPs often spoke about "putting my bit in for the world," "values of justice and equality," and "people's rights to participate in decision-making." This materialized not only through forums, but also backstage work trying to redress power imbalances—i.e. supporting "community action forcing the Council to come around," or contesting "anti–non-profit-sector" attitudes that hindered inclusion in policymaking. Their motivation stemmed from previous experience in social movements, community work, or non-profit organizations, and understanding "their struggles." However, this insider activism "can feel very uncomfortable because we are [government] employees."

In addition, the official PPPs studied here could seldom rely on formal power as they operated from the bottom of their organizational hierarchies. This can be challenging: "I can't call a Head of Service into account"; "I don't have power over any area, so the negotiation depends on interpersonal relations." Nonetheless, one PPP argued that "maybe this is an advantage, I am not a senior manager, so I can raise questions and do things that others can't"; "I do have the power to bring things to the table." Perhaps their lack of formal power has honed the micro-political know-how illustrated earlier. The capacity to work the backstage, build relational capital, and assemble processes thus becomes crucial for "spotting opportunities to pursue forum objectives that were unlikely to be achieved through official channels" (Barnes, 2009, p. 45).

This takes exhausting subtlety: "acknowledging sensitivities and being very careful that you don't upset certain people . . . takes a lot of energy." It requires patience: "sometimes spend months thinking about tactics to get around certain person or group." It needs perseverance: "I work and work and tweak my way until finally I get what I need." It also entails political knowledge to "play on existing interests" and find the right time for "rattling cages at the Council" or "rocking the boat with our colleagues." Finally, it also involves "twisting peoples' arms" when PPPs feel "forced to go around pushing people to work in certain ways." Despite mixed feelings about the thornier side of this "culture change" work, official PPPs relished the "pleasures of agency" (Newman, 2012, loc. 231). One explained: "I like finding the way through the maze, I enjoy the conflict bits, the bits that are frustrating and how you've got to sort of manage through people."

Emotion Work and Burnout

Previous sections illustrate the intensity of these official PPPs' world—an undercurrent of passion and frustration that springs into myriad actions, trials, and tribulations. Official PPPs noted that, in their job, the track from elation to despair is a one-stop journey. They often savored the relational milieu: "there is a lot of shit in this job, but there is a lot of good people." Occasionally, they relished the ecstasy of the forum aftermath. For instance, after large events culminating months of preparation, the atmosphere was so electrifying that team members couldn't sleep. Even deskwork time was often intense—while writing emails or policy documents, body language revealed mounting tension punctuated by sudden outbursts of "frustration" or laughter. At times of turmoil—e.g. post-elections—the texture of their emotional palette would thicken, turning frustration into despair and stories into tears. This unfolded in the backstage of their backstage—the toilet, the car. The frontstage remained the domain of emotional labour:

PPP 1: You are always performing in this job.
PPP 2: Yes, the other day my face was hurting from smiling so much. . . . keeping this level of enthusiasm and cheeriness is quite exhausting.

I witnessed the "burnout" of official PPPs over time: "I just don't know if I can carry on for much longer." They felt "overwhelmed and overstretched" and "scarred" by experiences. There was much self-questioning: "I'm going through a period in which I think my work is shit and doesn't mean anything." This "burnout" was not lost to other officials, who answered quite dramatically when asked if they would take the PPPs job:

COUNCIL OFFICIAL: I don't envy her, I think she's got possibly one of the worst jobs in the Council, and she's made a lot of enemies.
NON-PROFIT SECTOR REPRESENTATIVE: She is between a rock and a hard place, she sees injustice, people who stop things from happening and this is the deal about power play within a Local Authority.
NATIONAL HEALTH SERVICE OFFICIAL: I could not physically do it.
COUNCIL SERVICE MANAGER: I would commit suicide within six months.

Such strong expressions underline the intensity of official public participation work. PPPs shared stories of predecessors who, after forums collapsed, took "stress leave" and never returned. A PPP said that "it gets easier as you get a bit of life under your belt." But time kindled its own dilemmas: "I know where all the bodies are buried." Intense political work was taxing, although PPPs were sometimes humorous about it. In this conversation, an elected representative explained difficulties recruiting political candidates:

COUNCILLOR: Why would they want a job in which they'll have to work endless hours, for a modest salary and being attacked from all quarters?
PPP [LAUGHING]: Just like Community Planning Officers.

Over time, the fire of some activist PPPs would steadily dim. The prospect of "unfair" forum closures would eventually become a resigned affair: "do I want to fight to the bitter end, to go down all guns blazing? I don't know, because it's not worth it." In such cases, the frustrations, dilemmas, and struggles of the activist PPP could become catalysts for more administrative approaches. Engagement work can wear you down. Ups and downs can be unsettling even for those who enjoy "finding the way through the maze." The pressures of being wanted and unwanted can steadily add fuel to the "burnout." Arguably, Wyndland's ecology of participation provided a more hospitable environment for the administrative PPP, and somewhat nudged the activist PPP to weigh the pressures and pleasures of agency.

Professionalizing Official Public Participation in Scotland

Having offered an account of the backstage political work of official PPPs, the remainder of this chapter considers the professionalization and institutionalization of public engagement work more broadly.

In the sociology of work, professions are "exclusive occupational groups applying somewhat abstract knowledge to particular cases" and claiming to "control" certain "knowledge and skill" (Abbott, 1988, p. 8). The hold a profession establishes over certain tasks is known as "jurisdiction," which is maintained, extended, and refined according to a "knowledge system" capable of redefining "problems and tasks, defend them from interlopers, and seize new problems" (p. 10). In sum, a jurisdictional claim is a "claim for the legitimate control of a particular kind of work" (p. 60).

In Scotland, official PPPs seem nowhere near that level of professionalization. The PPPs studied here didn't claim to have the monopoly over engagement work, and actually trained others (e.g. officials, community representatives) in organizing participation. Nonetheless, I did observe attempts at developing a sense of professional jurisdiction. Their conversations often examined what it means to be "professional" in this field, the tools deemed suitable, and who does or doesn't perform "proper engagement." They also questioned the ability of others to assemble "legitimate" publics and provide "impartial" mediation among competing interests. And they remarked that "participation is not done properly" and "the field needs professionalizing."

PPPs understood their job as a political endeavour although, as did other policy workers (Colebatch, 2009), they faced demands to represent the political as technical and distort the mess of practice into ordered expert categories. Accordingly, they presented themselves as expert mediators between official and public spheres, foregrounding their process expertise, i.e. knowing how to assemble and perform publics, script participatory processes, facilitate deliberation, and translate myriad utterances into usable inscriptions (Escobar, 2014). However, their professional jurisdiction is contested as other actors stake claims on participatory practices. In Scotland, official PPPs arrive at domains with established engagement rituals (e.g. via councillors or community councillors) and, as seen in this chapter, struggle to develop new participatory spaces and deliberative dynamics. Consolidating professional jurisdiction will thus depend on their capacity to accomplish political work (e.g. "culture change") that enables them to incorporate, substitute, reshape, or displace existing practices.

Furthermore, they face challenges regarding their emerging professional status and identity within local government in Scotland (see Scott, 2012). For instance, as network-oriented agents, they often struggle to operate in hierarchical contexts—i.e. they lack power to summon senior officials, yet their job is to entangle them in participatory processes. They also sit uneasily within existing departmental structures because they don't belong to traditional policy silos (e.g. housing, education, etc.), but to the crosscutting realm of process. They are, therefore, a new type of policy worker in an evolving institutional landscape, and their professional status and identity are under development. Nevertheless, the official PPPs studied here (Community Planning Officers) are building informal networks across neighbouring local authorities and via platforms and events organized by the Scottish Government.[4] Assessing to what extent engagement work is becoming a professionalized field within public administration in Scotland is thus a task for future research.

Dilemmas of Institutionalizing Public Participation Work

Policy-makers deciding on building capacity for public participation face important choices. Some scholars argue that public authorities should become enablers of participatory and deliberative democracy (e.g. Sirianni, 2009). In that light, the choice is between building in-house capacity and buying services in the market. Cooper and Smith (2012, p. 22) note the distress of external participation consultants hired ad hoc by public authorities. They complain about lack of impact, a failure by officials to "understand the demands of participation," and "impediments caused by the broader structure and culture of public authorities." Wyndland's official PPPs share similar frustrations, but they can do something about it precisely because they are insiders.

Of course, institutionalizing engagement expertise can also foster tokenism and the proliferation of administrative approaches to the job. However, buying expertise externally establishes participation as an add-on, thus turning participatory practices into market commodities that can be sold as technical rather than political processes (e.g. Lee, 2015). Building in-house capacity brings new policy workers who, as I have shown, might seek to dislocate rules-in-use. External consultants, in contrast, face the challenge of working without trumping their commercial bottom line (Cooper & Smith, 2012, p. 29; Hendriks & Carson, 2008), and they are powerless after reporting the results of a process. In contrast, official PPPs enjoy public sector security, and can invest time building internal and external alliances. Kadlec and Friedman (2007) argue that forums must be followed by an activist phase in which PPPs try to make the process count. In Wyndland, that activism is not for the aftermath, but structured into the everyday work of the official PPP.

A new body of expertise is "a way of recognizing problems as well as a way of addressing them" (Colebatch, 2009, p. 32). If PPPs are the solution, what is the problem? If the point is to improve market research on policy products, then ad hoc external consultancy, or official administrative PPPs, may seem suitable. If the problem, however, is developing participatory practices that change governing culture, then official activist PPPs may be the way. Anyhow, partnership and participation remain empty signifiers rendered meaningful by their political ecology. Engagement is thus a contested domain of practice where agency, and its location, matters. This emphasizes the value of researching what participatory practices do to the institutions that host them.

In this light, the critique that official spaces for participation are prone to co-option can be countered with the argument that, precisely because of their official nature, they may enable clear links to formal decision-making and foster culture change. Of course, this depends on summoning participants who may question official agendas and engage in critical deliberation, as well as on having PPPs capable of scripting processes where that may happen. There are also questions about whether PPPs, being officials, can actually act as mediators between official and public spheres. In my experience, this depends greatly on their personal politics and loyalties, their approach to the job, and their evolving ecology of participation. All in all, given the criticism that participatory processes often lack connection to institutional decision-making, arguably, official PPPs accountable to elected bodies make lines of accountability and legitimacy clear and operational.

Conclusions

I have presented participatory and deliberative democracy in Scotland as a contested, fragile, and evolving assemblage that takes constant work. And I have sought to render the everyday political work of official PPPs visible. Accordingly, I illustrated that there is scope for manoeuvre—by officials, politicians, and citizens—when it comes to shaping a given ecology of participation. As Lowndes et al. (2006, p. 559) argue, institutions are malleable: there is "a degree of path dependence but actors can shape and bend institutional forces in new directions." Of course, that entails painstaking struggle to reshape rules-in-use as illustrated earlier, and the potential burnout of PPPs should not be underestimated. This also highlights how official PPPs can influence local participatory democracy and warrants further research into the consequences of administrative vs. activist approaches to public engagement work.

Studying the wanted/unwanted tension illustrated how various actors may react to participatory governance policy (i.e. Community Planning in Scotland) embodied and enacted by new cadres of official PPPs. The emerging picture features the perennial tensions between tradition and change. New participatory practices can unsettle established ways of working among public sector officials, politicians, and community representatives. Some may see their traditional roles challenged by the new participatory gospel, backed by national policies, and enacted locally by official PPPs. In this light, official PPPs appear as political workers advancing a culture change project ripe with tensions, ambiguities, and power struggles: a project both embraced and despised by people across the spectrum of official and public spheres. In that sense, the official PPPs' work forces negotiation amongst the diverse understandings of local democracy and public service that collide and coalesce in new participatory processes.

As Sullivan (2009, p. 65) argues, participatory governance policies "are themselves subversive acts, designed with the express purpose of unsettling the established relationships of politicians, the public and professionals in the pursuit of new ones." Consequently, Community Planning in Scotland can be seen as a disruptive intervention that problematizes local policy worlds. An intervention where official PPPs' practices shape, and are shaped by, an evolving ecology of participation. This, in turn, forges the activist PPP, or fosters more administrative approaches by virtue of puzzlement, disappointment, or exhaustion. The chapter highlights the risk of burnout faced by PPPs working for public authorities, and how it may be detrimental to a vibrant democracy if administrative approaches to public engagement work prevail over more "subversive" internal activism.

Consequently, deliberative scholarship must pay attention to the backstage work of PPPs, which sustains the frontstage of public forums (see Escobar, 2015). The chapter has offered examples of how participatory and deliberative democracy can be jeopardized by electoral and partisan dynamics and subservient to representative and bureaucratic institutions. In regions like Wyndland, the prospects for developing a coherent "deliberative system" (Parkinson & Mansbridge, 2013) can depend greatly on the political know-how, engagement skills, and personal commitment of people like the official PPPs shadowed here. Yet, as noted earlier, the institutionalization and professionalization of this field in Scotland is ambiguous and fragile, which can arguably hinder its development, thus placing this new cadre of officials in contexts where burnout is likely and support precarious—particularly in the current context of public spending cuts.

This chapter shows clearly that official PPPs do more than design and facilitate public participation processes. They are unstated political workers and culture change agents negotiating the cutting edge of evolving democratic practice. This has implications for decisions about employing in-house PPPs or outsourcing to consultants. It is not simply a matter of "what works best," but what works when, for whom, and to what purpose. Those who see public participation as part of the management toolbox of contemporary governance may favour buying expertise from the public engagement industry. In contrast, those who see participation as the driving force of a vibrant democracy may favour building engagement capacity into the everyday work of public administrations. What the Scottish example illustrates is that institutionalizing participation work can send powerful ripples across official and public spheres, at least when activist approaches are at play. There is much to learn about official PPPs across the world, particularly those carving up space for democratic innovation that may bridge elitist institutions and participatory practices.

Notes

1 Excluding time travelling or working on field notes afterwards.
2 This has been corroborated in subsequent workshops where I presented research find-ings. This "members-checking" stage in the research cycle helps to refine findings, gauge plausibility, and continue the grounded theorizing process (Schwartz-Shea & Yanow, 2009).
3 Survey currently underway at What Works Scotland, http://whatworksscotland.ac.uk.
4 See Scottish Government, Community Planning Conference 2015 Programme Changing Lives, Delivering Success; Turning Ambition into Action – Conference Programme, Wednesday, June 17, 2015, ISBN: 9781785444678, http://www.gov.scot/Publications/2015/06/5337.

References

Abbott, A. (1988). *The system of professions: An essay on the division of expert labour*. Chicago: The University of Chicago Press.

Abram, S., & Cowell, R. (2004). Learning policy—The contextual curtain and conceptual barriers. *European Planning Studies, 12*(2), 209–228.

Amelung, N. (2012). The emergence of citizen panels as a de facto standard. *Quaderni, 79*, 13–28.

Audit Scotland. (2013). *Improving community planning in Scotland*. Retrieved from http://www.gov.scot/Resource/0041/00418629.pdf.

Barnes, M. (2009). Alliances, contention and oppositional consciousness: Can public par-ticipation generate subversion? In M. Barnes & D. Prior (Eds.), *Subversive citizens: Power, agency and resistance in public services* (pp. 33–48). Bristol: Policy Press.

Barnes, M., Newman, J., & Sullivan, H. (2007). *Power, participation and political renewal: Case studies in public participation*. Bristol: The Policy Press.

Barnes, M., & Prior, D. (2009). Examining the idea of "subversion" in public services. In M. Barnes & D. Prior (Eds.), *Subversive citizens: Power, agency and resistance in public services* (pp. 3–13). Bristol: Policy Press.

Becker, H. S. (1993). How I learned what a crock was. *Journal of Contemporary Ethnography, 22*(1), 28–35.

Becker, H. S. (1996). The epistemology of qualitative research. In R. Jessor, A. Colby & R. A. Shweder (Eds.), *Ethnography and human development: Context and meaning in social inquiry* (pp. 53–71). Chicago: University of Chicago Press.

Bryman, A. (2008). *Social research methods* (3rd ed.). Oxford: Oxford University Press.

Bussu, S., & Bartels, K. P. R. (2013). Facilitative leadership and the challenge of renew-ing local democracy in Italy. *International Journal of Urban and Regional Research, 38*(6), 2256–2273. doi:10.1111/1468–2427.12070.

Chilvers, J. (2008). Deliberating competence: Theoretical and practitioner perspectives on effective participatory appraisal practice. *Science Technology, & Human Values, 33*(2), 155–185.

Clarke, J., & Newman, J. (1997). *The managerial state: Power, politics and ideology in the remak-ing of social welfare*. London: Sage.

Colebatch, H. K. (2009). *Policy*. Maidenhead: Open University Press.

Cooper, E., & Smith, G. (2012). Organizing deliberation: The perspectives of professional participation practitioners in Britain and Germany. *Journal of Public Deliberation, 8*(1). Retrieved from http://www.publicdeliberation.net/jpd/vol8/iss1/art3/.

Cowell, R. (2004). Community planning: Fostering participation in the congested state? *Local Government Studies, 30*(4), 497–518.

Craig, G., Mayo, M., Popple, K., Shaw, M., & Taylor, M. (Eds.). (2011). *The community development reader: History, themes and issues*. Bristol: Policy Press.

Czarniawska, B. (2008). *Shadowing: And other techniques for doing fieldwork in modern societies*. Malmö: Liber and Copenhagen Business School Press.

De Certeau, M. (1988). *The practice of everyday life*. Berkeley, CA: University of California Press.

DiMaggio, P. (1988). Interest and agency in institutional theory. In L. Zucker (Ed.), *Institutional patterns and organization: Culture and environment* (pp. 3–21). Cambridge, MA: Ballinger.

Durose, C. (2011). Revisiting Lipsky: Front-line work in UK local governance. *Political Studies, 59*(4), 978–995.

Durose, C., & Lowndes, V. (2010). Neighbourhood governance: Contested rationales within a multi-level setting—a study of Manchester. *Local Government Studies, 36*(3), 341–359.

Escobar, O. (2014). *Transformative practices: The political work of public engagement practitioners*. Doctoral thesis. Retrieved from https://www.era.lib.ed.ac.uk/handle/1842/9915.

Escobar, O. (2015). Scripting deliberative policy-making: Dramaturgic policy analysis and engagement know-how. *Journal of Comparative Policy Analysis, 17*(3), 269–285.

Feldman, M. S., Khademian, A. M., Ingram, H., & Schneider, A. S. (2006). Ways of knowing and inclusive management practices. *Public Administration Review, 66*, 89–99.

Fischer, F. (2000). *Citizens, experts, and the environment: The politics of local knowledge*. Durham, NC: Duke University Press.

Forester, J. (1999). *The deliberative practitioner: Encouraging participatory planning processes*. Cambridge, MA: MIT Press.

Foucault, M. (1980). *Power/knowledge: Selected interviews and other writings 1972–1977*. C. Gordon (Ed.). New York: Pantheon.

Freeman, T., & Peck, E. (2007). Performing governance: A partnership board dramaturgy. *Public Administration, 85*(4), 907–929.

Geertz, C. (1973). *The interpretation of cultures: Selected essays*. New York: Basic Books.

Goffman, E. (1971). *The presentation of self in everyday life*. Middlesex: Pelican Books.

Goss, S. (2001). *Making local governance work: Networks, relationships, and the management of change*. Basingstoke: Palgrave.

Hendriks, C. M., & Carson, L. (2008). Can the market help the forum? Negotiating the commercialization of deliberative democracy. *Policy Sciences, 41*(4), 293–313.

Huntington, S. (1968). *Political order in changing societies*. New Haven, CT: Yale University Press.

Kadlec, A., & Friedman, W. (2007). Deliberative democracy and the problem of power. *Journal of Public Deliberation, 3*(1). Retrieved from http://www.publicdeliberation.net/jpd/vol3/iss1/art8/

Lee, C. W. (2015). *Do-it-yourself democracy: The rise of the public engagement industry*. New York: Oxford University Press.

Lowndes, V. (2005). Something old, something new, something borrowed . . . How institutions change (and stay the same) in local governance. *Policy Studies, 26*(3), 291–309.

Lowndes, V., Pratchett, L., & Stoker, G. (2006). Local political participation: The impact of rules-in-use. *Public Administration, 84*(3), 539–561.

Mayo, M., Hoggett, P., & Miller, C. (2007). Navigating the contradictions of public service modernisation: The case of community engagement professionals. *Policy and Politics*, *35*(4), 667–681.

Newman, J. (2012). *Working the spaces of power: Activism, neoliberalism and gendered labour.* London: Bloomsbury Academic.

Newman, J., & Clarke, J. (2009). *Publics, politics and power: Remaking the public in public services.* London: Sage.

Nicolini, D. (2009). Zooming in and out: Studying practices by switching theoretical lenses and trailing connections. *Organization Studies*, *30*(12), 1391–1418.

Orr, K., & McAteer, M. (2004). The modernisation of local decision making: Public participation and Scottish local government. *Local Government Studies*, *30*(2), 131–155.

Ostrom, E. (1999). Institutional rational choice: An assessment of the institutional analysis and development framework. In P. A. Sabatier (Ed.), *Theories of the policy process* (pp. 35–72). Boulder, CO: Westview Press.

Parkinson, J., & Mansbridge, J. (2013). *Deliberative systems: Deliberative democracy at the large scale.* Cambridge: Cambridge University Press.

Pieczka, M., & Escobar, O. (2013). Dialogue and science: Innovation in policy-making and the discourse of public engagement in the UK. *Science and Public Policy*, *40*(1), 113–126.

Roberts, N. C., & King, P. J. (1991). Policy entrepreneurs: Their activity structure and function in the policy process. *Journal of Public Administration Research and Theory*, *1*(2), 147–175.

Schwartz-Shea, P., & Yanow, D. (2009). Reading and writing as method: In search of trustworthy texts. In S. Ybema, D. Yanow, H. Wels & F. Kamsteeq (Eds.), *Organizational ethnography: Studying the complexity of everyday life* (pp. 56–82). London: Sage.

Scott, K. (2012). Community planning in Scotland: Dilemmas of reconciling policy and practice in community development work. *Journal of Contemporary Community Education Practice Theory*, *3*(1), 1–10.

Shore, C., & Wright, S. (2011). Conceptualising policy: Technologies of governance and the politics of visibility. In C. Shore, S. Wright & D. Però (Eds.), *Policy worlds: Anthropology and the analysis of contemporary power* (pp. 1–25). New York; Oxford: Berghahn Books.

Sinclair, S. (2008). Dilemmas of community planning: Lessons from Scotland. *Public Policy and Administration*, *23*(4), 373–390.

Sirianni, C. (2009). *Investing in democracy: Engaging citizens in collaborative governance.* Washington, DC: Brookings Institution Press.

Stoker, G. (2004). *Transforming local governance: From Thatcherism to New Labour.* Basingstoke: Palgrave Macmillan.

Sullivan, H. (2009). Subversive spheres: Neighbourhoods, citizens and the "new governance". In M. Barnes & D. Prior (Eds.), *Subversive citizens: Power, agency and resistance in public services* (pp. 49–66). Bristol: Policy Press.

Sullivan, H., & Lowndes, V. (2004). Like a horse and carriage or a fish on a bicycle: How well do local partnerships and public participation go together? *Local Government Studies*, *30*(1), 51–73.

Taylor, M. (1995). Community work and the state: The changing context of UK practice. In G. Craig & M. Mayo (Eds.), *Community empowerment: A reader in participation and development* (pp. 99–111). London: Zed Books.

Wagenaar, H., & Cook, S. D. N. (2003). Understanding policy practices: Action, dialectic and deliberation in policy analysis. In M. A. Hajer & H. Wagenaar (Eds.), *Deliberative policy analysis: Understanding governance in the network society* (pp. 139–171). Cambridge: Cambridge University Press.

Warren, M. (2009). Governance-driven democratization. *Critical Policy Studies, 3*(1), 3–13.

Williams, P. (2012). *Collaboration in public policy and practice: Perspectives on boundary spanners.* Chicago: University of Chicago Press.

Wright, S., & Reinhold, S. (2011). "Studying through": A strategy for studying political transformation. Or sex, lies and British politics. In C. Shore, S. Wright & D. Però (Eds.), *Policy worlds: Anthropology and the analysis of contemporary power* (pp. 86–104). New York; Oxford: Berghahn Books.

Yanow, D. (2009). Dear author, dear reader: The third hermeneutic in writing and reviewing ethnography. In E. Schatz (Ed.), *Political ethnography: What immersion contributes to the study of power* (pp. 275–302). Chicago: University of Chicago Press.

8

NEGOTIATING PROFESSIONAL BOUNDARIES

Learning from Collaboration between Academics and Deliberation Practitioners[1]

David Kahane and Kristjana Loptson

Introduction

Collaborations between academics and practitioners have been pivotal in building, shaping, and legitimizing the field of public participation. There is increasing study of the professionalization of public participation, but relatively little attention to the role of academics on this shifting terrain. In this chapter, we draw on interviews with academics, practitioners, and academic–practitioners to examine how the norms and constraints of their different professional worlds are negotiated in the course of their work together.

Gaps and bridges between the worlds of academics and practitioners are a focus of study in management, public administration, and education (see, for instance, Bartunek & Rynes, 2014; Battaglio Jr. & Scicchitano, 2013; Beech, MacIntosh & MacLean, 2010; Empson, 2013; Kieser & Leiner, 2012; Kram, Wasserman & Yip, 2012; McNatt, Glassman & Glassman, 2010; Shani & Coghlan, 2014; Wasserman & Kram, 2009).[2] Scholars of public deliberation have paid less attention to these gaps and bridges, despite the fact that public participation is "one area in which the ivory tower has cultivated real world relevance—with researchers developing intimate connections with actual projects and practitioners, and in many cases, becoming scholar-practitioners or 'pracademics' themselves" (Lee, 2011, p. 1).

Our own interest in academic-practitioner collaboration derived from five years leading and contributing to Alberta Climate Dialogue (ABCD), a university-community project that convened citizens of Alberta, Canada, to deliberate on climate policy and that researched these processes and their influence.[3] Each of the three public deliberations that we held with government and NGO partners from 2012 to 2014 was designed collaboratively by academics and public deliberation practitioners, with academics playing different roles in each. As we reflected on this collaborative design and research, we became interested in other contexts where academics and practitioners work together on public deliberation exercises:[4] How do academics and practitioners regard one another and how is this shaped by institutional locations and norms? How do they see the proper division of roles in deliberation projects—around research design, process design, and implementation? What are the points of learning and friction? Exploring these questions casts light on the professional roles and self-conceptions of academics and practitioners, including around political commitment, norms of neutrality and objectivity, critical reflexivity, and negotiating professional boundaries. All of these themes are salient to broader inquiry into the professionalization of public participation.

Academics as Public Participation Practitioners

Changes in the field of public deliberation over the last two decades have shifted academics' involvement in public participation practice. Early in this period, research communities that focused on public deliberation were less developed within and across academic disciplines, and there were weaker networks between practitioners. Public deliberation initiatives were scattered and idiosyncratic: academics interested in public deliberation often resorted to designing and holding such processes themselves.[5] Now there is a more consolidated and visible community of practitioners made up of both consultants and organizations, gathered in bodies like the Canadian Community for Dialogue and Deliberation (C2D2), the International Association for Public Participation (IAP2), the National Coalition for Dialogue and Democracy (NCDD), and the Deliberative Democracy Consortium (DDC). Organizations like these include academics as well as practitioners, and the resulting networks enable researchers to gain personal experience of deliberative and collaborative methods and develop close relationships with the practitioners who run them. Researchers have ample opportunity to study processes without being extensively involved in design and facilitation, or can negotiate limited roles within processes.

Moreover, as research on citizen involvement has burgeoned in political science, sociology, communication studies, and other disciplines, research questions and methodologies have become more refined, and there may be more of a commitment to (or ideological investment in) definitions of research rigour that encourage academics to have an arm's length relationship with the exercises they study—we explore this further below.

How is this reflected in the public deliberation literature? The last decade has seen the emergence of important work on the professionalization of public deliberation (Chilvers, 2008, 2010, 2013; Hendriks & Carson, 2008; Lee, 2011, 2015), which adds to a strong existing literature on particular deliberative exercises (e.g. Abelson, Eyles, McLeod, Collins, McMullan & Forest, 2003; Andersen &

Hansen, 2007; Luskin, O'Flynn, Fishkin & Russell, 2014; Wojcieszak, 2012). There is even a small literature on the involvement of academics in deliberative exercises (Burchell, 2009; Chilvers, 2008, 2013; Gisler & Schicktanz, 2009; Powell & Colin, 2009). The broader role played by universities in the field has also been touched on by scholars like Carcasson (2014), who examines how campus-based centres can foster deliberative democracy. "Like most fields, our field suffers from a disconnect between theory and practice, and the work of local centers and institutes focused on deliberative practice offer a strong response to those gaps" (p. 2).

Within these literatures, there is a bit of attention to academic-practitioner identities and relationships. A Deliberative Democracy Consortium (2008) overview of projects and practices includes a brief section headed "Useful bridges have been built between academics and practitioners, but further attention is needed." Academic Peter Muhlberger comments:

> On the practitioner side, there's a feeling of expertness about deliberation, but that expertness is not tied to the theoretical infrastructure. On the researcher side, there's a need to come down from the theoretical heights and investigate things that might matter to practitioners.
>
> *(p. 36)*

In Albrechts's (2002) study comparing the perspectives of various experts involved in public engagement activities, he finds differences in responses between academics and practitioners, suggesting that their differing institutional contexts have significant impacts on how each group approaches public engagement. For instance, the practitioners he surveyed tended to have less trust in the political system than the academics, and thus more radical views in support of direct public participation. Academics were more trusting of the political system and believed that communicative and collaborative relationships with decision makers can help overcome structural barriers to public participation. A gap in perspectives is also identified by Lee (2011): based on interviews with academics and practitioners, she found that academics who study deliberative democracy were more likely to perceive it as a progressive, grassroots, political movement than the practitioners working in the field. Practitioners were more likely to distance themselves from liberal/progressive standpoints and to want to avoid alienating conservatives. Practitioners expressed discomfort with framing deliberative democracy as a social movement, because to them this implied leftist bias; they favoured more neutral, non-partisan framing such as "community of practice" and viewed themselves as part of a profession rather than a movement rooted in social activism (pp. 11–13).

Jason Chilvers's research (2008, 2010, 2013) comes closest to our own, as he studies actors involved in constructing and studying public dialogue and dialogue networks around science and technology in the UK. Chilvers (2013) interviewed 21 people in these networks including academics, practitioners, policymakers, and representatives of participation organizations. He maps four main expert roles

played in public engagement activities: "(a) *studying*, which includes researching, theorizing, evaluation, and reflection; (b) *practicing*, which includes designing,
facilitating, and reporting on dialogue processes; (c) *orchestrating*, which includes
commissioning, sponsoring, and guiding; and (d) *coordinating*, which includes networking, capacity building, and professionalization" (pp. 288–289). He emphasizes
that these public participation roles cannot be cleanly separated.[6]

The small amount of literature examining academic-practitioner identities and relationships suggests that there are gaps between the two groups that
merit further exploration. However, some scholars, particularly Chilvers, caution
against using rigid categories to understand the roles played by those in the field.
A number of participants interviewed for this chapter spoke to the complexity of the academic/practitioner distinction that we offered them in our interview script. Some felt that the distinction itself was "problematic," "blurry," and
"porous." Many of our interviewees emphasized that the roles of those involved
in deliberative exercises are fluid, and that research and practice are carried out by
both groups. They also pointed out differences within as well as across categories.
To a point, we acknowledge this. However, our experience in ABCD and our
analysis of our interviews convinces us that the distinction between "academics"
and "practitioners" serves a useful explanatory and heuristic purpose. People's
identities, capacities, and propensities are deeply shaped by the content of their
day-to-day work, and deliberation practitioners by and large have a very different work life than academics; face different financial incentives and pressures; are
assessed by peers, clients, and employers on different terms; and are surrounded
by different institutions and cultures. There are strong patterns to how academics and practitioners build their understandings of deliberation: practitioners do
so mainly through project development, design, facilitation, and other hands-on
work and reflection, while academics do so mainly through research literatures,
classroom teaching, and quantitative and qualitative research on deliberation projects. Academics are likely to have gained the majority of their work experience
from within a university setting and may have limited exposure to other work
environments, while practitioners tend to have more varied professional backgrounds. Further, when academics and practitioners interact, this is influenced by
their expectations and projections about one another's identities, capacities, and
propensities. So these differences of professional standpoints matter, even given
internal diversity and cross-cutting memberships.

For all of these reasons, we find it useful to explore the meeting points between
these discernible institutional communities when they collaborate on particular
deliberation projects and exercises, and to examine how they see one another,
how they divide work and roles, and how they negotiate challenges that relate
to their different professional milieus, capacities, propensities, and identities. With
this said, some of our interviewees clearly could not be segmented into one group
or another: these were academics whose research on public involvement had led
them to take on principal responsibility for designing and leading exercises for

clients in a professional role. Of the 14 people we interviewed, we categorize five as academics, five as practitioners, and four as "academic-practitioners."

Methodology

In addition to reflecting together on the ABCD experience, we reviewed literatures on researcher-practitioner collaboration in public participation and on the professionalization of public participation, seeking analyses of academic involvement in public engagement exercises and of roles played. Although our review of the literature was not exhaustive, it suggests that little has been written on these topics, with the exceptions discussed above. Once the literature review was complete, we conducted interviews with academics and practitioners involved in deliberative exercises. Participants were selected from within our network of acquaintances based on their work in the field of deliberative democracy as prominent practitioners and/or researchers. Six of those interviewed were significantly involved in ABCD, five not involved at all, and three involved at the margins. Our literature review and interviews focus on the experiences of public participation experts in Anglo-American contexts, especially North America, but with some input from the UK and Australia. We conducted 14 semi-structured interviews over Skype and telephone from February to June 2015 ranging in length from 30 to 90 minutes; these were audio recorded and transcribed.[7]

We asked participants to reflect on their roles within deliberative exercises, their approach to their work, their experiences around collaboration, and how decisions are typically made about the division of tasks around planning and holding deliberative events (see Appendix for interview guide). Transcripts were analyzed to identify common themes. We then used these themes to compare responses across participants. We paid close attention to similar and different experiences and perspectives expressed. Although the number of interviewees is relatively small, it is large enough to support an initial mapping and to guide further inquiry and reflection. Because we found the words of our respondents rich and evocative, we give their voices pride of place in the chapter, as contributions in their own right as well as ground for our analysis.

Tensions and Complementarities in Academic/Practitioner Collaboration

Our interview data is rich and we've had to restrain ourselves in the lines of analysis we're sharing here. In what follows we explore three dominant themes: the influence of different professional cultures on approaches to public participation work, especially in relation to questions of neutrality and objectivity; tensions that emerge from differing institutionally based priorities around research and evaluation; and perceived benefits of academic/practitioner collaboration.

Institutional Cultures and Their Influence on Understandings of Balance and Objectivity

Practice professionals' deep personal investment in their work was emphasized by both practitioners and academics. One practitioner highlighted normative stakes that go beyond the merely professional; the work requires a deep sensitivity to the hopes, fears, and vulnerabilities of deliberation participants, which

> calls all of your person into being. The word "professional" kind of connotes "well, I am a professional," but it is actually personal too. So it takes the personal as well as the professional: you as a person, your value set, your own vulnerabilities, your own baggage. And I think this is something important to talk about.
>
> *[P5]*

On the other hand, the distance of university-based academics from the exigencies of professional work in deliberative practice was perceived as valuable by a number of academic interviewees; this distance was seen as permitting a critical and less invested perspective on deliberative practice. One academic commented that academics are given more freedom to fail than practitioners are, and that this supports distinctive and important forms of learning [A3].

Our interviews suggest a tension between the nuanced knowledge that comes from enmeshment in practice and the critical perspective enabled by distance. An academic discussed how practitioners are a self-selecting group, believing deeply in the deliberative process. Because their careers have been devoted to this work, practitioners tend to have better intuitive and experiential knowledge of both the problems and possibilities of deliberation. However, because they are so embedded in deliberation practice, they lack critical reflexivity, "and that is where I think the academics can add some value. Especially trying to figure out where new kinds of processes fit into broader political systems" [A1].

An academic-practitioner pointed out, though, that academics' distance from the exigencies of actual deliberations can distort their understanding:

> There is a whole movement that is starting to talk about deliberative systems and is quite cynical about mini-publics and is in many ways discrediting the value of mini-publics. I think it is because they have so little experience in the field that they are able to think about the field in a big picture way that makes it easy to discredit aspects of the practice without actually understanding what is going on in the practice because of their very narrow experience with the practice. So I think the more exposure they have to the practice, the less likely they are to engage in that kind of undermining work. But there is no question that there are a lot of theorists who enjoy critiquing this activity without having any appreciation, or very little appreciation of what the activity is.
>
> *[AP2]*

One academic took a different view of academic critiques of practitioner work and pushed back in particular against the criticism that academic writing is inaccessible and out of touch with the realities and constraints faced by practitioners. This respondent suggested that the dismissal of academic critiques by practitioners is sometimes rooted in fundamentally conflicting interests, because part of what academics are saying is that rather than empowering publics, deliberations often serve the interests of the powerful. Because practitioners and policymakers can feel threatened by some academic critiques of deliberation, they are prone to dismiss these as irrelevant or poorly communicated.

> But I think the academics are saying "no, no, no, we are trying to raise more ethically critical points or more substantively critical points that are about power and politics and these kinds of things" and therefore they are saying things which maybe policy makers don't want to hear. They don't like the sound of it, and I think that is part of what is going on here, and that is the thing which doesn't often get dealt with, because this is again about politics and power, these sorts of questions which in nice cozy deliberative processes can sometimes get brushed under the carpet.
>
> *[A2]*

A number of other academics emphasized their own independence, as contrasted with the financial imperatives and pressures faced by deliberation professionals.

> I think that academics have an interesting role to play because we are, for the most part, immune to the kinds of forces that deliberation practitioners are vulnerable to, and we can play a role of what I want to call a "critical interlocutor." . . . But I don't think practitioners can because there is a lot riding on them in terms of economic forces. So as academics we can critique in the way that practitioners can't. And I have just heard from a lot of practitioners—if you talk to them they are very critical of a lot of things, but they often don't want to make that public because it can come back to haunt them, right?
>
> *[A3]*

An academic-practitioner made a related point:

> Consultants are in an invidious position, and I have been out there for [many] years, I really do know what it is like being a consultant. And being a consultant, you have to produce the goods that people who are paying you want you to produce, really. Unless you are so self-confident that you figure that if you don't someone else will have you anyway. But in the main, you have far more limitations than a group who come in as third party, come in as independent, and are clearly not beholden to anybody.
>
> *[AP1]*

So there are perceived differences between academics and public participation practitioners in terms of closeness to and investment in the work and in terms of financial pressures. There also is a set of professional norms in academia around proper objectivity, which academics contrasted with the priorities of practitioners.

> My goal is to understand how the world operates and how it can be changed: how it can operate differently. That is a very long-term goal, and everything I do feeds that goal. [A practitioner's] goal is to make this process as effective as possible and expand it as rapidly as possible, and to keep themselves employed. And there isn't a truth-seeking function in there. There is an improving the world function that we share; that is our shared commitment. But you know, the ends can justify the means. If they found out something embarrassing that they thought they could fix without anyone finding out about it, they would just fix it. I would have to report on it, so to speak.... what I kept stressing [to practitioners] was that the comparative advantage that I have developed over the years is that I am the academic researcher and evaluator, and you know, I have to maintain my neutrality and I answer to a professional set of ethics and standards for review.
>
> *[A4]*

Another academic reinforced this point:

> Academics have the luxury of working in an institutional setting where there is a culture of open debate and having an independent position and point of view, and we are allowed to try to speak out and hold people to account, and that is kind of part of our job. So yeah, it is pretty obvious then that the academics are going to have more freedom in that respect than a consultant that is doing [a big money] contract with government to actually get a process of national importance.... So, under those conditions, the contractor is going to some extent give the paymaster what they want. They are not going to come in and start kicking off about being critical about the fact that they are really picking particular lines of the story in terms of what is coming out from the public. I mean, I just don't think that that robust exchange is going to be there as much. I mean, that is my experience, and it is pretty obvious really.... my experience is that the power lines are drawn very much around funders and resourcing.
>
> *[A2]*

Yet what academics embrace as objectivity and truth seeking, some practitioners regarded as too lofty and pure an understanding of good deliberation. One practitioner saw this as shifting over time; at early stages of the field academics relied on Habermasian standards for deliberations, which frustrated practitioners who saw what was happening within deliberations as differing significantly from the pure theoretical understanding of the processes [P3].

This relates to a further current within the interviews regarding how different players focus on the process of deliberation as against its political outcomes. One practitioner contrasted the emphasis academics place on the results of the deliberation with the emphasis practitioners place on the experience of participants [P5]. In another's words, "I think practitioners are often hell-bent on the process, because that is what they do best, without maybe doing their deeper thinking about: how would you know if this was a successful enterprise, what would it look like, what would need to happen?" [AP2]. And a third interviewee suggested that many practitioners aren't

> politically savvy at all . . . some of them are sort of explicitly spiritually oriented, which is fine, but they are much more like "we can create a beautiful democracy on a small scale by bringing people together." And I actually think compared to them, a lot of academics are more hard-nosed about things like power.
>
> *[A5]*

A differing sensitivity to power was also touched on by a practitioner:

> I think that academic scholars don't all have the same view of power, and I think the same would be true of people in practice. So everyone has some understanding that power is the ability to coerce, I think everyone has some understanding of power as the ability to block, power as the ability to keep things off the agenda. It may be that some practitioners have a keener sense of how the framing of what is on the agenda affects the way power dynamics develop.
>
> *[P1]*

The contrast here is between a power-sensitive savvy about political impacts and a more pragmatic, constrained emphasis on process: one academic saw people's positioning as a function of circumstances rather than fixed professional or institutional roles. Practitioners, regardless of their institutional environments, are able to reflect in a critical way about their practice from a distance, but when it comes to actually doing their work, the political constraints surrounding the processes often impose a need for an instrumental approach to public engagement work. When academics enter into practice, they respond to the constraints in an identical way, becoming less reflective and more instrumental in their approach; they lose the critical distance that they might otherwise be expected to bring [A2].

Some interviewees emphasized the professional culture and institutional imperatives of academia and their impact on collaboration in public participation projects. A practitioner, speaking about the work of practice professionals, contrasted the social skills required for the work with the skills often emphasized and rewarded in academic settings:

> There is a high level of emotional intelligence in this work. You know, academics can have it as well as anyone else, but I think the difference of being an academic in general, and this is not true across the board, probably doesn't really elevate that. It is a very competitive world, it is "my brain is bigger than your brain, I am smarter than you are so I can analytically take this apart and score more points than you can." . . . you have got to bring your intellect into this stuff, but you have also got to bring your emotional intelligence, big time.
>
> *[P5]*

One interviewee remarked that practitioners tend to hold more of a normative commitment to the community service aspect of deliberations than academics do, since academics are pressured to balance teaching, research, and service.

> I am a critic in a lot of ways of academia, of publishing in top journals in the field. I feel as though we have so many journals now, and not many people actually reading these journals, but the whole incentive process is to publish in these journals. . . . but I would rather publish a practitioner piece that I know people are going to use . . . lots of people have talked about how the incentive process all around the academic research and certainly service, it depends partly on the institution, but generally service is going to be by far the red-headed step child of the three [laughter].
>
> *[AP4]*

The competitive and ego-driven character of academic environments was highlighted by other interviewees. Two academic-practitioners commented on how the institutional culture of academia cultivates non-collaborative habits and attitudes. One stated, "I think we have created in academia, not just a siloed world, but a world where it is me against the rest" [AP1]. The other argued that universities are highly non-deliberative environments,

> and also some of the people writing about deliberative democracy are some of the least collaborative people that you could possibly encounter and that is because they are part of a system that doesn't encourage collaboration, it encourages competition and hierarchy.
>
> *[AP2]*

The interview materials above show some of the intricacies and dilemmas that surround academic and practitioner understandings of objectivity, power, and personal investment in citizen participation work. A number of respondents characterized practitioners as oriented to the experiences of participants in deliberation and the relational nuances of practice, while academics were characterized as more distant, and their engagement with deliberation exercises mediated through professional cultures of objectivity. There was disagreement over the epistemic implications of these stances: to what extent does distance enable critical insight or astuteness about power, and to what extent does it lead to misunderstanding of the subtleties of deliberative work? As we will argue below, the friction between these professional stances can itself support effective practice and field learning.

Responses from interviewees to a draft of this chapter showed the difficulty of attributions of objectivity and critical distance to academics or practitioners. One academic-practitioner pushed back at the conceit that academia is a place of critical robustness and speaking truth to power, saying that while academic freedom is supposed to enable academics to engage in social critique, this is the exception, given a "pall of timidity" that has seized the academy. Meanwhile, a practitioner pushed back at the suggestion that practitioners are in thrall to funders and clients, pointing to professional norms and personal commitments that lead practitioners to push hard to ensure both integrity and astuteness about power in deliberative exercises.

Constructing Research and Evaluation

These frictions between perspectives and professional cultures extend to questions of research and evaluation, a pivot of collaboration between academics and practitioners. A number of our interviewees suggested that practitioners want ready to hand, useful research products that advance their professional work, whereas academics are preoccupied with innovation and new findings. One practitioner warned about

> allowing the organizational and scholarly agendas for putting on a good event, or an event that will yield significant data, to come ahead of the purposes of deliberation in the first place. I mean, this work is ultimately about a broad range of people having greater voice and power and addressing the problems that affect their communities, their families, their countries.
>
> *[P1]*

A practitioner contrasted the imperatives of academic careers (built around the quality of research) and practitioner careers (built on the quality of public engagement processes). For practitioners,

> our mindset is really about: how can we make this the best deliberation we can to achieve whatever the outcomes people are looking for, and to make it a really meaningful deliberation for the participants? So our starting

points, I think, are different. So when I am involved in a deliberation, even though I might have questions in my head about what happens if we do this, or do that, and how does it affect things, it is not my primary lens that I bring to the work. Whereas I think the researcher's primary lens is about the research question.

[P2]

A gap between academic institutional norms and building deliberations that serve participants was also noted in connection with research ethics. One academic-practitioner has opted to forgo the protocols of informed consent:

We don't need them to sign a form. And I kind of push on that pretty strong because, partly because these are real events, right? So we are not doing this for the research. We are doing it for doing it. We are also capturing the research to improve our practice in some senses. And I didn't want people to feel like they were being studied. So if everyone had to sign a release form for these events they would think "oh, they are here to study us, they are not here to actually help us solve this problem," right? So that is why I have always put research kind of a notch below in a sense.

[AP4]

An academic recognized that tensions between academic research and good participation practice can be tough for practitioners, who need to build public trust in a process under multiple constraints, including financial and political ones. These constraints are at the forefront of the practitioner's mind, and academic research is of secondary concern. Carrying out research and organizing the process "don't need to conflict, but sometimes some of the constraints need to be pushed back a bit for them to be compatible" [A1].

Another academic joined this chorus, saying practitioners are focused on how deliberation can address proximate concerns, while academics are more oriented to studying and spurring innovation:

Academics might have to deal with having a different agenda. Mainly, an agenda about wanting to develop original knowledge or otherwise, and the local community just wants to deal with what to do about the homeless shelter, or whatever. So there is a slight tension there. The academic needs to learn something new in order to get tenure, but not just that, but also because that is what they care about, that is what they love. And that community doesn't want anything that is original. In fact, if there is some good package that has been done somewhere else, that is what they want. They don't need some new invention. So I think there is some tension between originality and applicability.

[A5]

Interviewees also reflected on the different sorts of research questions that academics and practitioners want to address. One academic pointed to the privileging of quantitative research, and thus of particular exercises and sources of data:

> Part of the problem is that if you want to do high-level, high-quality research, you go where the good data is. And so that has left all of these new things to people who are risk takers, or are already tenured and can afford to do the kind of research that won't make it to the *American Political Science Review* because the data isn't there. So there is a little bit of a divide that is forced by the professionalization of political science. There is of course a divide between people who do more qualitative and quantitative work and this is a field where qualitative work is still the way you have to do it, you know, with a few exceptions. Yeah, I think it is hard to do. I tend to think that people who are more quantitatively oriented tend to be a little more skeptical of these processes because they are not doing the qualitative work to see what is going on. It is crowded out by the fact that they go where the data is.
>
> *[A1]*

A practitioner discussed how tensions arise about what counts as knowledge, and around emphasis on quantitative measurements of how participant attitudes change from before to after deliberation, measurements that may not capture their experiences adequately: "I think that sometimes what constitutes a good question for a scholar is not an identity with the question that someone working in community has" [P1].

These elements of our interviews point to divergences around how academics and practitioners understand and value *research*. The tensions become more acute when it comes to *evaluation*. As one interviewee notes,

> practitioners, when they are thinking about evaluation—which they do not do often enough [laughter]—but when they do think about evaluation and plan that into a process they typically veer off and think about some academic partner, reach out to somebody as an academic to be heading that part of things.
>
> *[P3]*

Evaluation processes bring to a head the questions of objectivity and bias discussed above: as one academic-practitioner said,

> to do an evaluation you really need to be an external person to the person who is doing all of the designing and so involved in the orchestrating and everything else. Like, I am seen to be biased. And although I really try to say "look this worked, this didn't" because I feel like that is the only thing that

will help, it is really not seen as me being independent, and you know, that is true. I am not independent, and I am part of the process, I guess.

[AP1]

Yet a number of interviewees said recruiting outsiders to evaluate participation is risky, in part because of the commercial imperatives of the participation profession. An academic noted that

There is a huge amount of pressure on organizers to get it right. So given that, you can see that they will be quite sensitive to criticism. And it is certainly ... academics style themselves as ... they can be sort of abstractly critical and even cynical about these processes without really knowing what they are talking about or looking very closely at what is going on. So I think that can be a source of tension and even distrust from the standpoint of organizers.

[A1]

The interviews turned up further areas of divergence around evaluation. For one thing, scholars' interest may not be in "evaluation" as construed by practitioners; in the words of one academic,

We are interested in more abstract questions, and in a sense I am getting my hands dirty by even doing an evaluation report, because an evaluation report sounds an awful lot like I am just answering the questions the practitioners want answered. I have to have good theoretical reasons for asking those questions if I am going to get publications.

[A4]

And yet this desire to connect evaluation to bigger questions can be problematic from the standpoint of practitioners:

The frameworks that those of us who have spent a lot of time, let's say, reading the literature on deliberation bring, are different than people who are just trying to figure out how to make a better decision [and this can be a problem] if the predetermined framework of the scholar is the evaluative criteria for what constitutes a robust public event.

[P1]

Academics also worry about objectivity when evaluation is treated as a device for legitimation rather than primarily as a tool for learning. One academic remarked on the pressures evaluators sometimes face to report their evaluation results very soon after a process has ended in order to demonstrate that it was "legitimate." This subverts learning because it fails to capture emergent outcomes and therefore does not fully reflect the impacts of deliberation [A2].

Further, interviewees noted tensions around how much time will be devoted to evaluation during deliberations.

> It is very practical. People are getting together in a church basement, or a school cafeteria, or a library, and they have three hours, or two and a half hours, and there is paper work to do [laughter]. So the question of how much time in the event is actually spent for evaluation is an issue.
>
> *[P1]*

Another noted tensions that arise when evaluations are onerous and time consuming:

> I think a fairly common tension is, you know, academics wanting to gather lots of data, and have people fill out long surveys and things like that, and the practitioners saying "wait a minute, they are going to be in this meeting for two hours and you want them to spend another half an hour filling out this survey?" That is a fairly typical kind of tension. . . . So it's funny, all of that kind of stuff as a subset of this preliminary conversation is: ok, what kind of information are we hoping to get from people about their experience and how are we going to do it?
>
> *[P3]*

To the above tensions and divergences, practitioners added concerns about the timelines of knowledge production in academia, norms around protection of data, and the vernaculars of academic research, all of which were perceived as unhelpful:

> you know there is some valuable information that you would love to be able to use to help the processes improve that you are working on, but the time lag, there is always a time lag, because of the constraints of publishing, I guess.
>
> *[P2]*

Another interviewee reinforced this, pointing out that timeframes, what counts as knowledge, and what is viewed as successful outcomes can differ between practitioners and academics [P1].

A further area of practitioner concern was the accessibility of academic research to practitioners and communities, remarking that many practitioners do not read the kind of journals that academics typically publish their results in, and furthermore, that they would not even know where to look to find these journals.

> It is often done, again, in ways that are hard to take and actually inform practice. So, you know, even the research that does get conducted, I think it is fairly distant for most practitioners. Partly because there is almost like

a translation divide between making the research meaningful for the users, the practitioners, and secondly, even just knowing that the research is out there, because most of us don't have the time or the access even to some of the journals where some of this stuff is starting to appear.[8]

[P2]

Some of the divergences between academics and practitioners around research and evaluation conform to stereotype: academics bring forth abstract research questions, chase good data, and publish scholarly analyses long after events, while practitioners want evaluation results on quick turnaround, resent extensive data collection that gets in the way of good process, and are interested in evaluating processes simply and quickly. But between the lines, more complex professional, political, and ethical dynamics are in play. A number of the practitioners we interviewed had critical questions about deliberation design and practice, and were frustrated that academic collaborators were not more willing or adept at investigating these in ways that yield usable insights; at the same time, a number of practitioners recognized the professional constraints and cultures that shape research and evaluation behaviours of academics. The academics we interviewed were not particularly reflexive about the burdens research activities placed on practitioners and their work, or about the epistemic norms implicit in academic models of objectivity and research production; they did share with practitioners a desire to advance a common field, and to bring a critical lens to practice. Academic-practitioners were most acutely aware of the tensions between these professional worlds, including (as seen above) in connection with norms of objectivity in evaluation and ethics review processes required for research. We will suggest in the next section that tensions in collaborations between academics and practitioners can support learning and innovation; but practices of research and evaluation may be more resistant to such learning-through-friction than other elements of practitioner and academic work.

Benefits of Collaboration

Even if we discount the financial demands and pressures that some interviewees suggested may push practitioners toward conventional or conservative methods, all of us are vulnerable to repeating what we know in our work—to routinization. New perspectives on practitioner methods are thus useful; they can come from many sources, but when academics bring well-grounded data and critical analysis, it can help practitioners to see their work in new ways, including in terms of political influence.

Concern about routinization, and the potential role of academics in seeding innovation, was brought up by a number of interviewees. One way to characterize this is as supporting practitioners—through critical questioning—to make good on core professional values. Practitioners have normative commitments to the integrity and influence of deliberative work, but can succumb to the very human tendency to notice those aspects of the work that manifest these values and be less perceptive about aspects that do not. Lee (2011), for example, points to the commonplace practitioner rejection of one-size-fits-all methods and their emphasis on tailoring processes to context; but she argues that the repertoire of participatory methods used in practice is limited and predictable. While academics can at times be lofty in their characterizations of "good deliberation," where they are respectful of practitioner expertise and attentive to the exigencies of practice, they can highlight decisions about projects and processes that strain against values practitioners affirm, and support thinking about how to better realize core values, and about political and systemic pressures that constrain the realization of these values.

On the other hand, engagement with practitioners can support better research by academics—not simply by providing data and experience that nuance abstract claims, but by challenging academic patterns of communication and analysis. Such engagement can also temper academic egos, including around self-attributed ability in skills like facilitation. Academics, too, are prone to the human tendency to notice those aspects of their practice that support their positive self-regard.

A key theme in the interview responses was how academics and practitioners can work effectively together, both within particular deliberation projects and more broadly. Several practitioners emphasized the importance of early alignment and also identifying possible areas of conflict ahead of time and "having really upfront conversations" [P4]. One reflected that

> like with any partnership, starting out with some discussion of goals. You know, why are you interested in . . . what do you want to achieve? Having a really frank exchange and figuring out what the other people's assumptions are about how this is supposed to work and why it is going to make an impact and all of those kinds of things.
>
> *[P3]*

This need for shared goals was echoed by another interviewee:

> I think success needs to be measured three ways. I think it should be measured by result . . . the process, and . . . the relationships that were built. Because you can have great results but destroy relationships in the process. That is not a good outcome. And similarly, you can have a great process, but if you get no results, that is not a good outcome. So I think a shared sense of purpose is . . . really important for both academics and practitioners.
>
> *[AP3]*

Another interviewee spoke about the importance of discussing differing objectives:

> I think some people come at a topic thinking "we are going to move the needle on a certain topic, we are going to move it in a particular direction"

and somebody else might think "we are going to move the needle but we are going to remain agnostic on the direction." I don't personally think that is very likely, but I do feel that people don't talk to each other about that tension.

[AP3]

A practitioner pointed to the further need, where there is divergence, to decide who in a collaboration has the last word, especially once a deliberation process is underway:

> My preference is to be collaborative but understand on the spot that there does have to be someone that is the decision maker. If a decision has to be made it should really be the facilitator who has to be responsible for the overall flow.
>
> *[P5]*

An academic–practitioner echoed this, emphasizing that holding a good process should always be given priority over research imperatives.

> One of the rules of thumb I had is that when you are engaged with the public, when people are showing up to a meeting, you have to be flexible, you know? You have to make it work. . . . So I don't allow the academic side to constrain us too much. If everything has to be exactly the same so it is kind of a representative sample and all that kind of stuff, then I think the realities of actual events is . . . as a practitioner, that need for flexibility, that need to adapt, that need for the individual facilitator if something is not working to be able to try something different for me kind of trumps the need for everything to be consistent to try to support the data in a way, right?
>
> *[AP4]*

It helps, in negotiating these areas of divergence, if collaborators recognize the differing pressures that academics and practitioners face. An academic said,

> I actually think the biggest problem is much more nitty gritty about how you get paid, what you get paid for and what you get evaluated for. So more understanding about that on both sides is helpful because most people don't know the other side faces and they can be much more sympathetic once they realize. They say, you know "why are you academic spending so much time on this paper that I don't care about" and the answer is partly that the academic loves it and wants to do it, and the answer is partly that the academic has to do it or they get fired. And once you kind of get to that place, it can lead to a more productive working relationship.
>
> *[A5]*

A practitioner spoke to the learning that comes from crossing over roles, and especially involvement of practitioners in research design and production.

> So I think the challenge is that academics need to be comfortable and open to having non-academic, whatever that means, people without PhDs, actually fully involved in research design and as researchers and writers. And I think the reverse is that practitioners have to be open to the fact that academics are not just in the ivory tower researching things, but they actually have a lot to contribute to process design and ongoing, like how the panel is implemented and things like the framing, how we get people to think deeply and critically about issues, how we present evidence, and so I think there just needs to be a real fluidity, and a real deep understanding that we are crossing borders with researchers being practitioners and practitioners being researchers. And I think being comfortable with that and maybe even having a conversation up front about that I think is really important because those are the things that prevent when we really see them as separate and as roles that are maybe not interchangeable. We cross over those roles in a really good process.
>
> *[P4]*

This quote encompasses the sense that we developed out of the ensemble of interviews: that the quality and self-reflexivity of work on public deliberation by both academics and practitioners is enhanced by collaboration that takes them onto each other's turf and into each other's activities.

Conclusion

We did this research to understand gaps and bridges between academics and practitioners working in the field of public deliberation and implications for collaborations between the two groups. In the interviews, academics, practitioners, and academic-practitioners pointed to a range of tensions arising from contrasting professional norms, incentives, and institutional constraints. Interviewees spoke of the freedom that academics have to be critically reflexive, but also of academics' non-collaborative tendencies; purist views of deliberation; equations of objectivity with distance from practice; and focus on innovation and good data over questions directly salient to practitioners and communities. Interviewees spoke of practitioners' emphasis on an empathetic mindset when doing their work; financial pressures that constrain them and make them sensitive to research critical of their work; their focus on good experiences for participants and clients rather than broader reckoning with power and influence; and their desire for accessible research that speaks to their practical challenges as professionals.

We hope our chapter can serve as a reminder to researchers that the potentials of public participation processes and the dispositions of the professionals who deliver them are not fully determined by a given professional ecology. Academics and practitioners can build relationships and projects that support critical reflexivity and, ultimately, challenge and change practice. At the limit, recognizing how critical reflexivity and political disagreement can arise from work across fields may temper strongly deterministic claims about the effects of professionalization on the work of public participation. Our analysis has acknowledged the strong effects of institutional norms, standards, practices, and incentives on how public participation professionals (and academics) do their work; these effects may shape the democratic meaning of public participation. And yet our interviews also bring out the room for movement in public participation practices as academics and practitioners negotiate institutional cultures, constraints, and dissonances.

Scholarship on the professionalization of public participation tends to emphasize the structures that shape the work of practitioners (Bherer et al., forthcoming; Chilvers, 2008, 2010, 2013; Hendriks & Carson, 2008; Lee, 2011, 2015); our interviews suggest elements of agency. Observing the effects of interaction across boundaries of institutional cultures and imperatives provides a counterweight to a scholarly tendency to treat professionalization as an iron cage for participation practice. Yet at the same time, recognizing this space for movement alerts us to the need for principles and guidelines of interaction across professions, as we assess the successes and limitations of these collaborations. The friction between professional fields is healthy and sustains reflective practice, but it needs to be deliberately contained and aligned by those involved. Developing such principles and guidelines is an important part of continuing collaboration between academics and practitioners.[9]

Academics are an important part of the story of the professionalization of public participation. Their contributions to convening, designing, and evaluating processes are significant and, as we have sought to bring out, carry a different set of cultures, norms, and practices into participation work. Tensions between the norms and conventions of academia and of public participation bring key features of each into relief. And out of these tensions come changes to practice, and to the degree of critical reflexivity academics and practitioners are able to direct at their own routines, practices, assumptions, and settings.

But to close on a more cautious note: public participation itself often promises that well-designed processes between diverse citizens can bring greater wisdom to public affairs and shift dominant practices. The literature on the professionalization of public participation reminds us that this is not always so. By analogy, it's an open question whether the right processes of collaboration between academics and practitioners in public participation work has emancipatory potential, or will themselves be subsumed by the dominant tendencies of their respective professions.

Appendix

Interviewees

- Academic Social Scientist [A4] Feb. 23, 2015, by Skype
- Academic-practitioner [AP2] Feb. 23, 2015, by Skype
- Public Engagement Practitioner [P2] Feb. 26, 2015, by phone
- Academic Social Scientist [A5] Feb. 26, 2015, by Skype
- Academic Social Scientist [A3] Feb. 26, 2015, by phone
- Public Engagement Practitioner [P3] Feb. 27, 2015, by phone
- Academic-practitioner [AP3] March 2, 2015, by phone
- Academic-practitioner [AP1] March 3, 2015, by Skype
- Public Engagement Practitioner [P1] March 6, 2015, by phone
- Academic-practitioner [AP4] March 11, 2015, by Skype
- Academic Social Scientist [A1] March 19, 2015, by Skype
- Public Engagement Practitioner [P5] March 25, 2015, by Skype
- Academic Social Scientist [A2] March 30, 2015, by Skype
- Public Engagement Practitioner [P4] June 5, 2015, by phone

Interview Guide

We're interested in how academics and professional deliberation practitioners work together when it comes to actually designing and facilitating citizen involvement exercises.

1. How has this division of labour in designing and facilitating exercises worked when you've collaborated? Who did what?
   i. How did this division of labour emerge?
   ii. What were the tensions? What learning did you do as you went?
   iii. Examples?

2. What led you to divide roles between academics and practitioners in the ways you did, when it came to designing and facilitating deliberation?
   i. Skills? Capacities? Knowledge? Interests? Costs? Resources? Availability of time?

3. Do you think academics and practitioners emphasize or value different things in setting up deliberation exercises? How did this play out in how you've worked together?

4. Given your experiences, what rules of thumb would you offer about how academics and practice professionals should work together in the design and facilitation of deliberative exercises?

    i. What questions should academics or practice professionals ask themselves about these collaborations, to make them go well?

    ii. What are the best roles for academics to play in delivering deliberative projects?

    iii. What characteristics do academics and practice professionals need in order to work well together?

5. Anything else you'd like to add?

Notes

1 We thank those who agreed to be interviewed for this project, and also our colleagues in ABCD for years of work together as academics and practitioners that have taught us so much. Thank you to the Social Sciences and Humanities Research Council of Canada and the Centre for Public Involvement for funding that supported us in writing this paper. And thanks to several interviewees who read a draft of this chapter and offered useful feedback—which reinforced our sense of the diverse views within as well as across the categories of academics, practitioners, and academic-practitioners.

2 The more conventional terminology in the field speaks of "researchers" and "practitioners," but from our perspective this begs questions about what constitutes research and who can generate research. We use the language of "academics" to emphasize the professional and institutional identities of those who both work in universities and focus their research, teaching, and/or public activities on citizen deliberation projects.

3 See www.albertaclimatedialogue.ca.

4 We take deliberative democracy or citizen deliberation to be a subset of public participation: practices of citizen engagement that foreground wrestling with alternative policies and courses of action, weighing trade-offs, and coming to joint decisions. For distinctions between participatory and deliberative democracy, see Bohman (1996), Gastil and Levine (2005), and Hendriks (2011). We also note that the practitioners and academics we interviewed were involved in sustained collaboration around citizen deliberation where citizens come together to address real problems and policy challenges in ways meant to influence action and political decisions (as distinct from deliberative settings created primarily for experimental purposes).

5 "One of the jokes I like to tell is that I always wanted to study deliberative practice but I couldn't find any so I had to make some." [AP4] Note: We have numbered our interviewees to correlate quotations with speakers, using A1–A5 (for academics), AP1–AP4 (for academic-practitioners), and P1–P5 (for practitioners).

6 We do want to note a divide among academics that affects their relationship to the public participation field. The academics we interviewed tended to express a normative commitment to the goals of deliberative democracy and saw their scholarship as helping to advance these goals (often by way of critique). A different current in academia has a more value-neutral understanding of its purpose, seeing deliberative exercises as arm's length objects of study. This latter current may tend to ally with particular methods like experimental models of deliberation, control group designs, and quantitative evaluation (see, for instance, Latimer & Hempson, 2012; Min, 2007); exponents of the former may more readily take on roles typically associated with public participation professionals.

7 Although all participants agreed to be named in this chapter and most agreed to have their names associated with particular quotes, we have decided to leave out the names of interviewees.

8 This perspective resonates with those noted by Burchell (2009), p. 55.

9 We intend to unpack the guidance about academic-practitioner collaboration arising from our interviews in a separate article.

References

Abelson, J., Eyles, J., McLeod, C. B., Collins, P., McMullan, C., & Forest, P. G. (2003). Does deliberation make a difference? Results from a citizens panel on health goals priority setting. *Health Policy, 66*(1), 95–106.

Albrechts, L. (2002). The planning community reflects on enhancing public involvement. Views from academics and reflective practitioners. *Planning, Theory & Practice, 3*(3), 331–347.

Andersen, V. N., & Hansen, K. M. (2007). How deliberation makes better citizens: The Danish Deliberative Poll on the Euro. *European Journal of Political Research, 46*(4), 531–556.

Bartunek, J. M., & Rynes, S. L. (2014). Academics and practitioners are alike and unlike: The paradoxes of academic-practitioner relationships. *Journal of Management, 40*(5), 1181–1201.

Battaglio Jr., R. P., & Scicchitano, M. J. (2013). Building bridges? An assessment of academic and practitioner perceptions with observations for the public administration classroom. *Journal of Public Affairs Education, 19*(4), 749–772.

Beech, N., MacIntosh, R., & MacLean, D. (2010). Dialogues between academics and practitioners: The role of generative dialogic encounters. *Organization Studies, 31*(9/10), 1341–1367.

Bohman, J. (1996). *Public deliberation: Pluralism, complexity and democracy.* Cambridge, MA: MIT Press.

Burchell, K. (2009). A helping hand or a servant discipline? Interpreting non-academic perspectives on the roles of social science in participatory policy-making. *Science, Technology and Innovation Studies, 5*(1), 49–61.

Carcasson, M. (2014). The critical role of local centres and institutes in advancing deliberative democracy. *Journal of Public Deliberation, 10*(1). Retrieved from http://www.publicdeliberation.net/jpd/vol10/iss1/art11/.

Chilvers, J. (2008). Deliberating competence: Theoretical and practitioner perspectives on effective participatory appraisal practice. *Science, Technology, & Human Values, 33*(2), 155–185.

Chilvers, J. (2010). *Sustainable participation? Mapping out and reflecting on the field of public dialogue on science and technology.* Harwell: Sciencewise Expert Resource Centre.

Chilvers, J. (2013). Reflexive engagement? Actors, learning, and reflexivity in public dialogue on science and technology. *Science Communication, 35*(3), 283–310.

Deliberative Democracy Consortium. (2008). *Where is democracy headed? Research and practice on public deliberation.* Washington, DC: Deliberative Democracy Consortium.

Empson, L. (2013). My affair with the "other": Identity journeys across the research-practice divide. *Journal of Management Inquiry, 22*(2), 229–248.

Gastil, J., & Levine, P. (Eds.). (2005). *The deliberative democracy handbook: Strategies for effective civic engagement in the twenty-first century.* San Francisco, CA: Jossey-Bass.

Gisler, P., & Schicktanz, S. (2009). Introduction: Ironists, reformers, or rebels? Reflections on the role of the social sciences in the process of science policy making. *Science, Technology and Innovation Studies, 5*(1), 5–17.

Hendriks, C. (2011). *The politics of public deliberation: Citizen engagement and interest advocacy.* Basingstoke: Palgrave Macmillan.

Hendriks, L., & Carson, L. (2008). Can the market help the forum? Negotiating the commercialization of deliberative democracy. *Policy Sciences, 41*(4), 293–313.

Kieser, A., & Leiner, L. (2012). Collaborate with practitioners: But beware of collaborative research. *Journal of Management Inquiry, 21*(1), 14–28.

Kram, K. E., Wasserman, I. C., & Yip, J. (2012). Metaphors of identity and professional practice: Learning from the scholar-practitioner. *Journal of Applied Behavioral Science, 48*(3), 304–341.

Latimer, C., & Hempson, K. M. (2012). Using deliberation in the classroom: A teaching pedagogy to enhance student knowledge, opinion formation and civic engagement. *Journal of Political Science Education, 8*(4), 372–388.

Lee, C. W. (2011). Five assumptions academics make about public deliberation, and why they deserve rethinking. *Journal of Public Deliberation, 7*(1). Retrieved from http://www.publicdeliberation.net/jpd/vol7/iss1/art7/.

Lee, C. W. (2015). *Do-it-yourself democracy: The rise of the public engagement industry.* Oxford: Oxford University Press.

Luskin, R. C., O'Flynn, I., Fishkin, J. S., & Russell, D. (2014). Deliberating across deep divides. *Political Studies, 62*(1), 116–135.

McNatt, D. B., Glassman, M., & Glassman, A. (2010). The great academic-practitioner divide: A tale of two paradigms. *Global Education Journal, 23*(3), 6–22.

Min, S. J. (2007). Online vs. face-to-face deliberation: Effects on civic engagement. *Journal of Computer-Mediated Communication, 12*(4), 1369–1387.

Powell, M., & Colin, M. (2009). Participatory paradoxes: Facilitating citizen engagement in science and technology from the top-down? *Bulletin of Science Technology Society, 29*(4), 325–342.

Shani, A. B., & Coghlan, D. (2014). Collaborate with practitioners: An alternative perspective-A rejoinder to Kieser and Leiner (2012). *Journal of Management Inquiry, 23*(4), 433–437.

Wasserman, I. C., & Kram, K. E. (2009). Enacting the scholar-practitioner role: An exploration of narratives. *Journal of Applied Behavioral Science, 45*(1), 12–38.

Wojcieszak, M. E. (2012). On strong attitudes and group deliberation: Relationships, structure, changes, and effects. *Political Psychology, 33*(2), 225–242.

9

MAKING CITIZEN PANELS A "UNIVERSAL BESTSELLER"

Transnational Mobilization Practices of Public Participation Advocates

Nina Amelung and Louisa Grabner

Introduction

In the last few decades, various "democratic innovations" have spread around the globe and particular public engagement instruments have become part of the standard repertoire in the toolboxes of policymakers and practitioners (Organisation for Economic Co-operation and Development [OECD], 2001; Saward, 2000). The critical literature on public engagement instruments has pointed to problems of technocratization of public participation processes on the one hand and the professionalization and commercialization of a growing "deliberative industry" involving consultants and public participation professionals on the other hand (Felt & Fochler, 2010; Lezaun & Soneryd, 2007; Saretzki, 2008). However, the transnational spread of particular public participation instruments testifies to the successful innovation and institutionalization process of selected instruments, such as participatory budgeting, scenario workshops, or citizen panel designs. In this chapter, our aim is to explore the specific phenomenon of the transnational spread and standardization of instruments to better understand how this phenomenon is shaped by the dedicated practices of public participation advocates. We draw attention to the practices of abstraction, theorization, and standardization that are involved in this phenomenon and to how they can have ambivalent effects. While these practices considerably favour successful global innovation, a potential threat to locally and culturally situated public participation remains. This threat arises due to efforts to package and translate standardized blueprints and their implicit presumptions about democracy and participation that ignore cultural specificities and identities. We introduce the concept of public participation advocates in order, first, to expand the focus from public participation professionals (see the introduction to this book) by also integrating other actors that only occasionally, or in a very specific context, or not even intentionally, nonetheless meaningfully contribute to the expansion of public participation instruments as their advocates, and second, to partly contest the notion of a community of public participation professionals and instead suggest an additional notion of fragmentation and isolation among public participation advocates involved in promoting the same instruments. Public participation advocates can include practitioners, consultants, politicians, academics, media, activists, and even critics. However, whom we see as belonging to the group of advocates is not defined with regard to specific categories of actor groups but rather with regard to specific practices and their impact on the instruments' development.

Adopting a perspective that focuses on the social collective creating, shaping, and modifying public engagement instruments in a manner of distributed agency sheds light on the supply side of the instruments, the social life linked to these instruments (Voß & Simons, 2014). Our specific interest in this chapter is in the transnational diffusion and standardization of public engagement instruments across countries. The study reveals the challenges of expanding transnational "democratic innovations" and the ambiguities of the standardization of public participation instruments concerning the specific conditions of their contextual (dis)embedding.

We ask: How do the dynamics of the transnational spread, circulation, and standardization of public engagement instruments occur across countries? How do they relate to or how do they even result from specific practices carried out by the particular actors involved? We propose an approach that identifies the actors involved in the formation and modification of public engagement instruments, grouping them according to their particular activities and how they contribute to specific sequences within the journey of mobilization and diffusion of these instruments. We trace these actors in our empirical case study, which examines the transnational spread and standardization of three relatively similar public participation instruments—the planning cell (PC), citizens' jury (CJ), and consensus conference (CC). Although they originated in different contexts, they have over time merged into an abstracted model based on common generic design principles of citizen panels (Amelung, 2012; Brown, 2006).[1] In our notion of these public engagement instruments, citizen panel designs

> share the same basic features: small group deliberation, random selection of participants, integration of external expertise and the production of a common recommendation for public decision-making. They all address the gap of institutional solutions for the integration of citizens in established systems of representative democracy.
>
> *(Amelung, 2012, p. 18)*

A trio of independently developed deliberative designs (PC, CJ, and CC) emerged without direct interconnections in different countries, in different "peer groups," and in "peer policy domains" such as urban planning, evaluation of political candidates, and participatory science and technology assessment. They appeared, with an astonishing similarity in their organizational designs, between the late 1960s and early 1980s in the United States, Germany, and Denmark. Separated networks of public participation professionals (all centered on core organizations and led by individual entrepreneurs) interested in promoting such designs started to push them beyond their initial application contexts. As a result, this trio of citizen panels began to share application contexts and certain deliberation issues, and, over time, became accepted as a standard option for policymaking (Amelung, 2012). Diverse other actors, such as the media and policymakers advocating citizen panels, helped to expand them as a kind of global "bestseller" that became established across different geographical, jurisdictional, and policy field contexts, with some degree of rivalry and competition among the various suppliers. Hence, concomitant with the proliferation of citizen panels were a diversity and plurality of implementations of the format, which prevented its clear recognition as a unified global standard. However, under umbrella designations such as citizen panels, the model and its variations became established in the toolbox of public engagement instruments in diverse destinations around the globe. More recently, we find a fragmented landscape of multiple adaptations and hybrids of citizen panels in practice and loosely linked networks of public participation advocates centered on their respective agendas.

The case of citizen panels examined here offers interesting insights into the diversity of actors shaping the innovation path of citizen panels constituted by distributed agency. Advocates develop, establish, expand, and maintain citizen panels in gradually promoting a one-size-fits-all solution. However, the ambiguities of de-contextualized (abstracted) models tend to interfere with the instruments' implementation in new destinations.

The chapter includes five sections. First, we begin by introducing our notion of public participation advocates promoting public engagement instruments. Second, we develop an analytical framework to study in particular the processes of the emergent transnational mobility and spread of the instruments, inspired by (transnational) diffusion studies. Third, we present our case study of citizen panels by following a heuristic of transnational diffusion (Drori, Höllerer & Walgenbach, 2014), which distinguishes the sequences of abstraction through theorization, the construction of equivalency across contexts, adoption and local enactment of the "global" model, and the rebound of locally enacted ideas onto the theorized templates for selected episodes of transnational spread. Fourth, we discuss the dedicated practices of instrument advocates that are required for transnational spread, and, finally, we conclude by noting the ambivalences of the standardization of public participation instruments.

Public Participation Advocates Promoting Public Engagement Instruments and the Emergence of "Universal Bestsellers"

Public participation advocates' contributions can enable their respective public participation models to become successfully established across single contexts and then potentially turn into "universal bestsellers." The global travel of public participation instruments has become a growing phenomenon in the past few decades (Ganuza & Baiocchi, 2012; Soneryd, 2008). Citizen panels (Amelung, 2012) have expanded around the world and have become part of the toolbox of public participation. We understand the institutionalization of such an apparently "one-model-fits-all-contexts" solution of public participation as standardization. We do not assume that actors necessarily pursue a global expansion of the model in a purposeful, strategic manner. Rather, we assume that dedicated practices, in a distributed manner, shape an instrument in a way that encourages its travel, under certain conditions, around the world. Generally, the travel of instruments does not result in identical reproductions but rather produces design variations with every local implementation and thus in fact results in a multiplicity of locally contextualized versions of the instrument.

Previous studies have identified several critical issues associated with these developments. The development of ready-made designs, which can become mobile, de-contextualized from their original context, translated and re-contextualized in new settings, is accompanied by changing meanings beyond the control of the initiating public participation professionals (Soneryd & Amelung, 2016). Another issue is related to the standardization and theorization of knowledge about methods, which can lead to a technocratic manner of interpreting public engagement instruments (Voß & Amelung, 2016). A third concern is the increasingly professionalized "deliberative industry" (Saretzki, 2008) involved in promoting public participation instruments, as these professionals may sometimes follow their own self-sustaining professional interests rather than contributing to authentic public participation.

We begin here by focusing on public engagement instruments while following social constructivist approaches regarding policy instruments. Such approaches suggest that the ideational or cognitive existence of policy instruments—imagined as abstract models and configured in instrument designs—cannot be separated from the social activities that mobilize them in their implementations (Voß, 2007a, 2007b). Public engagement instruments in that sense are assumed to have a life of their own. The process that leads to the making of instruments resulting in the development, proliferation, and establishment of public engagement instruments is based on the distributed agency of actors. Such a perspective—as illustrated elsewhere with an alternative example of the policy instrument of emissions trading—demonstrates the heterogeneous practices that constitute an instrument: "Scientific theory building, data production and publishing, political issue framing, agenda setting, coalition building, business development, marketing and lobbying, management of innovation networks, professional organization" (Voß & Simons, 2014, p. 3). However, there exists a wide diversity of "what" and "why" actors related to a public engagement instrument due to the multiplicity of their beliefs, promises, and interests related to the establishment of the instrument.

However, few studies have used specific public participation instruments as the entry point for systematically investigating how instruments are developed and made mobile, and by what type of actors, and for examining what kinds of distributed dedicated practices are employed to promote the instrument (but see for instance Ganuza & Baiocchi, 2012). The study of the complex dynamics of such instruments' establishment and travel reveals how these instruments are developed and shaped by epistemic communities of public participation professionals united by their shared knowledge about the instruments, such as public participation practitioners, scientific experts, and decision makers (Chilvers, 2008), but also by actors that might not belong to the community of public participation professionals. By introducing the idea of "public participation advocates," we intend to focus on these actors' dedicated working practices that contribute to the establishment and transnational spread of the instruments. This perspective will help to clarify the boundaries of what can be understood as the community or field of public participation professionals (see the introduction to this book) and to widen the scope in order to integrate those actors who are outside of this field. This includes those who do not share a common understanding of the purpose and specific rules of the field, but still help to promote the instrument. These actors might only serve as occasional advocates for an instrument, and their profession and expertise may not be narrowly linked to public participation. This wider approach will allow us to specify the role of, for instance, some sponsors, potentially the media, and even critics in the proliferation of public engagement instruments.

In this chapter, we follow the dynamics of heterogeneous dedicated practices that initially involve the mobilization of instruments in an iterative process that fosters these instruments' travel across organizations, across sectors, across regions, and across countries. Then, over time, there occurs a transnational spread and standardization of public engagement instruments. The following section introduces an analytical search heuristic to study the iterative processes of instrument mobilization alternating between abstractions and implementations of the instrument. This heuristic helps us to empirically identify the dedicated practices that favour, in a distributed and accumulative manner, the transnational spread and standardization of public engagement instruments.

Studying the Processes of Transnational Mobility and Diffusion of Public Engagement Instruments

The specific historical innovation journey of the case of citizen panels has been studied with respect to the mobility of knowledge from its origin up to its present form. Voß and Amelung (2016) reconstruct the complex historical evolution of citizen panels over time and consider that the development of citizen panels has reached a phase characterized by an increased production and circulation of knowledge about citizen panels and growing standardization of the models. For the purposes of this chapter, we briefly re-examine and simplify the complex and differentiated narrative of the entire history of the development of citizen panels by deconstructing it into selected episodes and smaller sequences and by reconstructing repeating patterns. We "zoom into" the process of the historical expansion of citizen panels over decades to focus on single transnational moves of the instrument across regions, and sometimes also across sectors or organizations.

In organization studies, recent research explores how ideas and models move across different levels, or across entities on the same level, or over time in a globalized world. Suggested dynamic patterns of diffusion (Strang & Meyer, 1993), which complement conceptual contributions from the sociology of knowledge, have been mobilized for the case of citizen panels by Voß and Amelung (2016). Abstraction through theorization, theorization and its ontological role of interpreting, projecting, and constructing social reality, the crucial role of experts as "legitimated theorists," and the influences of global models and bottom-up theorizing are key components in these concepts (Drori et al., 2014, pp. 9–11). "Global" and "local" are not assumed to be static categories, but are defined in relation to each other: "global and local are mutually constitutive: the so-called global is a collage of local practices, behaviors, and tastes, while the so-called local is increasingly constructed within the scripts drafted by global forces" (Drori et al., 2014, p. 5). Inspired by these ideas, we imagine the process of the transnational mobilization of public participation instruments, across regions, across organizations, and sometimes across sectors, in iterative loops. For the presentation of our case study, we draw on the chronology of four phases outlined in Drori et al. (2014, pp. 10–11): (1) abstraction through theorization, (2) construction of equivalency across boundaries, (3) adoption and enactment of the more "globally" theorized model, and (4) a rebound of the locally adapted and enacted model. We mobilize these patterns in order to match them with the characteristics of the dedicated practices of public participation advocates, which together contribute to the spread of public engagement instruments and, specifically in our case, of citizen panels.

Policy instruments have been conceptualized according to a general distinction between instrument design (or model) on the one hand and implementation on the other, taking into account that both dimensions of policy instruments are multi-related (Voß, 2007a, 2007b). Hence, their analytical distinction corresponds with our presentation of the different sequences in the mobilization loops. While enactment and adoption relate to the instrument's concrete implementation, the other three sequences relate to design or model considerations regarding the public engagement instrument. Abstraction through theorization means that an idea or model—for our purposes, a PC or CJ or CC—gets abstracted from being a particular problem-solution to a typified problem-solution. In order to move horizontally across transnational regions, and, potentially, sectors or organizations, equivalency across boundaries on a more macro level has to be constructed by identifying similarities and commonalities between entities or contexts. A more "globally" theorized idea or model then gets adopted and locally enacted through translation, adaptation, re-contextualization, or modification to fit the local context. In a subsequent phase, rebound effects from locally enacted models onto the theorized model may occur. These processes of local-global-intersected spread take place continuously like a spiral along the innovation process of citizen panels. In that sense, the instrument is in a constant state of flux. If one zooms out again from single moves, one can imagine the development as a continuous spiral, as repeating loops of de-contextualizations and re-contextualizations, which increase the layers of abstraction over time. These continuously repeating loops of de-contextualization and re-contextualization and the related practices take different shapes depending on whether they spread across organizations, sectors, or regions. We have chosen such a focus in order to understand the global dimension of standardization across substantially different contexts.

In our research, we collected data from various sources, including secondary and primary literature (such as documentation on citizen panel implementations, manuals, handbooks, and policy reports; information received from interviewees and from an archive on the work of the German academic who created PCs, Peter Dienel; as well as data from the Internet). We used transcripts from five semi-structured expert interviews with academics, practitioners, and consultants. In the related project, we conducted 30 interviews. Interviewees were selected according to the criteria of their being personally involved in working or having worked with (one of) the designs and of their work covering different time periods, geographical areas, and actor types. Interviewees were asked to describe the social life of citizen panels, their dedicated work, some of their reasons for using this design, and their understanding of the instrument. In order to analyze these materials, we developed conceptual propositions on various patterns and dynamics of instrument spread. Through an iterative process of pattern matching and abductive reasoning, and adapting codes and categories to the data with the help of the ATLAS.ti program, we arrived at a stable interpretation. We also benefited from previous research on the case of citizen panels that took place within the Innovation in Governance Research Group at Technische Universität Berlin (Amelung, 2012; Amelung & Grabner, 2013a, 2013b; Mann, Voß, Amelung, Simons, Runge & Grabner, 2014; Voß & Amelung, 2016).

Sequences in the Transnational Spread of Citizen Panels (Case Study)

In this section, we present selected episodes of transnational spread for each of the three instruments—the CJ, PC, and CC. We reconstruct the transnational spread in terms of global-local oscillation, that is, continuous linkages between local enactments and abstract conceptualizations of the instruments. For each instrument, we identify the different sequences that together constitute loops of mobility according to our search heuristic with four sequences, as described above. These sequences are carried out through diverse practices of the actors involved, which contribute to the mobility and spread of the instruments. In the selected episodes, we look at single loops in the case of each instrument, with a focus on initial shifts from one country to another and later rebounds onto the abstracted model of the instrument. In order to investigate the complex dynamics of transnational standardization, we identified sequences that took place in the initial phases of instrument development, whereas the rebound dynamics are taken from later stages in order to demonstrate the characteristic differences in rebound variations. We chose across-country shifts which were recognized in the literature as either "successes" (in the sense of effective reproductions of the instrument) or "failures" of transfers (for various reasons). The selected episodes follow the shifts, for the CJ, from the US to the UK; for the PC, from Germany to Spain and the US; and for the CC, from Denmark to the UK and Chile. The analysis results in the discussion of various exemplified patterns of the actors' dedicated practices of mobilization and transnational transfer of the instruments.

Abstraction through Theorization

As the first of the four sequences, abstraction through theorization emerged in a rather bottom-up way, deriving from tests and experiments with single implementations of the CJ, PC, and CC. In processes involving the gradual systematizing of knowledge and the explicating of the functions and promises of the instrument, models were created that became packaged in narratives and documented in publications. These packaged and edited ideas could thus begin to travel.

Citizens' Jury

The US-based political scientist Ned Crosby developed the CJ process in 1971 while writing a doctoral dissertation on social ethics.[2] The initial purpose was to create a process to enable citizens to discuss a public policy matter or to evaluate political candidates. Crosby founded the Jefferson Center in 1974, a non-profit organization located in Minneapolis, and conducted several local implementations, which were thoroughly evaluated in reports and documentation (Center for New Democratic Processes, 1986; Crosby, 1974). From 1974 to the mid-1980s, the fundamental principles of the CJ process were continuously tested and refined. Out of evaluations and reflections on implementations in heterogeneous settings, abstracted formulations of the model were derived. In 1995, Crosby outlined an abstracted template of the CJ procedure—with theoretical-normative accounts of deliberative democracy based on his own empirical experience—for a larger audience, which he saw as "one solution for difficult environmental problems," "to study specific public policy issues or to review candidates in an election" (Crosby, 1995).

Planning Cell

The German sociologist Peter Dienel developed a first draft of the PC model in 1969 when he was a member of the planning staff of the North Rhine-Westphalia state chancellery (Dienel, P.C., 1969). He created the process in order to enable citizen participation in planning processes (Dienel, P.C., 1980). Dienel sought to improve citizens' participation by creating techniques that encourage citizens' involvement in planning processes and that are compatible with the existing system of representative democracy (Interview # 1). Dienel released his approach by name for the first time in 1971, as the contextual framing of activating citizens towards planning issues found expression in the procedure's naming: the planning cell (German: "Planungszelle") (cp. Vergne, 2010, p. 3). Like the CJ, the PC model was theorized in publications during the 1970s and the following two decades (Dienel, P.C. & Renn, 1995). The design was refined and standardized in order to make it implementable for a wide range of issues and to circulate it as a concrete solution for planning processes: "To keep this technique replicable, the size of the group should be standardized. It seems favorable to have around 25 persons in each Planning Cell" (Dienel, P. C., 1980, p. 4).

Consensus Conference

In the late 1980s, the CC was initiated as a procedure for involving citizens in the assessment of science and technology policy in Denmark.[3] In 1986, the Danish Board of Technology (DBT) was established as a public body to assist the Danish parliament. The subsequently appointed first general secretary, Bo Carstens, in coalition with a social scientists' initiative (Reynolds, Soneryd & Szerszynski, 2008, p. 18), introduced and promoted the CC as a new approach for participatory technology assessment. According to Reynolds et al. (2008, p. 19), for the institutionalized use of the model in Denmark, "it mattered that the Technology Board was established . . . and that there were politicians interested in technology issues." In its first years, the DBT conducted 22 CCs in Denmark, on various environmental and technological policy issues (Andersen & Jæger, 1999, p. 334). The CC came to be characterized as a unique standard and problem-solving instrument that produces outcomes regardless of local conditions:

> There was a tendency in a [certain] period that [the] consensus conference was seen as a one-size-fits-all method. . . . But the fantastic thing with the consensus conference, which I think is a reason for that is, it's such a clear method. It's really a project in itself. . . . everything is really neatly laid out,

and I think that's, in that way it's a superb method. I cannot point ... [to] any
other method, which is as well guided from the start to the end.

(Interview # 2)

In sum, in these historically slightly different phases, practices of theorization and
abstraction shaped the very early stage of the instruments' development, carried
out by the pioneers of the instruments, their respective organizations, and supportive communities. In the specific cases, applied research-oriented academics
and staff from a parliamentary technology board developed independent, universalized rationales for each of the three models. "Inventors" systematized their
knowledge in order to match the model with suitable conditions for replication elsewhere. Publications and documentation with abstract descriptions of
the model made it possible to transport a typified problem-solution to various
contexts. Although all three instruments originated from independent contexts
and for different purposes (civic education, participatory planning, participatory
technology assessment), it is interesting how the models resembled one another
from the very beginning in regard to their key design features (externally provided expertise to inform citizen participants about the issue at stake, small group
deliberations to develop and exchange informed opinions, and final reports summarizing the results of the participants' discussion).

Construction of Equivalency across Boundaries and Entities

The exploration of equivalent conditions, in terms of both the context and design
principles, was a crucial step in finding corresponding situations that enabled
the models' transnational movement beyond their inventors' communities and
countries of origin. Constructing equivalency across situations and contexts was
empirically associated with various practices. Correspondence was determined by
theoretical considerations of the design principles. Storing and circulating design
knowledge was therefore a necessary precondition. Another relevant practice
established equivalence through the evaluation, classification, and appropriation
of problems and solutions or application contexts. Academic and practitioner networks, together with political allies, explored similarities and differences across
national boundaries.

Citizens' Jury

Dedicated practices of testing and displaying equivalence by newly evolving advocates are well documented for the CJ's travel from the US to the UK (Coote &
Lenaghan, 1997; Stewart, Kendall & Coote, 1994). In the early 1990s, the Institute
of Public Policy Research (IPPR) in the UK, a think tank dedicated to public
education, conducted a systematic theoretical comparison of the American CJ
model with the somewhat similar German PC and produced a compact synthesis

design of both approaches, with Ned Crosby and Peter Dienel as consultants (Stewart et al., 1994, p. 11). Equivalence became established through a systematic elaboration of the similarities and differences, as one of the protagonists at the IPPR, involved in the initial uptake of the model in the UK (Interview # 3), reports:

> What happened was that it was really something that was in the air; people were using the term, you know, "perhaps we should start thinking about citizens' juries", and when I started asking and said, "well what are they?", nobody knew the answer. . . . So we decided that we would do some research and see where it had come from, and we sent researchers out to the United States and to Germany to Peter Dienel and to the Jefferson Center.

The aim of the resulting publication, "Citizens' Juries: Theory into Practice," was to turn its title into a program. It described the UK model as "being developed to suit the particular conditions and expectations of the UK" (Coote & Lenaghan, 1997, p. 14). The IPPR's comparative investigation and reconstruction work formed the foundation for the subsequent spread of this model across the UK. However, while the personal conduits were striking, focal publications not only (theoretically) substantiated but also catalyzed activities to prepare for the construction of equivalence. The particular cases of the CJ and PC are intriguing, since dedicated efforts to construct equivalence across national or local boundaries increased after the IPPR's initiative. Dienel and Crosby, as the models' central advocates, first met in person in 1987 and started to reference each other's work and to act as advisors on the work of each other's centres (Crosby, 1995, 2007). In 1995, the PC and CJ were first internationally evaluated in an academic publication in direct comparison with one another, as equivalent models of citizen participation (Renn, Webler & Wiedemann, 1995).

Planning Cell

While the transnational transfer of the CJ to the UK was inspired by a systematic and theoretically sound evaluation of the US version of the CJ and the German PC, another pattern of extrapolating similarities emerged from the case of the diffusion of the PC model from Germany to the Basque region of Spain.[4] The case reveals an approach of creating equivalence between situational local problems and the model's appropriateness in terms of the solution it represents. Conflicts in the form of public protests regarding specific urban and rural planning projects in the Basque region of Spain triggered the exploration of the PC as a potential solution that could be used to overcome these obstacles. As "something with mediation and citizen decision" (Interview # 4), the PC was considered as a potential platform that would help to create understanding in the face of conflicting positions. A connection occurred due to a rather general comparison of problems in planning processes in the Basque region and the German region of North Rhine-Westphalia. Some of the driving forces in the Spanish case were local mayors and academics, who attempted to prevent the escalation of local conflict by looking for solutions in order to tackle the issues involved:

> and during their meeting also this question evolved, mediation and appease-ment of those decision processes . . . And this ombudsman said, it's an inter-esting story, we should have a closer look. We may invite this professor from Wuppertal, he should explain that in detail. And I already had been in con-tact with Jürgen Brand, who is a friend of mine, and told him to send me some information about the planning cell. . . . And then we somewhat cir-culated this here and informed the ombudsman and then we invited Dienel.
>
> *(Interview # 4)*

Hence, taking the diverse political situations in both regions into account, and in particular regarding the confrontation with an armed separatist organization in the Basque region, the construction of equivalence with the application context of the PC in the German region remains somewhat surprising. In this case, a for-mer student of the University of Wuppertal, Hans Harms, at that time employed by the University of San Sebastian, introduced the idea of the PC. Later, Dienel was invited to explore, together with the local interested parties (mainly local mayors and regional politicians), the compatibility of the PC with the specific conditions in the Basque country and the use of the PC in already highly politi-cized controversies (Font & Medina, 2001, p. 156, 2007).

Consensus Conference

The CC model spread outside Denmark due to its strong affiliation with an aca-demic community interested in evaluating European experiences of participatory technology assessment practices (Joss & Durant, 1995b). The CC model was also typified from a research perspective through comparisons of different local imple-mentations of the template in the early 1990s, as one exemplary advocate for the model states: "I did a comparison back in my PhD, a comparison of Dutch and Danish CCs" (Interview # 5). The model gained momentum in its transnational spread when its functional equivalence with contextual refinements adapted to new local settings began to be tested:

> after a period of several years the Danish experience began to attract interest elsewhere. Over the past few years, other observers have begun to explore the possibility of adapting the Danish model to suit different institutional and cultural contexts. The transferability of the consensus conference model is an important and interesting question in its own right.
>
> *(Joss & Durant, 1995b, p. 10)*

However, the transfer of the model to the UK was closely tied to the "public understanding of science" movement, which involved linkages between academic, political, and non-governmental organizations. The movement accelerated the diffusion of the CC model when the associated actors jointly engaged in determining the model's appropriateness:

> of course [the] UK differs from other European countries. . . . one important step . . . was that public understanding of science movement . . . so you have lots of policy makers, academics, scientists engaging in public understanding of science, the science museums and so on; and as a result of that increasing research capacity [was] being built up; they . . . [went] about critiquing some of the assumptions of the public understanding of science, as a result of which it turned, it got refined but also it prepared the ground for an alternative . . . such as consensus conferences.
>
> *(Interview # 5)*

The construction of equivalence was also facilitated due to the organizational embedding of the DBT and the flow of knowledge across European networks of technology boards closely linked to parliaments. As a consequence, a British parliamentary delegation travelled to Denmark to observe the practices carried out by the DBT and examined to what degree the Danish circumstances applied in the UK; it concluded that the model is the "only form of public consultation designed specifically to deal with technological and scientific issues" (House of Lords Select Committee on Science and Technology, 2000):

> during our visit to Denmark . . . [t]he DBT emphasized that different methods were suitable for different issues and different stages of technological debates. In some cases it was best to consult the public; in others, meetings involving scientific experts were more appropriate. Another important consideration was that the results of the DBT's work, including consensus conferences, were made available for the Danish Parliament to use as it saw fit. The DBT does not act as an arbiter, and its work with the public was not seen as "direct democracy", in the sense of abdicating responsibility for decisions to some kind of popular vote.
>
> *(House of Lords Select Committee on Science and Technology, 2000,*
> *chapter 5.23)*

In sum, equivalence could only be constructed based on circulating knowledge about the models and the contexts of their origins and connecting this knowledge with demands in different local contexts—which was often facilitated by organizations such as the IPPR or networks such as the European technology assessment networks that had the necessary resources and communication channels for this. Equivalence was then established by theoretical elaboration on the similarities and differences between the functions and features of the various models, as well as by understanding their particular characteristics in order to deconstruct and reconstruct them. Yet the different forms of constructing equivalence implied further editing and packaging towards the end of creating universal and standardized models, stripped of their "localness." These practices involved new actors beyond those in the initial application contexts: either actors motivated by their specific need to find and apply appropriate instruments for specific application contexts or actors driven by a more analytical interest to explore the participatory capacity of the instruments in order to test and transfer them more generally to a different country context.

Adoption and Enactment of the "Global" Model

While our illustrations of pertinent circulation and evaluation practices have shown how equivalence was constructed and maintained, the aim of this sequence is to delineate patterns of adoption and local enactment of the universalized, and then systematized and tested, models in different countries. The transnational spread of these models' implementations has been accompanied by their increased institutionalization. We will now follow the abstracted models' re-contextualization and de-contextualization, beyond their initial institutionalization, in new destinations.

Citizens' Jury

In the UK, the nationwide implementation of the adapted CJ version during the 1990s was initiated with the first five pilot CJ projects that were carried out and promoted by an alliance of actors including the IPPR, the Anglo-German Foundation, and the London Local Government Management Board. The UK King's Fund then organized and funded three more CJ projects in the domain of health care (McIver, 1998). Facilitation practices were accompanied by design variations. In the UK, the CJ model was often installed as a singular event instead of allowing for a set of iterated and parallel CJ implementations, which were more common in the US version (Davies, Wetherell & Barnett, 2006, p. 44). This and other variations in design became replicated and led to a new de facto standard in the UK context, distinct from the initial US model (which had even been formally fixed and standardized by a trademark in the meantime). The massive reproduction of the universal model in the UK led to further adoption dynamics, creating various adaptations of the model. Accordingly, the CJ model was widely implemented for various application instances and on several scales during the 1990s. By the beginning of the 2000s, more than 100 CJ projects had already taken place in the UK (Wakeford, 2002)—in the areas of waste disposal, education, genetic engineering, and more (Aldred & Jacobs, 2000; Dunkerley & Glasner, 1998). From the initial adoptions onwards, the growing interest in participatory models in the UK attracted new actors, including market research firms and consultants, the media, and political advocates. The model's uptake gained political support with Tony Blair and Gordon Brown, who referred to citizens' juries as a key tool of a "new type of politics" (BBC, 2007), in order to face the legitimacy problems encountered by government policies. The commissioning bodies included governmental bodies, health authorities, and NGOs (Joss & Durant, 1995a; Wakeford, Singh, Murtuja, Bryant & Pimbert, 2007, p. 334). However, the widespread enactment of the model also provoked critical debates. Consultants and market research firms using the CJ model have been severely criticized for triggering commercialization, dilution, and manipulation effects (Wakeford & Singh, 2008; Wakeford et al., 2007). In sum, a constellation of diverse advocates, such as consultants, think tanks, researchers in coalition with political advocates, and the media, promoted the adoption and enactment of the "globally" theorized model in the UK with their dedicated practices.

Planning Cell

In Spain, the evaluation and systematization of the planning cell as an appropriate problem-solution led to several implementations that have been discussed in evaluative reports (Dienel, P. C. & Harms, 2000; Font, 1996; Harms, 2000, 2005, 2007). The practitioners' experiences, elaborated on by academic reflections in publications, promoted the further transnational diffusion of the model. Simultaneously, local adoptions were dynamic processes involving contingent assets, such as the model's attribution with new qualities and local functions. In Spain, the PC became linked with the notion of democratic competence and civic education (Font, 1996, p. 148).

However, the inherent standardization features of abstract, (re)formulated umbrella templates of instruments can have ambivalent effects. While the typified templates (for example, reified in handbooks or policy guidelines) facilitate interaction among heterogeneous networks through mutual reference, the instrumental nature of the standardized template may impede local uptake, as an early adoption experiment in the US illustrates. Commissioned as the first PC project outside of Germany (in 1988) by the Department of Environmental Protection of New Jersey[5] and by protagonists of Dienel's PC network, the replication of the procedure in a different cultural and political context failed. Participants opposed the prescribed and externally imposed procedure, excluded the organizing researchers, and instead initiated a self-organized process to articulate a public statement (Dienel, P. C. & Renn, 1995, p. 135; Renn, Webler, Rakel, Dienel, P. C. & Johnson, 1993, pp. 204–208).

In sum, these adoption examples illustrate that creating abstracted models is not the only precondition for their "successful" dissemination. Adoption and implementation practices also require translations in order to relate the universal model to specific local conditions. This kind of appropriation work is most often done by local practitioners familiar with the specific implementation context (as was the case in Spain) and able to facilitate the models' implementation as an interpretation of the universal model that suits local demands.

Consensus Conference

The CC quickly spread within Europe and beyond. It particularly attracted the interest of academics and practitioners in the technology assessment community and came to be emulated as an established design by the beginning of the 1990s (Joss & Durant, 1995b). The first CC in the UK, held in 1994 on the subject of plant biotechnology, was organized by the Biotechnology and Biological Sciences Research Council (BBSRC) and the London Science Museum. The local uptake of the CC model in the UK became a remarkable multiplier for the further enactment and global spread of this model (Durant, 1995).

Another example of a failed implementation once again demonstrates the relevance of local sense making of universal models. We learn from Ureta's (2016) recent study of a CC on the management of patients' personal health records in Chile in 2003 about the locked-in side effects of standardization. Although the instrument gained substantial institutional support from Chilean state authorities, including the Chilean Ministry of Health, the Chilean Congress, and the National Council for Science and Technology, the adoption failed to manifest its democratic value. A representative of the DBT with the mandate to safeguard quality criteria during the organization and conduct of the CC insisted on the local adoption of the model in accordance with the DBT's standards: "No digression was accepted" (Ureta, 2016). Although the model was applied "correctly," it failed to produce the expected outcomes due to an overly rigid interpretation of standards, which did not leave any room for situational and culturally sensitive alterations (Ureta, 2016, p. 12).

In sum, a broad range of diverse advocates, such as consultants, think tanks, and researchers in support of political allies, and their dedicated facilitation, lobbying, and sponsoring practices promoted the adoption and enactment of the universally theorized models. The examples of all three instruments point to the adaptations required in order to adjust the ideas and structure of the model to new and different social and cultural contexts.

Rebound of Locally Enacted Ideas and Models onto the Theorized Templates

While the previous depiction of various sequences in the oscillating spiral of local-global dissemination of the models dealt with patterns of abstraction, equivalence composition, and enactment of typified versions of the models, we now complete the spiral with a description of the "rebound dynamics" for selected episodes of transnational spread. Different practices are examined that illustrate three different patterns of rebound from local adaptations onto the abstracted models.

Citizens' Jury

The relocation and re-contextualization of abstracted templates of citizens' juries in the UK were permanently accompanied by further evaluations and implementation and provoked counter developments and corrective normative maintenance of the model. The "do-it-yourself CJ" was developed in the early 2000s by Tom Wakeford and his colleagues from the Policy, Ethics and Life Sciences Centre at Newcastle University (PEALS) in the UK and explicitly opposed the state-led citizens' juries (Soneryd & Amelung, 2016). The inventors in this case emphasized normative principles of inclusion and empowerment. As a critical reaction to the CJ model that prevailed in the UK, academic efforts to refine the design led to the formulation of quality criteria for the CJ. Wakeford and colleagues offered the alternative design as a response to the recognized threat of a funding trap (Wakeford, 2002) and to the discontent with a perceived instrumentalization of the model by politics and with the methodological inadequacies of the CJ: "The element of the methodology I sought to improve was how as wide and inclusive a range of people [as possible] could set the subject of the jury's discussion" (Wakeford, 2012, p. 4). In the DIY version of the CJ, participants set the agenda of deliberations and choose the witnesses themselves. Also, the jury members compile the final report with recommendations. This splintering off from prevailing implementation practice in the UK as a rebound dynamic differentiated the landscape of available versions. Critical scholars and practitioners diverged from the original model as a countermovement seeking to preserve particular normative functions of the instrument, which represents one type of rebound onto the generalized model of the CJ.

Planning Cell

Other types of rebound are associated with specific constellations of actors and their dedicated practices. In the case of the PC, certain rebound effects became obvious because of regulation practices and networking activities. As a reaction to the increasingly occurring variations of PC implementations, the core network of PC practitioners in Germany began to harmonize their practices in order to create a meta-standardization that was intended to increase and maintain the legitimacy and credibility of the PC instrument. Already at an early stage, Dienel had endeavoured to establish a community around the German research centre for citizen participation and planning procedures at the University of Wuppertal.[6] A rebound effect of ongoing global-local iterations was manifested when PC experts developed and negotiated quality criteria to regulate the diversity of practices (Trütken, 2005). In 2007, the German protagonists that were implementing PCs came together to establish a network[7] in order to share their experiences in enacting the instrument, to develop joint quality standards, and to install them as a code of conduct. In 2008, a working group at Friedrich-Ebert Foundation brought PC practitioners together to advance the development of joint quality standards (Dienel, H.L., Vergne, Franzl, Fuhrmann & Lietzmann, 2014). Annual network conventions and networking activities with strategic allies (foundations, public administration bodies) functioned as platforms for the exchange of knowledge on how to implement the quality criteria. We qualify this enhancement as a meta-standardization, as a specific rebound effect, and as another rebound pattern.

Consensus Conference

Finally, the more recent globalization of the CC reveals a third pattern of rebound effects. While the CC came to be adopted, modified, and (re-)contextualized transnationally over time by different actors and their dedicated practices, the pioneering Danish organization, the DBT, remained the focal actor promoting a specific pattern of transnational spread. Unlike the pioneering advocates of the CJ and the PC, the DBT fostered the hybridization of the model for the purpose of implementing citizen engagement procedures on a European or worldwide scale. On an international level, the World Wide Views (WWV) (Blue & Medlock, 2014; Bovenkerk & Brom, 2012) are an example of the diffusion of a hybrid version of the CC model. The DBT, with its specific and longstanding design tradition, itself became the carrier of rebound effects. Informed by diverse global implementation practices and being embedded in a European technology assessment community, the DBT co-created a considerable number of European and international deliberation experiments. The WWV method, which was developed as a reconstruction of various models—the DBT refers for instance to deliberative polling, the citizen summit, the voting conference, and the CC—shows how hybridization, that is, the recompiling of model components in order to brand an "innovative" model designed to enter a new application context, represents a third type of rebound effect that can have a tremendous influence on the transnational diffusion of the model.

In sum, rebound dynamics, as a final sequence in the loop, are characterized by reflections on prevailing adoptions and by some actors' ambitions to change and direct those adoptions towards their own purposes, which result in specific modifications of the universal model for the instruments.

Discussion

In our case study of selected episodes of transnational spread of the CJ, PC, and CC, we followed specific sequential patterns, which in reality create a multiplicity of loops, resulting in the instruments being in a constant state of flux. The selected episodes focused on single loops for each instrument's development and demonstrated specific practices of mobilizations and transfers of the instruments. We identified dedicated practices carried out by the actors involved according to the specific dynamics of the transnational spread and standardization of the public engagement instruments. Although our selected episodes are to some degree exemplary, interesting patterns can be detected which should be tested on other cases for further verification.

We can summarize our main findings according to the four sequences of the mobilization loop. In our empirical study, it became obvious that different actors were not exclusively involved in single sequences. Rather, their involvement often became relevant across several sequences. In terms of the first sequence, "practices of theorizing" here does not so much mean academic theorizing alone, but also refers to the systematization of knowledge. The three instruments studied here developed from individual entrepreneurs (Ned Crosby, Peter Dienel, and Bo Carstens) embedded in organizations such as a think tank (Jefferson Center), a university department (FBPUW), and a parliamentary technology board (DBT), which provided the environment for bottom-up *theorizing and consolidation* of the models based on initial experiments and tests. Regarding the sequence of constructing equivalency across entities, we identify practices of *storing and circulating instrument know-how* and stories as well as practices of *classification and categorization* in order to pinpoint similarities. Personal, academic, and professional networks and focal publications facilitated, not only theoretically, but often through practical implementation reports or manuals, such as the IPPR's publications, and further systematization of the instruments by clarifying their functions, values, and purposes. Similarities in the cases studied were constructed across situational requirements (PCs), across models (CJs), or across organizational portfolios of parliamentary technology assessment institutions (CCs). Regarding the sequence of enactment and adoption, adoption successes and failures of transfers across countries were studied. The wide range of actors involved in refining the instruments throughout the course of the various implementations can be linked to practices of *facilitating and consulting* (academics and practitioners), practices of *governing and regulation* (mayors in the Basque country in the case of the PC), and practices of *public and political advocacy* (the British Parliament in the case of the CC; the BBC and British political leaders in the case of the CJ). As effects of standardization, extreme examples demonstrated the problems that resulted from transferring and re-contextualizing abstract models without embedding them in the specific local contexts (as shown in the transfer of the PC to the US, and in the transfer of the CC to Chile).

We identified three different patterns of rebound from local enactments as a final feedback on the development of the model (to complete a single loop): enhancement (PC), differentiation (CJ), and hybridization (CC). They serve as single examples, not as a comprehensive collection of potential rebound types. *Enhancement* took place when the core instrument advocates maintained the original model but established quality criteria in order to optimize it or to prevent it from dilution, and to gain legitimacy. *Differentiation* refers to the separation of a new version from the original model as a spin-off in order to preserve or expose particular functions of the public engagement instrument. The contestation of critics (academics in the case of the DIY CJ) resulted in the creation of a new specified design. *Hybridization* here means reassembling model components—potentially also as rebounds from other models—in order to brand an "innovative" model designed to enter a new application context. Although the three patterns have in common the fact that the actors involved in the rebound sequence were those who assume ownership and responsibility in designing, shaping, and promoting specific models, they differ in regard to the specific effects that they have on the instrument. The pattern of enhancement is intended to protect and improve the model and thereby manifests the universalization of models in order to establish superior models. The patterns of hybridization and differentiation reinforce the dynamics of the diversification of instruments. While differentiation in the example discussed was a reaction to the previous "misuse" of the CJ instrument, hybridization in the example of the WWV emerged with the motif of creating an innovation to shape a new arena for public engagement.

Standardization—understood here as various forms of institutionalization—involves dynamics of isomorphism and diversification, due to distributed agency, which results in a multiplicity of various independent developments. In the cases studied, individuals and specific organizations working in the contexts of applied sciences, consulting, and parliamentary technology assessment that act as entrepreneurs to establish their respective design schools played a central role. However, political advocates and the media also performed a critical role in fostering the popularity of the instruments. Interestingly, critics also contributed to the further institutionalization of diverse forms of citizen panels. Over time, the instruments disengaged from their dedicated areas of application and subsequently became subsumed under the umbrella term of citizen panels.

Conclusions

This chapter offers an empirically oriented, constructivist approach to the dedicated practices of actors in the field of public engagement advocating for specific instruments and enabling their transnational diffusion. We have therefore prioritized the identification of specific practices relevant to transnational diffusion and have left as an empirical question the identification of the specific actors associated with these practices. We assume that, in other cases, different types of actors may be relevant. When new instruments are developed and "design schools" become established around specific inventors (as analyzed in the first two sequences), we can speak of communities of public participation professionals that dedicate their professional lives to promoting and spreading specific designs. Although the respective communities of public participation professionals might still influence some destinations, the instruments' uptake is beyond their control. Paradoxically, as soon as these models become mobile, are enacted in new contexts, and to a certain extent contribute to the standardization of public engagement instruments, diverse forms of fragmentation occur. Fragmentation becomes visible with regard to the *coherence of instrument designs*—as demonstrated in the various forms of failed transfers, but also in regard to the diverse types of rebounds—as well as in terms of the *actor networks* that advocate the instruments in their new destinations. Implementation, regulation, and lobbying practices are instead also carried out by new public participation professionals advocating the instrument permanently but also ad hoc after the instruments begin to travel. Shared beliefs and interests, which might still unite the initial "design schools," become diversified. In particular, ad hoc advocates such as political lobbyists or the media may use the instrument as a means to an end (for instance, to create a showcase for a specific policy strategy), which may strongly contradict the purposes of some permanent advocates such as certain practitioners and academics (for instance, embracing an instrument for commercial interests or to prove a specific theoretical claim). Hence, what unites these advocates are their diverse dedicated practices in promoting the instrument—although for different reasons—which result in the institutionalization and diversification of citizen panels. Notably, these practices cannot be coherently associated with specific actors' groups or communities. Thus, the investigation of the dedicated practices involved in promoting a packaged model in new contexts and making it a "universal bestseller" reveals the productive aspects as well as the constraining frictions at play and hence, the complex ambivalences of standardization.

Acknowledgments

The underlying project "Innovation in Governance" (grant number 01UU0906) from which the writing of this chapter derives was funded by the German Federal Ministry for Education and Research (BMBF). Responsibility for the contents of this chapter lies entirely with the authors. The authors would like to thank Dzifa Ametowobla, Linda Soneryd, Joan Font, Kostas Smagas, and Laurence Bherer and her colleagues for valuable comments on earlier versions of the chapter and Linda Soneryd for sharing an interview transcript with us. Furthermore, we are grateful to all our colleagues in the Innovation in Governance Research Group at TU Berlin, which laid the foundations for this study, and in particular we benefited from the work with Jan-Peter Voß, Carsten Mann, Arno Simons, and Thomas Crowe.

List of Interviews (anonymized)

Interview # 1: Interview with public participation advocate for PCs from Germany, 02-03-2010, conducted by Nina Amelung

Interview # 2: Interview with public participation advocate for CCs from Denmark, 27-03-2012, conducted by Nina Amelung

Interview # 3: Interview with public participation advocate for CJs from the United Kingdom, 10-03-2008, conducted by Linda Soneryd

Interview # 4: Interview with public participation advocate for PCs from Spain, 03-12-2010, conducted by Nina Amelung

Interview # 5: Interview with public participation advocate for CCs from the United Kingdom, 15-06-2012, conducted by Nina Amelung

Notes

1 The chosen framing of this study with the use of the term "citizen panels" has certain implications. Other umbrella terms have been used, such as mini-publics (Fung, 2006) or deliberative forums (Saward, 2003), to categorize the phenomenon of similarity across a specific set of different instruments. Deliberative polling is often mentioned in connection with the three instruments chosen here (Brown, 2006). After initially starting with a wider collection of instruments, we selected the three discussed here due to the stronger historical cross-referencing between them compared to other instruments.

2 According to Vergne (2010), Ned Crosby stated his thoughts in his 1973 (unpublished) doctoral dissertation *Concern for All*, written for his PhD at the University of Minnesota.

3 The model originated in the US, where it was frequently used by the National Institute of Health (NIH) as a tool for medical assessment, starting in 1977. The US CC model, however, was based on expert and stakeholder involvement and had been adopted in Denmark from 1983 onwards, followed by the formulation of a Danish lay panel version (Reynolds et al., 2008, p. 17ff.).

4 A comprehensive overview of the first Spanish PC experiences between 1992 and 1999 can be found in Font and Medina (2001, p. 157).

5 The objective of the project was to give the citizens of Hunterdon County, New Jersey, the opportunity to design the regulatory provisions for an experimental sludge application project on a university research farm located in Franklin Township in New Jersey (Renn et al., 1993, p. 204).

6 German: Forschungsstelle für Bürgerbeteiligung und Planungsverfahren an der Universität Wuppertal (FBPUW).

7 "Qualitätsnetz Bürgergutachten", formerly "Planungszellenprotagonisten".

References

Aldred, J., & Jacobs, M. (2000). Citizens and Wetlands: Evaluating the Ely citizens' jury. *Ecological Economics*, *34*(2), 217–232.

Amelung, N. (2012). The emergence of citizen panels as a de facto standard. *Quaderni*, (79), 13–28.

Amelung, N., & Grabner, L. (2013a). *Report on design controversies in the innovation of citizen panels*. Berlin: Technical University. Unpublished.

Amelung, N., & Grabner, L. (2013b). *Report on the constituency formation and dynamics in the innovation of citizen panels*. Berlin: Technical University. Unpublished.

Andersen, I. E., & Jæger, B. (1999). Scenario workshops and consensus conferences: Towards more democratic decision-making. *Science and Public Policy*, *26*(5), 331–340.

BBC. (2007, September 6). Brown defends new citizen juries. *BBC News*. Retrieved from http://news.bbc.co.uk/2/hi/uk_news/politics/6980747.stm

Blue, G., & Medlock, J. (2014). Public engagement with climate change as scientific citizenship: A case study of World Wide Views on global warming. *Science as Culture*, *23*(4), 560–579.

Bovenkerk, B., & Brom, F. W. A. (2012). World Wide Views on global warming: Evaluation of a public debate. In T. Potthast & S. Meisch (Eds.), *Climate change and sustainable development: Ethical perspectives on land use and food production* (pp. 95–99). Wageningen: Wageningen Academic Publishers.

Brown, M. B. (2006). Survey article: Citizen panels and the concept of representation. *Journal of Political Philosophy, 14*(2), 203–225.

Center for New Democratic Processes. (1986). *Preliminary report on the citizens panel on transplants and public policy.* Retrieved from http://jefferson-center.org/wp-content/uploads/2012/10/Organ-Transplants.pdf

Chilvers, J. (2008). Environmental risk, uncertainty, and participation: Mapping an emergent epistemic community. *Environment and Planning A, 40*(12), 2990–3008.

Coote, A., & Lenaghan, J. (1997). *Citizens' juries: Theory into practice.* London: Institute for Public Policy Research.

Crosby, N. (1974). *The educated random sample. A pilot study on a new way to get citizen input into the policy-making process.* Retrieved from http://jefferson-center.org/wp-content/uploads/2012/10/National-Health-Care-Plan.pdf

Crosby, N. (1995). Citizens juries: One solution for difficult environmental questions. In O. Renn, T. Webler & P. M. Wiedemann (Eds.), *Fairness and competence in citizen participation: Evaluating models for environmental discourse* (pp. 157–174). Berlin: Springer.

Crosby, N. (2007). Peter C. Dienel: Eulogy for a deliberative democracy pioneer. *Journal of Public Deliberation, 3*(1). Retrieved from http://www.publicdeliberation.net/jpd/vol3/iss1/art7/

Davies, C., Wetherell, M. S., & Barnett, E. (2006). *Citizens at the centre: Deliberative participation in healthcare decisions.* Chicago: University of Chicago Press.

Dienel, H. L., Vergne, A., Franzl, K., Fuhrmann, R. D., & Lietzmann, H. J. (2014). *Die Qualität von Bürgerbeteiligungsverfahren: Evaluation und Sicherung von Standards am Beispiel von Planungszellen und Bürgergutachten.* Stuttgart: Franz Steiner Verlag.

Dienel, P. C. (1969). Der Soziale Pluralismus Als Planerisches Problem. *Stadt- Region- Land,* (8), 31–44.

Dienel, P. C. (1980). *New options for participatory democracy.* Wuppertal: Forschungsstelle Bürgerbeteiligung und Planungsverfahren, Univ. Gesamthochschule.

Dienel, P. C., & Harms, H. (2000). *Repensar la democracia: Los núcleos de intervención participativa.* Barcelona: Ediciones del Serbal.

Dienel, P. C., & Renn, O. (1995). Planning cells: A gate to "fractal" mediation. In O. Renn, T. Webler & P. M. Wiedemann (Eds.), *Fairness and competence in citizen participation: Evaluating models for environmental discourse* (pp. 117–140). Berlin: Springer.

Drori, G. S., Höllerer, M. A., & Walgenbach, P. (2014). The glocalization of organization and management: Issues, dimensions, and themes. In G. S. Drori, M. A. Höllerer & P. Walgenbach (Eds.), *Global themes and local variations in organization and management: Perspectives on glocalization* (pp. 3–24). London: Routledge.

Dunkerley, D., & Glasner, P. (1998). Empowering the public? Citizens' juries and the new genetic technologies. *Critical Public Health, 8*(3), 181–192.

Durant, J. (1995). An experiment in democracy. In S. Ross & J Durant (Eds.), *Public participation in science: The role of consensus conferences in Europe* (pp. 75–80). London: Science Museum.

Felt, U., & Fochler, M. (2010). Machineries for making publics: Inscribing and describing publics in public engagement. *Minerva, 48*(3), 219–138.

Font, J. (1996). Los núcleos de intervención participativa (NIP): Análisis de tres experiencias. *Gestión y análisis de políticas publicas,* (5–6), 143–150.

Font, J., & Blanco, I. (2007). Procedural legitimacy and political trust: The case of citizen juries in Spain. *European Journal of Political Research, 46*(4), 557–589.

Font, J., & Medina, L. (2001). Los consejos ciudadanos en España. In J. Font (Ed.), *Ciudadanos y decisiones publicas* (pp. 153–159). Barcelona: Ariel.

Fung, A. (2006). Varieties of participation in complex governance. *Public Administration Review, 66*(s1), 66–75.

Ganuza, E., & Baiocchi, G. (2012). The power of ambiguity: How participatory budgeting travels the globe. *Journal of Public Deliberation, 8*(2). Retrieved from http://www.publicdeliberation.net/jpd/vol8/iss2/art8/

Harms, H. (2000). Apuntes Críticos y Criterios Prácticos para la Resolución Participativa de Conflictos Ambientales. *Cuadernos Bakeaz*, (96). Retrieved from http://www.accioecologista-agro.org/IMG/pdf/Participacion.pdf

Harms, H. (2005). Die Planungszelle in Spanien und Darüber Hinaus. In H. Harms (Ed.), *Die Befreiung der Politik* (pp. 116–118). Berlin: Springer.

Harms, H. (2007). *Dictamen Ciudadano.* Report for the city of Ibarra, Ecuador. Unpublished.

House of Lords Select Committee on Science and Technology. (2000). *Science and technology— Third report.* London: UK Parliament. Retrieved from http://www.publications.parliament.uk/pa/ld199900/ldselect/ldsctech/38/3801.htm

Joss, S., & Durant, J. (1995a). The UK national consensus conference on plant biotechnology. *Public Understanding of Science, 4*(2), 195–204.

Joss, S., & Durant, J. (1995b). *Public participation in science: The role of consensus conferences in Europe.* London: NMSI Trading Ltd.

Lezaun, J., & Soneryd, L. (2007). Consulting citizens: Technologies of elicitation and the mobility of publics. *Public Understanding of Science, 16*(3), 279–297.

McIver, S. (1998). *Healthy debate? An independent evaluation of citizens' juries in health settings.* London: King's Fund.

Mann, C., Voß, J. P., Amelung, N., Simons, A., Runge, T., & Grabner, L. (2014). *Challenging futures of citizens panels: Critical issues for robust forms of public participation. A report based on an interactive, anticipatory assessment of the dynamics of governance instruments.* Berlin, Technische Universität Berlin.

OECD. (2001). *Citizens as partners: OECD handbook on information, consultation and public participation in policy-making.* Paris: OECD.

Renn, O., Webler, T., Rakel, H., Dienel, P. C., & Johnson, B. (1993). Public participation in decision making: A three-step procedure. *Policy Sciences, 26*(3), 189–214.

Renn, O., Webler, T., & Wiedemann, P. M. (1995). *Fairness and competence in citizen participation: Evaluating models for environmental discourse.* Berlin: Springer.

Reynolds, L., Soneryd, L., & Szerszynski, B. (2008). CARGO: Comparison of approaches to risk governance (Contract Number: FP6–036720), deliverable 6, risk deliberation. *European Commission Community Research.* Retrieved from http://www.cargoproject.eu/docs/project-deliverables/wp3_risk_deliberation.pdf

Saretzki, T. (2008). Policy-Analyse, Demokratie und Deliberation: Theorieent-Wicklung und Forschungsperspektiven der "Policy Sciences of Democracy." In F. Janning & K. Toens (Eds.), *Die Zukunft der Policy-Forschung: Theorien, Methoden, Anwendungen* (pp. 34–54). Berlin: Springer.

Saward, M. (2000). *Democratic innovation: Deliberation, representation and association.* London: Routledge.

Saward, M. (2003). Enacting democracy. *Political Studies, 51*(1), 161–179.

Soneryd, L. (2008). *The spread of ideas and the travel of "public deliberation" methods.* Conference paper presented at 2008 EASST Conference, Rotterdam.

Soneryd, L., & Amelung, N. (2016). Translating participation: Scenario workshops and citizens' juries across situations and contexts. In J. P. Voß & R. Freeman (Eds.), *Knowing governance: The epistemic construction of political order* (pp. 155–174). Basingstoke: Palgrave Macmillan.

Stewart, J., Kendall, E., & Coote, A. (1994). *Citizens' Juries*. London: Institute for Public Policy Research.

Strang, D., & Meyer, J. W. (1993). Institutional conditions for diffusion. *Theory and Society*, *22*(4), 487–511.

Trütken, B. (2005). Qualitätskriterien für die Durchführung von Planungszellen. In P. C. Dienel (Ed.), *Die Befreiung der Politik* (pp. 141–143). Berlin: VS Verlag für Sozialwissenschaften.

Ureta, S. (2016). A failed platform: The citizen consensus conference travels to Chile. *Public Understanding of Science*, *25*(4), 499–511.

Vergne, A. (2010). *Das Modell Planungszelle—Citizens Juries: Diffusion einer Politischen Innovation.* Unpublished manuscript.

Voß, J. P. (2007a). *Designs on governance. Development of policy instruments and dynamics in governance.* Doctoral dissertation. Retrieved from http://doc.utwente.nl/58085/1/thesis_Voss.pdf

Voß, J. P. (2007b). Innovation processes in governance: The development of "emissions trading" as a new policy instrument. *Science and Public Policy*, *34*(5), 329–343.

Voß, J. P., & Amelung, N. (2016). Innovating public participation methods: Technoscientization and reflexive engagement. *Social Studies of Science*, *46*(5), 749–772. Published online. doi: 10.1177/0306312716641350.

Voß, J. P., & Simons, A. (2014). Instrument constituencies and the supply side of policy innovation: The social life of emissions trading. *Environmental Politics*, *23*(5), 735–754.

Wakeford, T. (2002). Citizen's juries: A radical alternative for social research. *Social Research Update*, (37), 1–5.

Wakeford, T. (2012). *Teach yourself citizens' juries: A handbook* (2nd ed.). Retrieved from http://www.academia.edu/11223382/Teach_Yourself_Citizens_Juries

Wakeford, T., & Singh, J. (2008). Towards empowered participation: Stories and reflections. *Participatory Learning and Action*, (58), 6–10.

Wakeford, T., Singh, J., Murtuja, B., Bryant, P., & Pimbert, M. (2007). The jury is out: How far can participatory projects go towards reclaiming democracy. In P. Reason & H. Bradbury (Eds.), *The Sage handbook of action research: Participative inquiry and practice* (pp. 333–349). New York: Sage.

10

LEARNING TO FACILITATE

Implications for Skill Development in the Public Participation Field

Kathryn S. Quick and Jodi R. Sandfort

One of the manifestations of professionalization trends in public participation is the growing demand for people to have the facilitation skills to convene participatory processes. Indeed, alongside a growing number of full-time, professional facilitators, more and more people are expected to facilitate competently as part of their everyday work. Formal facilitation training programs have proliferated as one way of conveying facilitation skills for public participation professionals and others, yet many people recognize that facilitation is also learned through practice. Given the expectations that people should facilitate well, and the nuances and judgment involved in that work, it is important to understand how people learn this complex craft.

That is the subject of this chapter, an ethnographic study of a group of people who went through a training program to professionalize their skills in facilitation and then transformed that knowledge into practice. We describe the particular training model—workshops on learning the Art of Hosting and Harvesting Conversations That Matter (hereafter abbreviated as "hosting")—because it is an innovative approach to facilitating and training that is inherently of interest to scholars and practitioners working on the professionalization of public participation. Introduced in Denmark, hosting approaches to facilitation are now being used in at least 41 countries (Holman, Devane & Cady, 2007; Wheatley & Frieze, 2011). Thousands of people have now been trained in hosting across the globe (Art of Hosting, 2016).

Hosting merits critical attention from anyone interested in the professionalization of facilitation and the growing "consultancy industry" of facilitators (Hendriks & Carson, 2008) merely because of its growing popularity. However, the types of learning that we characterize are not exclusive to a hosting orientation to facilitation. Literature on other approaches to public participation and facilitation, as well as our own teaching and practice, suggest that the patterns we describe in this study are commonplace and applicable in a wide variety of facilitated public participation contexts, regardless of whether the facilitators espouse "hosting" or not. This chapter illuminates how facilitators learn both about discrete techniques, concepts, and artefacts and about the situated knowledge necessary to apply these things in particular settings and particular process designs.

The Stakes for Learning to Facilitate

Facilitators with special competence play increasingly central roles in supporting collective capacity for public participation (Bingham, Nabatchi & O'Leary, 2005; Escobar, 2011; Moore, 2012; Polletta & Chen, 2013). They play an especially essential part in shaping the discursive exchange and group dynamics required for high-quality deliberation,[1] which is increasingly identified as a preferred approach to decision-making in public policy and administration (Cooper, Bryer & Meek, 2006; Roberts, 2004). The skills and judgment expected of people in facilitation roles imply that they play a demanding, central part in the success of public participation.

A diverse array of individuals have and desire these skills, both trained professionals specializing in facilitation or engagement and others, such as community organizers, public and non-profit managers, and political leaders, who facilitate in the context of a broader scope of work (Lee, 2011; Leighninger, 2006; Ryfe, 2007). Indeed, a "consultancy industry" of professional facilitators appears to be growing in size and influence, and concerns have been raised about how commercialization of these skills affects the quality and integrity of the participation processes these practitioners support (Hendriks & Carson, 2008). Schools of public policy, public administration, and planning increasingly recognize a demand for professionals with abilities to convene democratic processes and seek ways to train their students in these skills (Leighninger, 2010).

At the same time, many who see the value of participation feel poorly equipped to design and implement participation processes (Nabatchi & Leighninger, 2015, p. 228). It is no wonder that becoming a masterful facilitator feels like a daunting challenge. Facilitation is a complex ability, demanding skill and judgment in the design and implementation of engagement efforts. John Forester suggests that skilled facilitators are doing

> *not just* the pragmatic work of facilitating a discussion, but the critical pragmatic work of thinking through the procedural design, thinking through the politics and ethics, the normative structuring, of that discussion in the first place. . . . A critical pragmatism must be attentive not just to getting agreements or "getting things done!" but to the legitimacy and transparency and accountability of that pragmatic production of agreements, deals, and consequences. The critical pragmatist, we see, must attend to expertly informed outcomes and to equitably structured processes as well.
>
> *(Forester, 2013, p. 19, emphasis in original)*

In this chapter we respond to critiques that prior scholarship has not sufficiently captured this complex craft, particularly facilitators' own views of what they do and how they are enlisted in participatory processes (Cooper & Smith, 2012; Hendriks & Carson, 2008). Some previous interpretive research has described the knowledge and judgment brought to bear by facilitators implementing participatory processes (e.g. Forester, 1999; Healey, 2009) or evaluating their success (Mansbridge, Hartz-Karp, Amengual & Gastil, 2006). We complement these scholars' work with an interpretation of facilitators' accounts of their learning and work. We describe not only what the facilitators in this study are taught to do, but also how they learn to practice.

To investigate both *what* and *how* facilitators learn, we first review the skills and techniques that facilitators are typically expected to have. We then describe some distinctive features of the hosting approach to facilitation and explain how we collected and analyzed data from practitioners. After illustrating how they transform and utilize facilitation knowledge in their professional practice and within a community of facilitators, we conclude with some implications of this study for supporting the professional development of facilitators.

What and How Facilitators Learn

What do facilitators learn? Research on participatory processes (Bryson, Quick, Slotterback & Crosby, 2013; Forester, 1999; Jacobs, Cook & Delli Carpini, 2009; Mansbridge et al., 2006), handbooks for facilitation professionals (Baker & Fraser, 2005; Creighton, 2005; Escobar, 2011; Kaner, 2007; Schwarz, Davidson, Carlson & McKinney, 2005; Sunwolf & Frey, 2005), and online resources for practitioners[2] (IAP2.org, ncdd.org, publicconversations.org) identify multiple areas of competence required of facilitators. All emphasize skills for managing discursive exchange and group dynamics, with some also suggesting that expertise in the policy content area is not necessary and that neutrality about the outcomes is desirable. These identify several key tasks of the skilled facilitator, including

- Selecting the processes best suited for accomplishing the task at hand, combining prior planning with improvisation to respond to emerging dynamics
- Establishing and enforcing ground rules and group norms, particularly maintaining a respectful, open, and inclusive environment
- Supporting diverse participation and managing potential problems of exclusion, power, and associated conflict
- Helping the group work toward its objectives, in part by focusing on relevant topics and managing time
- Enhancing the development of mutual understanding, for example through asking clarifying questions, rephrasing statements, and supporting diverse perspectives

Formal training for facilitators typically emphasizes effective techniques and concepts for accomplishing these tasks. This kind of instruction is well suited to communicating explicit and expert knowledge, which are content areas that can be articulated, codified, or stored as forms of de-contextualized, technical knowledge (Scott, 1998; Yanow, 2004). While valuable, these modes of instruction and the discrete skills conveyed are not sufficient to create skilled facilitators. The judgment described earlier by Forester (2013) also involves eliciting and activating "tacit" knowledge—the practical knowledge often implicit in a situation (Polanyi, 1966).

Facilitators develop this knowledge through acting, testing their intuitions and perceptions, and reflecting on results. For example, when facilitators interpret and work with the emotions surrounding a policy issue and dialogue (e.g. hope, urgency, fatigue), they are assessing what a setting demands from their facilitation skills, which aspects of their knowledge to bring to bear, and how to do so. They are exercising what theories of pragmatism describe as "practical inquiry" or "practical judgment," by drawing on their broad, generalizable bases of knowledge and frameworks to interpret and act in ways situated in the particular context (Nicolini, Gherardi & Yanow, 2003; Suchman, 1987). They orient that work to the ends they wish to achieve, in an iterative, interactive cycle of redefining the policy challenges and solutions (Healey, 2009; Schön & Rein, 1994).

This "learning-in-action" (Argyris & Schön, 1996) or "knowing-in-practice" (Orlikowski, 2002) is not a matter of received knowledge that facilitators can access through traditional training models. Nor is it merely a cognitive process. Eliciting the relevant features of particular contexts and exercising practical judgment are situated in practice, an embodied experience in which understanding is elicited through practical engagement with objects or problems situated in particular environments (Dewey, 1925; Yanow, 2004). Learning theories suggest that these capacities are better developed through interacting in and reflecting on settings iteratively (Forester, 1999; Kolb, 1984; Schön, 1983; Thomas & Brown, 2011). Lave and Wenger (Lave & Wenger, 1991; Wenger, 1998) describe these processes as "situated learning," an element of their theory that learning is inherently social, occurring through "communities of practice" in which individuals learn through being exposed to, taking up, or modifying practices in exchanges with others. The Art of Hosting community's approach to training facilitators is unusual because it incorporates learning through practice, reflection, and the intentional creation of a community of practitioners.

The Art of Hosting

The intentional practice of learning through reflection is just one of several features of hosting that make it particularly well suited to our analysis of how people learn to facilitate. People trained in the Art of Hosting are taught a suite of techniques and patterns, and hosting is more of an assemblage of practices than a method. In hosting training workshops, trainers explicitly encourage practitioners to select among, sequence, and modify techniques to adapt to the contexts in which they work. Experienced and new hosts are invited to participate in an Art of Hosting "community of practitioners" to continue to learn and produce knowledge. Indeed, hosting knowledge is supported and generated through an open source, democratic philosophy in which the methods and ideas draw upon pooled knowledge, facilitation techniques, and frameworks, developed by others willing to share them at no cost within the community.

Hosting's orientation towards learning and shared knowledge goes beyond trainings and the community of practitioners, however. One of the explicit espoused values of hosting is to promote learning among all involved in a deliberative setting. This value is expressed in the premise for the Art of Hosting approach, as expressed by a leading group of scholars and practitioners of facilitation, "Learning together makes us all stronger, better equipped to serve the growing needs [for a] shift in how human beings organize themselves to accomplish meaningful purpose" (Holman et al., 2007, p. 56). All participants at events are presumed to have wisdom about the problem at hand, and the point of the hosted setting is to encourage learning through the interactions. Thus with support from the hosts, participants discover the key issues, define the content of the agenda, and have responsibility for both the direction and quality of the conversation. Quick and Feldman (2011) have asserted that diverse public engagement processes produce different kinds of political communities, some in which participants are alienated, some in which the parties are atomized, and some which are inclusive, meaning that diverse participants co-produce the means as well as the outcomes of their public participation processes. Viewed through this lens, the philosophy of the Art of Hosting is inclusive. This has implications for what hosts learn to do, for how they practice, and for how they learn to host.

Notably, hosting practitioners play a distinctly de-centered role as facilitators. The skills traditionally expected of facilitators, described above, place them in a central role: they are the actors who design the process, set forth ground rules, mediate conflict, manage time, guide who speaks, and filter what is and is not relevant. In contrast, hosts play a convening role: the word "host" signals their position of issuing a gracious invitation and providing a comfortable space for participants to interact. Hosting has been characterized as a form of leadership in which "the heroes go home" and the job of a leader is to convene the conversation, to invite people to share their insights and develop new understandings, and ultimately to enable participants to organize and direct themselves (Wheatley & Frieze, 2011). Hosts' roles are to legitimate the wisdom of the collective, to cultivate inquiry and experimentation by participants, and to sense and lead movement to "the learning edge" in the group (Holman et al., 2007, p. 86). They create a "container" (Isaacs, 1999) or "hold the space" (Senge, 2006) within which inquiry, negotiation, and dialogue can occur.

Research Methods

Studying a group of facilitators with any common training background provides a good sampling frame for analyzing how large groups of individuals respond to and use a particular set of facilitation techniques. Our study participants were the core trainers and all the training participants in two cohorts of a three-day, introductory workshop about hosting. These trainings were sponsored by a foundation in Minnesota, a state in the upper Midwest of the United States. The foundation sought to foster a cadre of people skilled in participatory leadership to support community-based problem solving in the region. Participants were invited to be trained at no cost and then to donate three days of their time to hosting participatory processes.

It is important to place this study population in a broader context of the professionalization of facilitation practice. Some participants in the training and study are full-time public participation professionals who might be hired as facilitation consultants or recognized as the go-to people within their organization for facilitation work. Many others, however, identify themselves primarily as leaders of an organization, advocates, or policy specialists for whom facilitation is just a part of their tasks, or one of the ways to accomplish their work. They are active in a variety of professional fields in the non-profit, public, and private sectors. Over one-third had been facilitating for 21 years or more at the time of the training. They are primarily white (80%), female (70%), and highly educated with a graduate degree (80%), which is reflective of the larger population of facilitators in the United States (Polletta & Chen, 2013).

We observed the training programs in-depth and, five to eight months after the training, interviewed the two trainee cohorts and their trainers (69 persons) about what and how they learn to facilitate. Studying a group of individuals trained in the same facilitation practices, by the same trainers, and in the same place allowed us to analyze learning variation and explore the influences of other factors (i.e. their previous experience, field of practice, and personal preferences). We utilized a multi-sited ethnographic approach (Gupta & Ferguson, 1997) to both construct a thick account of study participants' learning processes in this locale and embed it in a broader context of increasing practitioner interest and scholarship about public participation and facilitation practices.

Our interviews combined a standardized set of questions with follow-up probes to elicit study participants' practice stories and their interpretations of them (Holstein & Gubrium, 1995). We explored how they understood the Art of Hosting in relation to other facilitation experiences they had had, their understanding of specific practices or concepts from the training, and whether and how they were using what they had learned. When interviewing the five trainers who had participated in both cohorts, we explored their theories about how training participants take up the Art of Hosting practices and concepts, what is easiest and most difficult for newcomers to learn and implement, and the supports or barriers to ongoing learning. These trainers have high credibility within the hosting community: at the time of these workshops, each one had been practicing hosting and serving as a steward of the international Art of Hosting community for at least several years.

In addition to these interviews, we collected data from multiple other sources. As participant observers, the authors took part in the training and participated in the local community of hosting practitioners. Through field notes, we problematized our own processes of learning alongside the study participants (Dewalt & Dewalt, 2002; Marcus, 1998). In addition, we gathered data from three policy deliberations that were hosted by individuals from our study population of hosting practitioners. All three concerned the redesign of the direction and design of public services by public or non-profit organizations. We observed these public participation settings and, two to eight months later, conducted interviews about how the meetings had been facilitated with nine facilitators (all from our original population of hosting trainees) and with 23 non-facilitator meeting participants.

We analyzed the data from field notes and interviews inductively and iteratively using thematic coding in a grounded theory development process (Glaser & Strauss, 1967). The multiple sources enabled us to identify common phenomena or patterns occurring across multiple interviews, observations, or texts and thereby to strengthen our inferences regarding patterns within the case (Yanow & Schwartz-Shea, 2015). Through analysis of the field notes and interviews, we uncovered three learning processes through which the study participants transformed knowledge on the way to becoming capable of critically pragmatic facilitation. From this rich data set, we have selected accounts from the participants about these learning processes and illustrations of how they applied what they had learned in policy deliberations.

Learning to Facilitate

Learning Explicit Facilitation Techniques

The Art of Hosting trainings use a combination of traditional and innovative pedagogical methods. Unlike many traditional facilitation trainings, the workshops are not oriented to mastering a set of "best practices" or teaching a set of prescribed steps or an ideal process design for facilitating participatory processes. Instead, the workshops introduce skills which practitioners are invited to select from or to modify for the particular participation processes they facilitate. However, the training begins with teaching explicit skills and competencies, each introduced in a one- to three-hour block. They are presented as internally coherent, fairly discrete, and clearly named parcels of explicit knowledge, many of them introduced from sources that are already available elsewhere. Trainers circulate and display reference materials at trainings, and trainees receive a guidebook summarizing these techniques. This part of the training involved transmitting explicit techniques; when we asked study participants five to eight months after their training about what aspects of the training were most memorable to them, the vast majority cited at least one of these specific techniques.

In learning how to facilitate, our study participants were more successful in applying the techniques they had learned in the training if they had understood them well. Novices, whom we define as those with up to three years of facilitation experience prior to the training, were more likely than more experienced practitioners to express a need for additional training or tools to make the techniques and patterns easily available for reference. However, study participants with at least three years of previous facilitation experience (including Adam, Ann, Bridget, Melissa, Rosalyn, Sarah, and Sonya) found it easier to recall and evaluate particular techniques and concepts from the training and were able to describe how they had—or would—use them. For them, the specific techniques were not only easy to grasp, but frequently also already familiar.

An illustration of the impacts of facilitators' acquisition of these techniques in public participation settings comes from the use of World Café (Brown & Isaacs, 2005). It is the single take away from the training that they are most likely to bring into their subsequent facilitation practice (Sandfort, Stuber & Quick, 2012). Indeed, in Minnesota, the US state where we conducted our study, the World Café technique is now so frequently used by public and non-profit organizations and in community meetings that even people who have not been formally trained in hosting refer to it by name. It is an easy and appealing technique to understand and use to facilitating intensive small group interactions and exchanges of ideas. It occurs through having groups of four to five people consider a predetermined series of questions, with participants mixing into new groups for each question, sharing what was discussed at their previous table as input for each stage of discussion. Designed for exploration of ideas rather than decisions, World Café does not support coordinated, ongoing action, but is frequently used to reset or open a dialogue about a policy issue.

Kyle, a practitioner introduced to World Café through the training, thought it might be a solution to a problem facing a human services network where he provided facilitation support. Believing that the technique "pulls people into the experience, rather than kind of pushing them away," he thought it could engage ethnic and racial groups that had previously been absent or silent in their annual planning process. He understood, however, that he could not unilaterally introduce the technique, but needed to co-develop it with people in the lead organization in order for it to work well. After working with their director to craft good questions for the World Café, they tried it out and found that the director and meeting participants subsequently judged that the annual planning process generated more information, connections among participants, and a sense of ownership than did prior approaches.

A statewide dialogue about significant declines in local and state funding streams and how to address their potentially alarming implications for service delivery levels and coordination makes clear the policy application of the World Café technique. A group of local government associations sponsored a series of six meetings throughout the state, involving more than 400 staff and elected officials. Sponsors consistently identified their primary goals as building relationships and trust across jurisdictional boundaries so that leaders could learn from each other. To accomplish those purposes, they hired Cindy, an experienced facilitator trained in hosting, who designed a session utilizing an adapted World Café technique, which included sharing a meal, sitting at pre-assigned small tables to maximize a diversity of perspectives, telling stories, and working through a series of carefully designed questions.

The meeting sponsors interviewed later felt that using World Café techniques had been an excellent alternative to what one (Tai) characterized as the traditional format of "listening sessions" that employ a central facilitator mediating a single, large-group dialogue. Another (Jay) observed that the World Café method provided respondents "the opportunity to answer however they would like to answer as opposed to a more directed approach that might ask a very specific question." They reported that they and the participants had learned from one another, enjoyed interacting with others, and also acknowledged that building more durable relationships across jurisdictions takes time.

The reactions of non-facilitator participants are also telling. World Café was not difficult for them to grasp, and their reactions were positive. For example, Naomi observed that it was "energizing to have that type of conversation with people who were in similar situations in local government." Like those who had taken the hosting training, however, they also cautioned that a one-time conversation, although novel and pleasant, was not enough to address the challenging realities of local institutional change. Hannah, another participant, described this as "the turf issue and how strong it is." Phil, also a participant, stated, "The only problem is with the brainstorming and the ideas and everything, with personnel and financial resources lacking, are the agencies able to even do some of this stuff?" The facilitators, sponsors, and participants all recognized that to produce convergence on policy directions and actions, World Café alone is not enough.

Recognizing Patterns of Group Dynamics

Learning to host involves more than deploying learned techniques. The Art of Hosting community encourages facilitators to pick and choose so that they blend the individual techniques into a design suited to the particular participation processes they will facilitate. To learn how to play a role of "holding the container" for the participatory process, facilitators are introduced in their training to a number of "patterns," which describe commonly experienced group dynamics. These patterns name dynamics that facilitators recognize from their prior experience, making their knowledge of them visible and practical, helping them to make sense of complex or ambiguous group dynamics. Patterns also are meant to help facilitators improve how they design participation processes, become more comfortable with surprises, and improvise to deal with problems or take advantage of opportunities. Not all hosting trainees were able to use the patterns. For example, Derrick, who described himself as a more "concrete thinker," found that guidance on general group dynamic patterns was not enough to help him design participation events and wished for "a flowchart to help me understand when to use specific tools." As one trainer (Kurt) hypothesized, people are so familiar with a "linear worldview" in which "one method or approach is always the best," that it is difficult to adjust to a more "circular" or holistic sensibility about how to design and improve facilitation as it is unfolding.

For many other hosting trainees, however, the patterns were very helpful. In particular, many experienced an "Aha!" moment of recognition when introduced to the "chaordic path," a concept developed by Hock (1999) to characterize the movement back and forth between chaos and order as necessary for channeling groups' innovation potential. Rosalyn, an experienced facilitator, reflected after being introduced to the idea in the training, "I love the chaordic path! It is an elegant summary of so much of what I've been looking at over the course of my career." Another highly experienced facilitator, Cristina, immediately began using it in a challenging project in which it was difficult to stay focused and complete tasks with youths. The chaordic path helped her to understand the group's dynamics differently, describe the "dance between chaos and order" to the young people, and be more intentional in her interventions. A third, Tracy, who was facilitating deliberative conversations among the leadership team at a major university about organizational policies, drew upon the chaordic path to impress upon the participants that they were trying to reach closure prematurely and instead needed to stay for a while in a more chaotic, but creative, mode.

Another way of making sense of group interactions is through awareness of individual identities, positionalities, and power dynamics. The trainers and written Art of Hosting materials refer to the importance of recognizing the influence of "our individual characteristics and unique history" on "our individual realities and the actions we take in the world." Study participants' individual reactions to this were diverse. A few strongly critiqued the training for not doing enough to enact an awareness of identity, power, and privilege in participation processes, the facilitation role, or the training workshop itself. Nora, Fernando, and Cecilia asserted in interviews that they would not adopt hosting's de-centered approach to facilitation because it does not help them address power dynamics in intercultural settings in the ways that they wish. However, others who also view the world through a lens of identity intersections (e.g. of race, class, gender, sexual orientation) have expressed quite the converse. Sarah, Steve, Tami, and Sonya all told us stories about using the hosting stance of "holding space" for participatory processes to redefine the group's work to include power relations associated with race, class, place of origin, and religious identity, and to reorient their convening role attending to, interrogating, and trying to address power inequalities.

Getting on the Mat

Pedagogically, both the training workshop and the ongoing facilitation work are explicitly designed to support learning through practice. Novice and experienced facilitators learn continually through immersion in and application of the material. In the workshop, the techniques, patterns, and overall hosting paradigm are iteratively explained, directly experienced, and evaluated. It is an immersive practicum that runs as a lived experience of a hosted conversation. For example, trainees learn Open Space Technology, a technique through which groups generate their own agenda topics for discussion in break-out groups (Owen, 1997), by using it to set topics and organize small group work during the training.

In addition, the trainers repeatedly invite training participants to "practice" and to "get on the mat," through an analogy to the learning-by-doing approach of martial arts, in which the discipline of practice is a way of becoming comfortable with and embodying knowledge. The invitation to the training advised that it was "not for spectators," and while some study participants found this uncomfortable because their personal style was to take an observing rather than an active role, they consistently acknowledged the value of physically experiencing and doing the practices to learn. One of the trainers (Andre) coached them through this, insisting that practitioners need to "get out of our heads and do. We can only move forward if we practice." By experimenting with manipulating group structures and dynamics, experiencing being hosted and hosting, and discussing those dynamics, the trainees learn through experiencing and reflecting in and on the very things that they hope to later practice.

This practicum element of the workshop seemed to directly enhance trainees' recollection of and attachment to the techniques. For example, trainees are trained in peer circle process (Baldwin & Linnea, 2010) through an opening check-in. For participants in the first training cohort of people in our study, the opening circle unexpectedly took several hours to complete. When we asked members of that group what stood out to them in their memories of the workshop, their recollection of circle technique was particularly acute. Eight of the 29 participants in the first training cohort emphasized to us the lessons they learned from the circle "that took so long" or "went on and on" about both the benefits of making a deep connection through this storytelling technique and the risks of losing control of its pacing. Actively working with the techniques, as either facilitators or participants, enabled people to remember specifically how the approaches are structured and what can result.

Other impressions of techniques were more specific to individuals' particular experience of them. For example, Ann recalled Open Space Technology because she "was able to suggest an agenda item of my own ... passion and bring a group together around it, which was very helpful." Jonathan, a younger participant, remembered the Open Space Technology technique because he and some peers had used it to convene a dialogue about "leadership" and "succession planning" by younger professionals, two issues that had been concerning them. Similarly, study participants recalled most vividly the training content that they had subsequently applied to a work or personal project, recounting that they learned it both by practicing and by using it in a context reflecting their "own concern and passion" (Jacob).

The trainers consistently refer to everyone present, themselves included, as "co-learners." This signals that everyone is learning from others and capable of helping others to learn. For example, trainers quickly invite training participants into co-teaching roles: volunteers receive brief coaching from a trainer in a given technique and then find themselves introducing the engagement technique to others in the training. Our data indicate that study participants learned content more deeply by teaching it, like one trainee (Erica) who told us, "I remember doing the ProAction Café [an innovation developed by Art of Hosting community members that combines elements of Open Space Technology and World Café] because I volunteered to head the demonstration up."

When training participants are hesitant to jump in, the workshop leaders stress that repeated practice builds "courage," and in fact encourage them to sustain their learning after the workshop by continuing to stay "on the mat" through ongoing "practice." One trainer, Kerry, explained, "If people come out of the training . . . feeling inadequately prepared to really use these tools, what helps is a framework of, 'We're practicing.' I think that helps." Andre, a founder of the Art of Hosting community and trainer in these workshops explained:

> These are arts that you can spend a lifetime in learning. If you've gone to 1–2 trainings, you are still learning. I am still a student of this even though I have been doing this constantly for 20 years. I want to temper the perfectionist in us all, saying we go to a training and then we need to be able to do everything. Impossible! Practice makes the master, or makes mastery.

Another way in which experienced hosts embody the ethic of ongoing learning through practice is to make their own process visible to newcomers during the training workshops. A workshop exercise might including the trainers pausing to consult with one another, in the presence of the whole group, and discuss the dilemmas they are facing in implementing a planned activity or the reasons for making adjustments. In the first training cohort we observed, for example, there was extensive discussion in front of the whole group about how to respond to the opening circle that "went on and on."

Their modeling has direct implications for what trainees subsequently do when facilitating public participation. Study participants told us that they have taken the example of these senior practitioners to be more open-ended and transparent with participants in conversations they convene. In a community policy roundtable about priorities for maintaining a rural road system, for example, the participants began to discuss one of several policy alternatives in great depth.

The facilitator, Nicole, became concerned that they were not only neglecting exploration of the other alternatives, but running the risk of not having time to accomplish other business she had planned for the day. Nicole paused the dialogue to voice the dilemma she was encountering about what direction to take, and worked with the group to decide together how to proceed and to take shared responsibility for managing the time to accomplish what they decided.

Post-Training Application

Study participants did not equally take up the message that they should continue to "get on the mat" and stay on it through ongoing practice. While people very consistently understood intellectually the ideas of ongoing learning and continually practicing, there was less uniformity in how much they were acting upon that aspiration. Trainees with previous experience facilitating were both more likely to recall specific lessons from the training and to have subsequently applied it. In our interviews, they offered many examples of how they had used the practices in their work, across a broad range of settings, including staff meetings, organizational strategic planning sessions, and community meetings about educational improvement, public health, and rural sustainable development. They easily described many ways in which they had applied and adapted the techniques, consistently indicating attentiveness to their contexts. For example, Edgar, a practitioner who works in American Indian communities, described his adaptations as "indigenizing" what he had learned to work in those settings; he then observed that "indigenizing," which he defined as selecting and adapting techniques to do the work you want to do, is a central feature of the hosting approach in any setting.

The training model specifically encourages this kind of adaptation. As one of the trainers (Kerry) related, acquiring the techniques is only the tip of the iceberg. She described the move to a "deeper understanding of the tool" in terms of several levels:

> Level one is, I can go out and do a World Café or an open space. Level two is, I know how to design a World Café or open space into a project. Then I think there's even another level, which is, I have enough understanding of group process and of how communities work that I can start to adapt, meet people where they're at, take them through a journey, and hold energy.

Another important factor in application of learning is related to venue appropriateness. Novices and experienced facilitators offered different explanations of how this mattered. Experienced individuals could easily describe a technique, even if they had not yet applied it, because they were actively imagining and seeking practical settings in which to apply it. Several were eager to try out techniques but, as Laurie put it, had not yet found "the right setting" to do so. For example, Cindy and Judi each wanted to try Open Space Technology but had not yet been able to because of time constraints. Fernando was waiting to try ProAction Café, in which participants request intensive help from others on an agenda item of their choosing until he would be facilitating a gathering of people who knew one another well.

Novice facilitators were more likely to attribute their difficulties with implementing hosting approaches to an unsupportive boss, being in a hierarchical organization, or pressure to default to familiar approaches due to urgency. The workshop trainers expected that numerous practitioners, especially novices, would evoke a variety of barriers to explain what prevented them from implementing what they learned, particularly these kinds of external constraints. However, trainers pointed to a volitional component of novices' ability to apply their training as well. For example, when Kerry invited novice practitioners to co-host an event a few weeks after the training, she observed some were "getting it in their bones" and ready to jump in, while others were in "in a critique mode, a stand back mode" in which they were not ready to take in and use the hosting approach. Other trainers similarly suggested the more important factor in post-training application what the training offered was individual practitioners' internal readiness to practice, their willingness to get on and stay on the mat. As Alisha observed, "Some people are willing to go experiment and practice. Not everyone has that nature."

In public participation settings, participants as well as facilitators need to be willing to "get on the mat" and not be in "stand back mode" for a hosting approach to work. While not all participation settings are equally amenable, facilitators' willingness to push a group to try something new seems to relate to their own level of experience. A novice facilitator, Dana, described trying to introduce a hosting sensibility into a forestry-oriented community organization she frequently works with. She had planned to use Open Space Technology for a policy deliberation meeting, but judged during the meeting that it was not going to work and scaled back to a more conventional brainstorming process with post-it notes. She attributed the non-workability of a hosting approach to having colleagues who do not like "process" and are "more comfortable being out in trees than sitting around a boardroom table."

In contrast, Bridget, who has over 20 years of experience with group processes, also encountered resistance when she tried to adopt a hosting approach to facilitation. Unlike Dana, however, she prevailed. Bridget described combining elements of two techniques she had learned from the hosting training to organize a policy deliberation among stakeholders with strongly held and conflicting views about the use of antibiotics in food production. When she suggested some hosting oriented options to her fellow conference planners, some worried that it would create more uncertainty. To them, less centralized facilitation control meant that "vested interests would hijack the conversation." Bridget pushed back, encouraging the team to "trust the wisdom of the group." This stance was not specific to her relationships with these individuals, with whom she had not previously worked. It came from her confidence in the value of the approach of giving the group space to work things out and of her ability to provide a "container" to help them. She convinced her co-conveners to try what she suggested, and as it turned out, a third round of conversation spontaneously sprung up over the lunch hour because the first two rounds of Open Space Technology had worked so well.

Intriguingly, while the more experienced facilitators whom we interviewed readily articulated ideas about how well hosting could work in different settings, they did not agree about the criteria for evaluating feasibility. Features that some speculated would be barriers to a hosting approach—such as working with internally diverse groups, low-income rural people, politically conservative audiences, or in projects focused on quick products—did not stand in the way of others using a hosting approach to facilitation in precisely those conditions. This implies that some aspects of judgment about what is appropriate may be reflections of personal styles or perceptions. Generally, however, experienced facilitators were able to interact with contexts in a different way from the novices, notably by challenging and reshaping contexts rather than being constrained by them.

Engaging in a Community of Practice

One way in which the Art of Hosting explicitly supports ongoing practice and learning is by encouraging individuals to form or join in a "community of practitioners." Taking part in the community of practice takes various forms, including being part of formal local networks of trainees, participating in the international listserv, working with others in co-facilitation teams, or documenting innovations in the training workbook, which is constantly updated. The local networking opportunities enable people to stay connected with other practitioners, build a regional identity for the Art of Hosting, or find partners with whom to co-host.

Importantly, gatherings of the community of practitioners are hosted settings that provide opportunities to experience and practice hosting. A senior trainer in our study, Andre, described the opportunities to host and be hosted in his local community of practitioners as "practicing, practicing learning." In the community we study, practitioners frequently extend calls for assistance in facilitating events that also provide opportunities for mutual learning. For example, Kerry, another trainer, invited all participants in the first cohort to co-host an event a few weeks after their training, to provide an opportunity to continue practicing. Other study participants have supported each other's individual practice or professional development by checking with each other or by teaming up frequently, like Tamara and Cristina, who have been co-facilitating a women's interfaith dialogue circle that they started together after meeting at the training.

The communities of practitioners are also means for co-producing and exchanging new knowledge, as individuals experiment with the techniques and patterns and freely share their learning with the community. During our study period, there were two explicit manifestations of collectively produced, new knowledge. ProAction Café had just become part of the standard training. Conversely, the first cohort we studied was the first to try out a technique for gathering themes and ideas from storytelling; it has been developed further and is now routinely part of workshops used around the world.

However, some trainees did not feel "at home" in the Art of Hosting community. Sometimes this pertained to the location and rhythm of interactions, such as when people found it hard to recapture the strong connections they had felt with the group during the training, or when individuals outside the metropolitan area could not regularly participate in gatherings. Very often, however, their non-participation came from not feeling as if they belonged. An example is Jonathan, a policy specialist who used facilitation in his work but did not identify himself as a "professional facilitator," like those whom he perceived as being most active in the community. Other newcomers felt the community of practitioners was so amorphous in its definition that it was confusing. While veterans felt strongly that they meant to be inclusive, Clare told us that she and other newcomers had felt intimidated, disoriented, or envious about how to become an "insider" in the community. One trainer, Alisha, acknowledged that she frequently heard that it was "hard to figure out to access," and suggested that the blanket invitation and open-endedness of the community of practitioners paradoxically served as "barriers" to participating.

Some practitioners parlay their learning about building an ongoing community of facilitation practitioners into comparable efforts to build communities among the participants in the public participation efforts they facilitate. For example, three training participants in our study (Eve, Carolina, and Rick) subsequently worked with 30 people from public and non-profit agencies involved in HIV/AIDS service delivery networks, specifically with an eye to reshaping the community of providers to better respond to new client needs, delivery models, and changing regulatory and funding parameters. They oriented the three days of meetings to strengthening connections among providers and devoted the entire final day to discussions about system redesign and the next steps participants should take as a community. However, our observations and interviews with participants (Olivia and Eric) indicate that while some new connections and collaborations were created, participants did not perceive a clear way forward. Indeed, in the eyes of some (Brianna and Charles), long-standing tensions between large-scale providers of one-stop services and smaller providers of culturally competent services to particular communities were not addressed and were perhaps even exacerbated by the invitation to be part of a collective community. These results echo many of the same dynamics occurring in the Art of Hosting community of practice. While the relationships forged through events are significant, they might not be enough to make and sustain long-term policy or systems change or to overcome the feelings of some that they are not "at home" in the collective community.

Learning Processes in Developing Facilitation Skill

Despite agreement among the training participants and trainers that the workshop provided clear explanations of the techniques and concepts, study participants took up the ideas conveyed in the training to different degrees. Many individuals exercised practical judgment about how to apply facilitation practices in diverse circumstances, but some were barely using the techniques and patterns. While both groups frequently pointed to features of the contexts in which they work, close analysis of their accounts suggests that learning processes help explain some of the differences in their abilities to apply the hosting approach. Those who were using the techniques and patterns had experienced several kinds of changes: in themselves, in how they approach and facilitate, and sometimes also in how they identify themselves as members of a broader facilitation community. Those who were not using the techniques and patterns did not undergo these changes. These changes involved learning through at least one of three types of transforming facilitation knowledge: *metabolizing*, *situating*, or *co-producing* (Table 10.1).

TABLE 10.1 Transformations of Knowledge in Learning to Facilitate

Practice settings for learning	*Related theories of knowledge*	*Transformation of facilitation knowledge*
Introducing facilitation techniques and sense-making patterns in facilitation training	Acquiring explicit and eliciting tacit knowledge	***Metabolizing facilitation knowledge:*** incorporating or eschewing facilitation techniques or patterns
"Getting on the mat" as an immersion practicum during facilitation training. Using patterns for designing and improvising participation processes. Cultivating a stance of ongoing learning through practice.	Situating knowledge and exercising practical judgment	***Situating facilitation knowledge:*** applying or adapting knowledge of facilitation in particular contexts through ongoing practice
"Co-learning," de-centering expertise, and creating new knowledge together in the facilitation training, in an ongoing community of practitioners, and in public participation settings. Innovating through experimenting and sharing new facilitation knowledge.	Learning socially in a community of practice and de-centering expertise to co-produce knowledge	***Co-producing facilitation knowledge:*** exchanging and creating facilitation knowledge through ongoing co-learning with other practitioners and participants in participation processes

Metabolizing Facilitation Knowledge

We use the word *metabolizing* to describe the embodied processes of knowledge transformation, in which individuals take in and absorb or eschew knowledge about facilitation. Metabolizing involves acquiring explicit and implicit knowledge through a variety of mechanisms, including formal training, assimilation of new knowledge with previous knowledge, and learning through practicing. Metabolizing is a process that individuals manifest in various ways, and successfully metabolizing is not the same thing as successfully becoming an Art of Hosting practitioner. It is not merely cognitive, but also an embodied experience acquired through practicing and ongoing evaluative and volitional processes. As individuals are introduced to and try on new techniques, patterns, or identities as hosts, they consider whether they work for their own personal styles or needs. They accept or reject taking that knowledge into their own practice. These processes are present in our data in accounts where study participants recalled learning through training and practicing, their evaluative statements about whether or not they liked or felt prepared to use different parts of the material, and their observations about what was hard or familiar to them about the approach.

Training participants took up hosting approaches to different extents following the training. Examining their accounts allows us to unpack trainer Kerry's observation, when novices gathered a few weeks after training, that some people were "getting it in their bones," while others were in "a critique mode, stand back mode." Workshop trainers and participants' accounts suggest that getting it "in the bones" is a cognitive, embodied, *and* volitional process. Kerry herself attributed the differences among those she observed both to "understanding" and whether the individuals were accepting or measuring and critiquing.

What we know from the literature on learning-in-action, knowing-in-practice, and the embodied nature of learning (Dewey, 1925; Kolb, 1984; Orlikowski, 2002) was repeatedly borne out in trainers' observations about the importance of learning by "getting on the mat," participants' higher recall of the knowledge they had most deeply experienced in the training, and their desire for more opportunities to practice and apply what they had been introduced to through the training. Similarly, for participants in public participation meetings, the fact that World Café is one of the practices that they could most easily and directly experience probably contributes to that particular method being their most prominent impression of what they identify, and sometimes subsequently try to apply themselves, as an "Art of Hosting" approach.

Our study of participants' accounts adds a volitional component to prior understandings of the acquisition through practice of knowledge about facilitation. The differing experiences of Dana and Bridget in trying to apply and adapt hosting approaches among skeptical peers point to the significance of the facilitator's own choice to resolve discomfort or embrace their comfort with the practices. Dana, a novice, was unwilling to push her colleagues through their discomfort with "process," despite her strong relationships with them, and dropped back to a more directive facilitation style and expedient decision-making technique. Bridget, a far more experienced practitioner of group processes, offered a contrasting account of encouraging her reluctant colleagues to "trust the wisdom of the group." This was not an assertion about what she thought would happen, or her post hoc analysis of what did happen, but rather a statement of belief in the practices. The trainers emphasized an individual's internal willingness to metabolize the learning, like Alisha's assertion that people's willingness to experiment with the practices depended on their "nature."

But while these trainers were explaining metabolizing facilitation knowledge in terms of a fixed feature of people's dispositions—their inherent "nature"— trainees emphasized the volitional component of their learning as they described themselves more actively critiquing hosting approaches to facilitation for fit with their personal style. Identity played a salient role in this aspect of metabolizing knowledge, sometimes in terms of people identifying with the practices and sometimes in terms of whether they felt they belonged or did not among a circle of practitioners. Wenger (1998, p. 149) asserts the influence of a "profound connection between identity and practice" in how people situate learning in part through a "negotiation of ways of being." An example of this aspect of metabolizing knowledge lies in the study participants who opted out—who declined to take on the hosting approach in their own practice—because of their reactions to what they regarded as an inadequate treatment in the training of the power, domination, and identity dynamics of public participation. They rejected the hosting approach altogether—in effect spitting it out rather than metabolizing it—because it neglected their knowledge, embodied in their own lived experience, of the relevance of individual standpoints and the power that personal identity and experience embody.

These individuals did not metabolize knowledge of hosting because, having tried it on through the training, they determined it did not fit them and their work. Conversely, for those who did accept hosting approaches, identity also played a part in their ability to take them up. Numerous individuals were not participating in the community of practitioners because they did not identify as a "professional facilitator," while others were confused by how to become an "insider." An important consequence of this perception was they were inhibited from engaging in additional opportunities to learn through ongoing practice and exchange with practitioners.

Sometimes people's willingness to mobilize and apply facilitation knowledge changes over time, with the benefit of additional time for reflection and exposure to additional settings in which to consider how it would work for them as well as participants. We distinguish their evaluating the fit of hosting approaches to facilitation with their identity and style—which we define as metabolizing this facilitation knowledge—from their evaluation of its fit with the needs, constraints, and opportunities of particular participation settings—which we characterize as situating this facilitation knowledge in particular contexts. We turn next to that learning process, but first note that metabolizing facilitation knowledge appears to be foundational in the sense that it is a baseline for and must initially precede other kinds of learning that need to occur for trainees to become skilled, pragmatic facilitators. Practitioners cannot use particular facilitation approaches and techniques without taking on—sufficiently understanding *and* deciding to accept—explicit and implicit knowledge about those forms of facilitation. An additional type of transformation of knowledge is developing judgment about how to use that knowledge in particular participation settings.

Situating Facilitation Knowledge

Situating describes how facilitators develop and exercise practical judgment about how to use their knowledge of facilitation in particular contexts. Situating requires placing their facilitation knowledge in a setting, integrating it into the context, and in so doing potentially transforming or modifying the knowledge. A form of learning developed through experience, these processes involve evaluating the context and the likely implications of different facilitation techniques, sequencing of work, or use of particular concepts. Situating facilitation knowledge is done in anticipation of, during, or following facilitating, and frequently involves adapting explicit knowledge to better deploy it in a particular context. It is not merely a reading of the presenting context, however, but also is influenced by individual facilitators. Given variations in individual styles and skills, different practitioners make varying judgments about what to do. These processes reveal themselves in our data in individuals' accounts of how they chose particular techniques or approaches in response to a context; their evaluative statements about how it worked or what they might do differently if they were to facilitate again; and their stories of adjusting content from the training, previous knowledge, and the presenting context.

The participants in this study spoke repeatedly about what they had learned through trying out the techniques in different settings. Edgar's account of adjusting and improvising how he "indigenized" hosting techniques to work with different communities suggests that experiencing hosting is not just a way to use the skills or knowledge acquired in training. It is also an opportunity for ongoing learning and reflection about what the techniques do, consistent with theories about the development of professional knowledge through reflection in and on action (Argyris & Schön, 1996; Forester, 1999; Schön, 1983). In our data, having multiple opportunities for situated learning, by trying out and observing the consequences of applying the knowledge in different settings—both in the training workshops and in subsequent public participation efforts—was essential to learning.

The idea of learning through practice implies a "use it or lose it" dynamic in maintaining knowledge and keeping it available for use; this is reinforced by one of the founders of the Art of Hosting asserting that he is "still a student" and that "practice makes the master." This stance not only cultivates humility, but also keeps the learning and application fresh. In addition, the commitment to ongoing practice includes a strong element of deepening learning through situating facilitation knowledge in new contexts. The trainer (Kerry) who stated that gaining a "deeper understanding" of hosting approaches to facilitation involves "hav[ing] enough understanding of group process and of how communities work that I can start to adapt, meet people where they're at," is attesting to the importance not only of repeated practice but also of adaptation and improvisation.

Veteran facilitators recounted using knowledge acquired through the training in a variety of issue areas. They did not just recall the techniques. They also had developed theories, or sometimes questions, about how techniques would work for particular conditions or purposes. Kyle, for example, was explicit that using World Café to involve marginalized groups in the human services planning process was not merely a question of using the right technique, but of fitting it into the context by building trust with the organization's director and co-developing the World Café questions with her. Other facilitators who attested they want to use a technique had not found "the right setting" for it. In this situation, the barrier to transforming their knowledge into action was not whether they had metabolized it, as they understood and accepted the knowledge. Rather, they had judged it not appropriate for the contexts they were acting within.

The ability to situate facilitation practices appropriately into contexts has real implications for public participation, as illuminated by our study of the policy discussions subsequently facilitated by these trainees. Participants in the deliberation about local government financing suggested that the choice of method was not well suited to their needs when they commented that the World Café conversations and brainstorming were enjoyable and "energizing," but doubted they were enough to get traction and be pragmatic about problems like turf battles and limited resources.

Co-Producing Facilitation Knowledge

Metabolizing and situating facilitation knowledge are not merely individual processes. *Co-producing* facilitation knowledge occurs when practitioners acquire, test, and generate new and renewed facilitation practices through engagement with other practitioners. We describe this as "co-producing," in contrast with the emic term used within the hosting community, "co-learning," to draw attention not merely to the shared experience of continual learning but also to the shared generation of new knowledge about facilitation. In our data, co-producing facilitation knowledge emerges in trainers' and participants' accounts of how learning with others through the training or subsequently facilitating together, in innovations or shifts in practices discovered through the community, and in explicit encouragement to participate in the community of practitioners.

The Art of Hosting model intentionally supports the co-production of facilitation knowledge in several ways. Trainers cultivate the idea that all participants are "co-learners," style the training workshops as opportunities to co-produce the workshop and practice together, identify their social interchanges as being part of a "community of practitioners," and explicitly invite others to be part of the community. The original theorization of communities of practice holds that such intentionality is not necessary for learning to occur, as learning inevitably occurs through contact with others engaged in the same practice (Lave & Wenger, 1991; Wenger, 1998). However, hosting practitioners' intentionality about their community and co-learning does several kinds of work.

Notably, hosting practitioners' references to co-learning, and veteran hosting practitioner Andre's characterization of the work done in his local community of practitioners as "practicing, practicing learning," illuminate the view that hosting *is* learning: to practice hosting is to practice learning, and to co-host is to co-learn. The invitation to participate in a community of practitioners—of co-learners and co-producers of knowledge—also reflects the distinctive and democratizing philosophies that hosting practitioners have about participation. Those beliefs are that all people in the room have wisdom, that deliberation enables the sharing of knowledge, that facilitators and others aim to de-center the authority of their position and expertise in the room, and that participants ideally will co-produce the participatory processes as well as the decision outcomes.

The intentionality of co-producing knowledge in the Art of Hosting community has a close affinity with the co-producing paradigm of some public participation processes. This is described in terms of participants "co-learning" through deliberative dialogue (Innes & Booher, 2010; Roberts, 2004), facilitators and participants "inclusively" co-producing the design of a decision-making process and policy outcomes (Quick & Feldman, 2011), or consumers and providers "co-producing" public service priorities and implementation (Bovaird, 2007). In the hosting setting, co-learning and co-producing knowledge are not merely about trainers' modeling facilitation for others to see or about generating new knowledge about facilitation. Co-learning is actively encouraged and occurs among all participants (hosts and non-hosts alike). Calls to "co-learning" in training workshops thus evoke a role for facilitators as participants in a somewhat unscripted participatory process in which they cede control of the agenda, are hosted by participants stepping up to lead practice sessions, and learning from the particularities of emerging experience in the workshop.

Involving trainees in designing and running their own training and ongoing community models enacts this philosophy. Participants are embodying the same inclusiveness (Quick & Feldman, 2011) that they aim to enable in a hosting approach to facilitating participatory processes. Part of what hosting facilitators are practicing and modeling through co-producing knowledge and co-facilitating—in the training, in their community of practitioners, and in their subsequent co-hosting of participatory processes—is the essence of the hosting approach. They are de-centering the traditional role of a facilitator who defines the agenda, directs the flow of conversation, and decides who speaks in favour of a convening facilitator who shares authority (Wheatley & Frieze, 2011). By design, learning to host—metabolizing the skill to convene "meaningful conversations" and situating hosting techniques in context-appropriate ways—involves devolving authority to co-produce the means and ends of democratic processes with the participants.

It also has practical consequences for co-producing new knowledge: styling the hosting training workshop and gatherings of the community of practitioners as immersive, co-learning environments encourages experimentation and participation, which enhance the circulation of new ideas. New knowledge generated becomes available to others involved in facilitation because participants harvest their learning and share it through accessible platforms such as websites and list-servs. This learning model is akin to the work of participants in online gaming environments (Thomas & Brown, 2011) and open source computer engineering circles (Lerner & Tirole, 2001), who co-produce new knowledge by freely sharing intellectual property, confronting challenges, and creating solutions together.

Similarly, having trainers in the hosting workshops make their judgments visible and open to interventions by the other people, as occurred in our case study setting when they paused the training to discuss what was happening and how to handle the opening circle process that was going "on and on," also calls out and accelerates knowledge co-production. More experienced hosting practitioners made their knowledge explicit and understandable to others, partially addressing the frustration of some novices that they did not gain enough information about how to select, use, and adapt the techniques in designing and enacting an engagement effort. This approach models and invites others to constitute themselves as "co-learners" of facilitation. The invitation to continuous co-learning invites practitioners to be humble and to engage in ongoing reflective practice and learning about facilitation.

Together, metabolizing, situating, and co-producing facilitation knowledge concretize the processes our study participants undertake in learning to practice the skill, judgment, and "critical pragmatism" (Forester, 2013) of facilitating. While we have distinguished three learning processes, they are not strictly mutually exclusive in terms of their mechanisms or consequences. *Practice* is central in all three processes of learning to facilitate: facilitators learn their craft by practicing it. Individuals learn by metabolizing facilitation knowledge, acquiring explicit knowledge, and developing implicit knowledge through practicing and accepting or eschewing it for their own practice. They also situate their facilitation knowledge, exercising practical judgment about themselves and the contexts in which they work. In situating their facilitation knowledge, they practice, select, and adapt what they know about facilitation with a pragmatic view toward what they are trying to accomplish in particular participation settings. Moreover, they co-produce facilitation knowledge with others, renewing the resources and practices available by practicing, innovating, and sharing facilitation approaches with others.

Building Capacity for Public Participation

We conclude by addressing the implications of this study for the professionalization of facilitation and for the quality of public participation. The three types of knowledge transformations we identify occurring, and the value of learning through practice, have broad applicability beyond the community of "hosting" practitioners in this study. What can we gather from their learning processes that can support better facilitation and ultimately enhance societal capacities for robust public participation?

We make three suggestions. All are informed by our observations of how much emphasis the study participants placed on learning through practice and on building their craft through the seasoning of the individual facilitator and the community of facilitators:

1. *Designing training for facilitators to be an experiential practicum, such that trainees learn by doing, is an effective pedagogical approach to building capacities for facilitating participation.* Since conducting the fieldwork for this research project in 2011 and 2012, both authors have applied this lesson consistently and successfully in our own teaching of public and non-profit managers. We find that the immersive experience our students gain by practicing participatory leadership in the classroom is profoundly beneficial. It accelerates the process of our students' metabolizing, situating, and co-producing knowledge to be effective facilitators of public participation, collaboration, and inclusive decision-making.

2. *Would-be and seasoned facilitators need ongoing facilitation opportunities to sustain and develop their craft.* Creating and sustaining infrastructure for facilitators to continue practicing and learning together will help public participation professionals and others to continue to develop facilitation skills and innovate. This might occur through professional associations or less formal communities of practice.

3. *"Co-learning," a distinctive feature of what and how hosting facilitators learn, is a promising framework for building other kinds of facilitation skills and for enhancing societal capacity for participatory processes.* The study participants' many references to co-learning make legible that for many of these facilitators, learning *is* the practice and product of facilitation. The last point has intriguing implications for building capacity for public participation, because one sign of a productive participatory process is that the participants learn: they change their minds, gain new understandings, or generate new options (Deyle & Slotterback, 2009; Innes & Booher, 2010). Foregrounding learning as a means and end of facilitation—as the Art of Hosting does—appears particularly promising for building capacities to facilitate some of the normatively desirable outcomes of public participation.

While the focus of this chapter has been on processes through which facilitators learn, there also are implications for how *non-facilitators* learn to participate and contribute to democratic decision-making. Hosting may be a particularly apt facilitation approach to encourage participants to be "co-learners" and "co-producers" in inclusive, deliberative processes (Innes & Booher, 2010; Quick & Feldman, 2011; Roberts, 2004). That is, it explicitly encourages co-learning among participants by de-centering the facilitator's traditionally pivotal role in favour of a convening host (Wheatley & Frieze, 2011). By design, learning to host—metabolizing the skill to convene "meaningful conversations" and situating hosting techniques in context-appropriate ways—involves devolving authority to co-produce the means and ends of participatory processes with the people being hosted. Public participation processes have many purposes, and design should follow from those purposes (Bryson et al., 2013). We suggest that building facilitators' capacities to enact inclusive and de-centered authority will be particularly valuable, especially when the primary goals of participatory processes include understanding emerging problems, gaining new perspectives, generating creative solutions, or building community connections to sustain problem solving.

That is, the knowledge transformation processes of metabolizing, situating, and co-producing knowledge through hosting do not merely support, but also enact a particular form democracy. In the hosting context, the immersive, co-production environment of training and ongoing "practicing together" is not a "simulation" of democracy. It is not merely a mechanism for building hosts' capacities to support democratic processes in other venues. It is itself a radically democratic practice, with critical implications for the qualities of participation. The purposeful intent of hosting is to create an emergent, reflective space for building inclusive community and for learning to participate better. This makes the hosting paradigm, and the union of training with subsequent practice in a continuous stream of learning that engages hosts and participants, a powerful means and ends of enhancing participatory democracy.

Acknowledgments

Critical Policy Studies published a related paper in 2014. We thank our many study participants for their generosity in sharing their time and insights with us. We also gratefully acknowledge the contributions of Nicholas Stuber, Ahna Minge, and Leslie Watson to this research project.

Notes

1 Deliberation, as distinguished from other forms of public participation, involves multidirectional communication, engaging a diverse array of perspectives, and developing and evaluating options together (Fischer & Forester 1993, Fung & Wright, 2003; Innes & Booher, 2010).
2 Commonly used online resources for practitioners include the websites of the International Association for Public Participation (IAP2.org), the National Coalition for Dialogue and Deliberation (ncdd.org), and the Public Conversations Project (publicconversations.org).

References

Argyris, C., & Schön, D. (1996). *Organizational learning II: Theory, method, and practice*. Reading, MA: Addison Wesley.

Art of Hosting. (2016). *Art of Hosting and harvesting conversations that matter*. Retrieved from http://www.artofhosting.org/

Baker, L. L., & Fraser, C. (2005). Facilitator core competencies as defined by the International Association of Facilitators. In S. Schuman (Ed.), *The IAF handbook of group facilitation: Best practices from the leading organization in facilitation* (pp. 459–472). San Francisco, CA: Jossey-Bass.

Baldwin, C., & Linnea, A. (2010). *The circle way: A leader in every chair*. Oakland: Berrett-Koehler.

Bingham, L. B., Nabatchi, T., & O'Leary, R. (2005). The new governance: Practices and processes for stakeholder and citizen participation in the work of government. *Public Administration Review, 65*(5), 547–558.

Bovaird, T. (2007). Beyond engagement and participation: User and community coproduction of public services. *Public Administration Review, 67*(5), 846–860.

Brown, J., & Isaacs, D. (2005). *The world café: Shaping our futures through conversations that matter*. Oakland: Berrett-Koehler.

Bryson, J. M., Quick, K. S., Slotterback, C. S., & Crosby, B. C. (2013). Designing public participation processes. *Public Administration Review, 73*(1), 23–34.

Cooper, E., & Smith, G. (2012). Organizing deliberation: The perspectives of professional participation practitioners in Britain and Germany. *Journal of Public Deliberation, 8*(1). Retrieved from http://www.publicdeliberation.net/jpd/vol8/iss1/art3/

Cooper, T. L., Bryer, T. A., & Meek, J. W. (2006). Citizen-centered collaborative public management. *Public Administration Review, 66*(s1), 76–88.

Creighton, J. L. (2005). *The public participation handbook: Making better decisions through citizen involvement*. San Francisco, CA: Jossey-Bass.

Dewalt, K. M., & Dewalt, B. R. (2002). *Participant observation: A guide for fieldworkers*. Walnut Creek, CA: AltaMira Press.

Dewey, J. (1925). *Experience and nature*. Chicago: Open Court.

Deyle, R., & Slotterback, C. S. (2009). Group learning in participatory planning processes: An exploratory quasiexperimental analysis of local mitigation planning in Florida. *Journal of Planning Education and Research, 29*(1), 23–38.

Escobar, O. (2011). *Public dialogue and deliberation: A communication perspective for public engagement practitioners*. Edinburgh: UK Beacons for Public Engagement.

Fischer, F., & Forester, J. (Eds.). (1993). *The argumentative turn in policy analysis and planning*. Durham, NC: Duke University Press.

Forester, J. (1999). *The deliberative practitioner: Encouraging participatory planning practices*. Cambridge, MA: MIT Press.

Forester, J. (2013). On the theory and practice of critical pragmatism: Deliberative practice and creative negotiations. *Planning Theory, 12*(1), 5–22.

Fung, A., & Wright, E. O. (2003). *Deepening democracy: Institutional innovations in empowered participatory governance*. New York: Verso.

Glaser, B. G., & Strauss, A. L. (1967). *The discovery of grounded theory: Strategies for qualitative research*. Chicago: Aldine.

Gupta, A., & Ferguson, J. (1997). *Anthropological locations: Boundaries and grounds of a field science*. Berkeley, CA: University of California Press.

Healey, P. (2009). The pragmatic tradition in planning thought. *Journal of Planning Education and Research, 28*(3), 277–292.

Hendriks, L., & Carson, L. (2008). Can the market help the forum? Negotiating the commercialization of deliberative democracy. *Policy Sciences, 41*(4), 293–313.

Hock, D. (1999). *Birth of the chaordic age.* Oakland: Berrett-Koehler.

Holman, P., Devane, T., & Cady, S. (2007). *The change handbook: The definitive resource on today's best methods for engaging whole systems.* Oakland: Berrett-Koehler.

Holstein, J. A., & Gubrium, J. F. (1995). *The active interview.* Thousand Oaks, CA: Sage.

Innes, J. E., & Booher, D. E. (2010). *Planning with complexity: An introduction to collaborative rationality for public policy.* New York: Routledge.

Isaacs, W. (1999). *Dialogue and the art of thinking together.* New York: Random House.

Jacobs, L. R., Cook, F. L., & Delli Carpini, M. X. (2009). *Talking together: Public deliberation and political participation in America.* Chicago: University of Chicago Press.

Kaner, S. (2007). *Facilitator's guide to participatory decision-making* (2nd ed.). San Francisco, CA: Jossey-Bass.

Kolb, D. A. (1984). *Experiential learning: Experience as the source of learning and development.* Englewood Cliffs, NJ: Prentice Hall.

Lave, J., & Wenger, E. (1991). *Situated learning: Legitimate peripheral participation.* Cambridge: Cambridge University Press.

Lee, C. W. (2011). Five assumptions academics make about public deliberation, and why they deserve rethinking. *Journal of Public Deliberation, 7*(1). Retrieved from http://www.publicdeliberation.net/jpd/vol7/iss1/art7/

Leighninger, M. (2006). *The next form of democracy: How expert rule is giving way to shared governance and why politics will never be the same.* Nashville, TN: Vanderbilt University Press.

Leighninger, M. (2010). Teaching democracy in public administration: Trends and future prospects. *Journal of Public Deliberation, 6*(1). Retrieved from http://www.publicdeliberation.net/jpd/vol6/iss1/art2/

Lerner, J., & Tirole, J. (2001). The open source movement: Key research questions. *European Economic Review, 45*(4–6), 819–826.

Mansbridge, J., Hartz-Karp, J., Amengual, M., & Gastil, J. (2006). Norms of deliberation: An inductive study. *Journal of Public Deliberation, 2*(1). Retrieved from http://www.publicdeliberation.net/jpd/vol2/iss1/art7/

Marcus, G. E. (1998). *Ethnography through thick and thin.* Princeton, NJ: Princeton University Press.

Moore, A. (2012). Following from the front: Theorizing deliberative facilitation. *Critical Policy Studies, 6*(2), 146–162.

Nabatchi, T., & Leighninger, M. (2015). *Public participation for 21st century democracy.* San Francisco, CA: Jossey-Bass.

Nicolini, D., Gherardi, S., & Yanow, D. (2003). *Knowing in organizations: A practice-based approach.* Armonk, NY: M. E. Sharpe.

Orlikowski, W. J. (2002). Knowing in practice: Enacting a collective capability in distributed organizing. *Organization Science, 13*(3), 249–273.

Owen, H. (1997). *Open space technology: A user's guide.* Oakland: Berrett-Koehler.

Polanyi, M. (1966). *The tacit dimension.* London: Routledge.

Polletta, F., & Chen, P. C. B. (2013). *The gendered public sphere: Accounting for women's variable participation in settings of political talk.* Unpublished manuscript.

Quick, K. S., & Feldman, M. S. (2011). Distinguishing participation and inclusion. *Journal of Planning Education and Research, 31*(3), 272–290.

Roberts, N. (2004). Public deliberation in an age of direct citizen participation. *American Review of Public Administration, 34*(4), 315–353.

Ryfe, D. M. (2007). Toward a sociology of deliberation. *Journal of Public Deliberation, 3*(1). Retrieved from http://www.publicdeliberation.net/jpd/vol3/iss1/art3/

Sandfort, J. R., Stuber, N., & Quick, K. S. (2012). *Practicing the art of hosting: Exploring what art of hosting and harvesting workshop participants understand and do.* Minneapolis, MN: Center for Integrative Leadership, University of Minnesota.

Schön, D. (1983). *The reflective practitioner: How professionals think in action.* London: Temple Smith.

Schön, D., & Rein, M. (1994). *Frame reflection: Towards the resolution of intractable policy controversies.* New York: Basic Books.

Schwarz, R., Davidson, A., Carlson, P., & McKinney. S. (2005). *The skilled facilitator fieldbook: Tips, tools, and tested methods for consultants, facilitators, managers, trainers, and coaches.* San Francisco, CA: Jossey-Bass.

Scott, J. C. (1998). *Seeing like a state: How certain schemes to improve the human condition have failed.* New Haven, CT: Yale University.

Senge, P. M. (2006). *The fifth discipline: The art and practice of the learning organization.* New York: Doubleday/Currency.

Suchman, L. (1987). *Plans and situated action: The problem of human-machine communication.* Cambridge: Cambridge University Press.

Sunwolf & Frey, L. R. (2005). Facilitating group communication. In S. A. Wheelan (Ed.), *The handbook of group research and practice* (pp. 485–510). Thousand Oaks, CA: Sage.

Thomas, D., & Brown, J. S. (2011). *A new culture of learning: Cultivating the imagination for a world of constant change.* North Charleston, SC: CreateSpace Independent Publishing Platform.

Wenger, E. (1998). *Communities of practice: Learning, meaning, and identity.* Cambridge: Cambridge University Press.

Wheatley, M., & Frieze, D. (2011). *Walk out, walk on: A learning journey into communities daring to live the future now.* Oakland: Berrett-Koehler.

Yanow, D. (2004). Translating local knowledge at organizational peripheries. *British Journal of Management, 15*(S1), S9–S25.

Yanow, D., & Schwartz-Shea, P. (2015). *Interpretation and method: Empirical research methods and the interpretive turn* (2nd ed.). New York: Routledge.

11

CONCLUSION

Do the Institutionalization and Professionalization of Public Participation and the Enthusiasm for Participatory Processes Guarantee Greater Democratization?

Laurence Bherer, Mario Gauthier, and Louis Simard

The growth and diversification of public participation practices over the past 35 years have led to the creation of a new occupation: that of the public partici- pation professional (PPP). PPPs are individuals working in the public, private, or community sectors to design, implement, and/or facilitate public participation processes. What are some of the challenges of this new craft? How is this new pro- fessional field structured? Is the growing importance of this new profession result- ing in the development of higher-quality participatory processes? How much do public participation professionals influence the implementation of participa- tion mechanisms? The various contributions that we have assembled in this book allow us to identify a few main research findings in this regard, centering around the causes of the rapid development of the profession, the PPPs' influence on the dissemination of practices, and the fragility of this field of practice despite its rapid professionalization. In this conclusion, we also suggest three potential avenues for future research in order to further our knowledge about PPPs and about the effects of the professionalization of public participation. We will see in particular that this professionalization has been preceded by a trend toward institutionaliza- tion and the proliferation of participatory spaces in various spheres of society.

The Main Findings

What Are Some of the Factors Underlying the Rapid Professionalization of Public Participation?

The rapid development of the profession is closely linked to the proliferation of participatory spaces in a number of spheres of society, that is, to the increase in the demand for participation. Several factors have led to this increased demand. The cause that is most often mentioned in the studies presented in this book is the adoption by public authorities of laws, regulations, and practices that make participatory arrangements mandatory. This impetus from public authorities, which is generally accompanied by specific procedures, is especially marked in France, where the development of the field of public participation professionals mainly resulted from the institutional offer from public authorities. These formal innovations took advantage of the experience of the militants of the 1960s and 1970s, who transformed themselves into public participation professionals/consultants and were then replaced by a second generation of PPPs, who, without having experienced the social struggles of the 1960s, profited from the new market opportunities created by the state. The development of the field is thus said to be mainly due to the shift from a bottom-up process—where participation arose from protests—to a top-down trend of the ordering of participation by public authorities. Of these public authorities, local governments are often the most important sponsors of participatory processes. This is the case especially in France, the UK, and Quebec. The international dissemination of mechanisms such as citizens' juries also stems from municipalities' partiality to this type of mechanism, especially in Spain, as Amelung and Grabner show. Associated with the institutionalization of public participation is a second factor, which is linked to the major reforms that the state has undergone in the past 30 years. In the name of the greater accountability of the actors involved, the New Public Management (NPM) focused on partnerships and collaboration between public authorities and stakeholders, including citizens. This soon led to the need for experts in collaborative design, in order to implement and facilitate these new participatory arrangements. In the same way, the government austerity and state disengagement policies of the last decade made the use of participatory processes and PPPs necessary. Caroline W. Lee maintains that the development of these participatory tools was essentially used to manage social protest in a context of "hard choices." PPPs found themselves in the uncomfortable situation of defending a profession with a strong democratic ethos while at the same time being "complicit" in the acceptance of these austerity reforms. The third factor is more closely related to the internal dynamics of the field of public participation, which has experienced a succession of phases of renewal, with, for example, the development of alternative methods of conflict resolution and mediation as part of an overall approach centered on consensus and the search for mutually satisfactory solutions. The enthusiasm in academic circles for deliberative democracy has also fostered the emergence of a new generation of participatory mechanisms that some PPPs have taken advantage of. Finally, we cannot ignore the series of societal changes that have served as the backdrop for the increase in the demand for participatory services and for the rapid professionalization of public participation. And here we can point to the growing public protests against megaprojects, which have systematically questioned the approaches taken by the major proponents and governments responsible for these projects on a worldwide scale. The controversies surrounding the use of the new information and communication technologies (NICT) resulting from scientific advances must also be seen as driving forces in the institutionalization of public participation and in the structuring of the field of PPPs in the West as a whole. In sum, the need to deal with the series of major, but often contested, state reforms has made the use of participation experts increasingly important in order to come to terms with the participatory turn and thus the implementation of participatory processes. This trend has also spread to other actors, including private proponents, NGOs, and trade unions, which have also seen in participatory mechanisms a way of handling public criticism as well as the apathy and lack of interest of their members. The popularity of the participation movement in very different sectors of society has enabled PPPs to prosper, to create a number of market niches, and to offer a range of participatory services.

The Effects of Professionalization on Standardization and Innovation

The rise of PPPs as the actors at the center of participatory processes poses the question of what effects their activities have on the practice of public participation: are they able to favourably influence participatory arrangements, or must they follow the agendas of the sponsors of participation? This issue raises the question of the PPPs' role in the implementation of innovative practices. The various chapters that make up this book clearly show that PPPs not only carry out participatory processes but also influence the way that participatory designs are applied. Moreover, they help other actors to understand the ins and outs of public participation. The discussion on how the principle of impartiality is applied, as presented in the chapter by Bherer, Gauthier, and Simard, shows the amount of time and effort that some PPPs have to devote to their clients to get them to adopt a more open and more inclusive attitude. Others would rather not accept mandates from clients that do not wish to be influenced. This desire to change the attitudes of the sponsors of participation is also evident in the testimony of "official PPPs" (PPPs who are civil servants), as cited by Escobar, who see themselves as agents of change that can help to transform other actors and the culture of their organization. But these PPPs are not all willing to assume this role to the same extent. The most committed among them not only act during participatory forums but also make an effort to help their employers to combat prejudices about, for example, "incompetent" citizens and "anti-capitalistic" NGOs, by working within public administrations. This capacity to influence others is also due to a characteristic feature of PPPs, that is, the way that they learn their profession by going through a series of incremental processes of trial and error and correction or, in other words, "learning by doing." As Quick and Sandfort emphasize, acquiring the skills and judgment needed to act with empathy requires continual effort on the PPPs' part. It is in fact a "complex craft." To be able to disseminate the knowledge that they have gained in their practice, PPPs need to be proactive and to take advantage of opportunities to learn through various means (training, handbooks, mentors, etc.), to be able to then adapt what they have learned to different contexts, and to discuss and co-produce this new knowledge with other PPPs. In other words, PPPs need to be reflexive by activating and eliciting their tacit practical knowledge. This reflexive capacity, however, is difficult to acquire and remains one of the greatest challenges of the profession, as Chilvers indicates. The power relationships associated with participatory processes (also found in the case of civil servant PPPs) and the context of commercialization that affects the activities of most PPPs represent important obstacles to innovation.

The contributions featured in this book are ambivalent in regard to institutional incentives designed to encourage innovation on the part of PPPs and their sponsors. These incentives may in fact create the conditions for innovation and experimentation, but if they are too authoritative, the "innovative" participatory design becomes a dominant norm that tends to suppress other forms of experimentation. The dissemination and adaptation of a participatory design then turn into standardization, the negative effects of which are underscored by Amelung and Grabner: (1) the risk of losing sight of the guiding principles of a participatory mechanism in the process of local adaptation; (2) technocratization of the mechanism (the procedure becomes more important than the objective of the mechanism); and (3) the dissemination of the mechanism is tied to commercial interests and not to a search for the greater authenticity of public participation practices. The studies brought together here give several examples of the detrimental effects of institutional incentives. On the one hand, major financial and institutional incentives, such as those offered by the Tuscan Authority for public participation, clearly affect the PPPs' practices: the participation mandates funded by the Authority prioritize the use of mini-publics, and this has had the effect of strongly developing this practice, which was not very well known up to that point. PPPs are however very critical of this imposed choice, because mini-publics not only require a great deal of resources but also tend to make the practice of public participation more rigid. The findings are similar in the UK, where Chilvers notes that Sciencewise's preferences for citizens' juries led it to primarily use large survey and marketing firms, which significantly restricted the innovation process. The smallest firms were gradually disqualified from competing, and participatory approaches that did not meet Sciencewise's evaluation criteria were progressively eliminated. This is a clear case of commercialization having an adverse effect on innovation. In response to such domination, some British academics and NGOs in fact set up their own type of citizens' juries, called "do-it-yourself" citizen juries. According to Amelung and Grabner, this counter proposal was an attempt to prevent the political instrumentalization of participatory mechanisms by promoting an autonomous and inclusive type of citizen jury that civil society, and not professionals, would be responsible for implementing.

Despite the Rapid Development of the Profession, the Practice Remains Fragile

Several of the analyses in this book reveal a paradox: although over the last 20 years PPPs have been able to take advantage of the enthusiasm for participatory practices to strengthen their expertise and skills in the design and facilitation of these mechanisms, the future of this practice still seems uncertain. The PPPs' practices remain fragile and are far from being stabilized. This is what a number of PPP leaders in their field have said in the US: they feel that, in a context rife with citizen apathy and cynicism about public policies, the changes are not coming fast enough, and there has been a proliferation of "fake" participatory processes that have had little effect on decision-making or in empowering communities.

What are the reasons for this continued fragility? Several of the chapters explicitly or implicitly mention the strong competition between PPPs in terms of the types of participatory services that they offer and the participatory approaches that they prefer. The rapid development of the participation market has attracted a series of players with different backgrounds that want to take advantage of the growing demand in this field. The methodological approach that studies not only individuals and organizations with a strong professional identity in the area of public participation but in fact all the firms that obtain contracts in this sector—see the chapters on Quebec and France—offers clear evidence of such a trend. The case of Quebec shows that these firms are certainly not competing on a level playing field, as the big public relations and engineering firms that have entered the participation market have far greater resources and means to impose their vision of public participation than do the small firms specializing in participatory services. The data collected in France show a similar tendency, since for a large majority of the consultants surveyed (75%), public participation is a secondary activity within the wide range of services that they offer. We may thus assume that they devote less time and expertise to participation services, which undoubtedly has an impact on the quality of their engagement and on the reflexive scope of the practice of public participation for them. The important role that communications and public relations firms play in the provision of participatory services in Quebec, France, and the US indicates that this is a very desirable market. Caroline W. Lee's example at the beginning of her chapter on the closing of America-Speaks, an organization recognized in the United States and worldwide, testifies to the effect of strong competition. In this regard, the preferences for particular participatory designs by influential institutions such as Sciencewise in the UK have had the effect of favouring certain firms. Jason Chilvers shows that the decision to opt for forms of mini-publics that use random selection—citizens' juries in this case—has enabled large survey and marketing firms to enter the public participation market, to the detriment of more experienced players in this field, who are often freelancers. The resources required for such mechanisms favour larger firms. And it is the same type of selection in favour of communications firms that occurs in the case of the major participatory exercises organized by the Commission Nationale du Débat Public (CNDP) in France, which require a huge investment in communications activities.

The fragility of this field is also evidenced by the lack of shared norms within the profession as a whole, especially concerning the issue of impartiality, as demonstrated in the chapter by Bherer, Gauthier, and Simard. This issue raises the question of how PPPs see their role as third-party actors positioned between the sponsors of participation and citizens. Whom are PPPs actually working for? Several of the chapters mention that this is a crucial issue for PPPs. This is in fact the case for some of the PPPs interviewed in the UK, Italy, and Quebec. They would like to have impartiality viewed as a central principle in the profession in the hope that some questionable practices would then no longer be associated with the field, such as public relations or lobbying practices that many PPPs feel should not be included in public participation activities or offered by firms in these sectors. They do not want to see public participation so readily tied to all the advocacy services now being offered by the new political professionals discussed in the introduction to this book. Impartiality is not only an issue in the context of commercialization, but also affects PPPs working in the civil service. Oliver Escobar's research on these official PPPs indicates that PPPs are often seen by other civil servants and elected officials as hampering their usual practices. The proximity between all these actors puts official PPPs in a very tricky situation, a fact that is recognized by some elected officials and civil servants, who would not want to be in the PPPs' position. "I don't envy her, I think she's got possibly one of the worst jobs in the Council, and she's made a lot of enemies," says one of the elected officials interviewed by Escobar, in referring to a certain PPP. The opposition is equally strong between PPPs who are concerned with the effect that participatory processes have on the final decision made by the sponsors of participation and PPPs who feel that the objectives of participatory mechanisms should be to create better citizens and foster collaboration. Such opposing concerns have strongly divided not only the small community of PPPs in Italy but also PPPs in the US, some of whom reject the practice of the art of hosting, which they feel is too consensual or not political enough. Ultimately, PPPs are not only divided over the type of participatory design that they should choose. An even more important issue is that the structuring of the profession and of the participation industry means that very different and strongly opposing approaches to action are competing with one another, which underscores the fragmentation of the practice of public participation: that is, there are a number of actors marked by a lack of hierarchy and by strong competition over the principles, rules, and practices that should guide actions in this field.

Potential Research Avenues

As we emphasized in the introduction, PPPs are often relatively invisible actors, who are difficult to inventory and study, especially because they are referred to by an impressive variety of names, the firms operating in this field do not always explicitly publicize their services, and there are as yet few organized professional networks of PPPs. The various studies in this book testify to the methodological solutions that researchers have had to develop to reach this community. Two main types of approaches were used to study PPPs. The first type of approaches are ethnographical in nature, and include observing PPPs in conferences and seminars, professional associations, and training sessions (Lee; Mazeaud and Nonjon; Quick and Sandfort) or through participant observation of teams of PPPs (Escobar). This method enables researchers to study PPPs within a given space. This work is then supplemented with documentary research, interviews, and online discussions with PPPs. The second type of approaches, in cases where there are no professional organizations of PPPs or only relatively inactive ones, involves researchers interviewing PPPs by using a "snowball" technique to enable them to identify other such professionals. This investigative approach is often complemented with other data collection methods, such as documentary research and systematic analysis of the websites of participation firms. Because the findings presented here come from some of the first research programs on PPPs, many other potential research avenues could still be explored to learn more about the role of PPPs and the impact of professionalization. In the following paragraphs, we suggest three main approaches that we feel should be given priority in order to further our knowledge in this area.

The Role of Major Public Participation Organizations in the Standardization and Dissemination of Practices

Although it is not central to their analysis, several chapters mention the important role that some leading public participation organizations play in the legitimization of the practice, the development of know-how, and the dissemination of participatory practices. We are thinking in particular here of the role of the BAPE in Quebec, the CNDP in France, the Tuscan and Emilia-Romagna authorities for public participation in Italy, Sciencewise in the UK, and AmericaSpeaks in the US. These organizations may have different mandates, but they have all played a role in fostering the recognition of public participation. As Chilvers pointed out, this kind of organization has the capacity to build and structure the practice of public participation: "Such actors were recognized for their roles in speaking for, overseeing, coordinating, and professionalizing the public dialogue field, which included networking, knowledge transfer, developing guidance, training, and building capacity" (2012, p. 296). The Italian PPPs also noted that the creation of the two authorities specializing in public participation has greatly helped their profession to gain recognition. The problem is that we know very little about the role played by these organizations and how they make a difference (compared with a situation where there is no such organization). We can hypothesize that their role varies according to their status. The BAPE, the CNDP, Sciencewise, and the two Italian authorities for public participation are public agencies established by governments with the mandate to organize participatory forums in accordance with the provisions of the legislation that created them. This legislation usually sets out clear rules for the implementation of participatory arrangements, but also gives public agencies room to manoeuvre in terms of putting participatory tools in place (Bherer, Gauthier, and Simard). We can also hypothesize that their autonomy and resources allow these public organizations to interact with many actors, in serving as a reference for them by providing examples of ways of implementing public participation, by writing guides and reports, by organizing networks, etc. Furthermore, the rules and practices implemented by this kind of public organization can help to encourage actors such as public or private sponsors to change their behaviour in terms of how they formulate policies or develop projects. The analyses offered in the chapters of this book suggest that the dynamics created by these public agencies can have a direct effect on the way that public participation works. The cases of Quebec and France show that the BAPE and CNDP have directly or indirectly contributed to the development of the participation industry. In fact, the institutionalization of the public participation field is seen not only in the legislation that created participatory settings or public agencies dedicated to public participation, but also in the adjustment that the actors make to the new context created by these laws. The former AmericaSpeaks or similar NGOs such as Involve in the UK or the Institut du Nouveau Monde in Quebec do not have the same power and resources as public agencies to incite actors to change their behaviour. Nevertheless, their reputation and the efforts they put into promoting public participation, their continued existence over time, and their involvement in numerous cases over the years can also give them a role as a guiding force, a force that can influence PPPs in their practice and help to institutionalize principles and practices. An international comparison of all these organizations would allow us to identify the conditions and resources needed for the dissemination of innovative participatory processes and the improvement of participation practices.

Further Study of the Diversity of PPP Profiles

The contributions in this book show that PPPs are far from being a unified group that should be considered as a coherent and homogeneous whole. They in fact differ in a number of ways. First, the studies presented here agree that PPPs come from a variety of educational backgrounds and have had a wide range of work experiences that have led them to become PPPs. There are clues that suggest that both their educational backgrounds and career profiles influence the way that PPPs carry out their work. Some PPPs' militant past or their expertise in certain areas such as communications and public relations are said to tend to affect their view of public participation. More specifically targeted and comparative studies are needed to help us to better understand this link and how it influences the PPPs' preferences for certain types of participation mechanisms. A second difference has to do with the niches that PPPs have developed within the participation industry. These niches may be related to the kinds of clients that PPPs target, the sectors that they prefer to work in, or the types of development projects for which they accept mandates. These niches are especially visible in the case of public participation firms that benefit from the contracting out of public participation, but there may also be specialization in terms of skills for PPPs that work in the other main areas of expertise described by Chilvers (2012) and presented in the introduction. Further study is necessary to accurately map the participation industry. Finally, another difference concerns how the PPPs' main areas of expertise are connected to the types of organizations that they work in. The little research that has been done on PPPs has mostly concentrated on firms that obtain mandates from the sponsors of participation, as this is where the largest group of PPPs is found. There has still been relatively little exploration of PPPs working in other types of organizations. Oliver Escobar's research, including the study discussed in this book, shows that the role of PPPs working in public administrations is a delicate one that warrants greater—and more specific—attention. Because of their proximity to actors with considerable political power and influence (elected officials and other civil servants), these PPPs have the potential to become very important agents of change. They can for example ensure that the results of participatory exercises are more closely linked to decision-making. It is because the nature of their work means that they have to confront traditional working practices that official PPPs experience the strong pressure described by Escobar and often feel powerless in the face of so much resistance. Similar studies have been conducted in France, a country that is notable for its high level of institutionalization of participatory democracy. More research is needed to give us a better understanding of the effects of the internalization of participatory services. It would also be interesting to learn more about the PPPs' strategies in the face of adversity, a subject that Escobar examines in his chapter in showing how PPPs deal with their relations with other public participation actors. Another reality that is not often investigated but is broached in some of the chapters is the special place that some fundraisers and foundations occupy in the ecology of participation (to use Jason Chilvers's expression). In both the US and the UK (especially in the case of citizens' juries: see the chapter by Amelung and Grabner), there are organizations that believe that participatory processes can make a positive contribution to community life and are ready to fund this type of exercise, without being directly involved in it. So they are neither clients nor sponsors that directly benefit from public participation, but they do play a role in helping to disseminate and legitimize participatory processes.

Toward a Reflexive Collaboration between Academics and Practitioners

The chapters in this book show the different kinds of duos that PPP form with other public participation actors, that is, in their relations with elected officials, civil servants, private proponents, professional associations, and large participation organizations, as well as with other members of the profession. As several of the contributions have highlighted the role played by academics in legitimizing participatory mechanisms, we feel that it is important to take a closer look at the conditions needed for collaboration between academics and practitioners (without of course ruling out the need for further study on the other kinds of interactions). The interest manifested by researchers in democratic innovations and in experiments with different forms of deliberation shows that special ties have developed over the years between the academic sector and the sphere of practice, especially in connection with the work of PPPs. As Kahane and Loptson note in their chapter, "Academics are an important part of the story of the professionalization of public participation." The idea for this book in fact originated in a symposium involving academics, PPPs, and representatives of influential NGOs in the public participation sector (AmericaSpeaks, the Institut du Nouveau Monde, and Involve).[1] In his text, Chilvers stresses the importance not only of seeking out the best public participation practices but also of applying the notion of a "reflexive participation," that is, one that "seeks to open up, anticipate, and be continually responsive to the exclusions, underlying purposes, politics, framing effects, uncertainties, unintended consequences, social implications, and effects of public participation." The contribution by Kahane and Loptson shows that this rallying call should involve not only PPPs in the strict sense but also academics, who have been profoundly engaged in this sector through their actions, writings, and research. Some have officially acted as PPPs, but even those that have not been professionally engaged to such a degree need to recognize that they are also actors in the field of public participation. In such a context, research on deliberation and participation must accord a growing place to reflection on ways of improving this collaboration, especially in taking up Kahane and Loptson's suggestion to formulate principles and guidelines. And here we are not so much recommending a potential research avenue as calling for deeper reflection on the conditions needed to strengthen the ties between research and practice.

To conclude this book, let us mention that several of the contributions seem to indicate that the development of the field of public participation has arrived at a crossroads, in the sense of a decisive stage or an important moment when PPPs must make a choice in the light of the road already travelled and the road that lies ahead for the profession. While, for some, the professionalization of public participation has resulted in a major step backwards, due to the greater constraints and the standardization of public participation mechanisms and practices, for others, it represents an opportunity for innovation. For still others, like Caroline W. Lee, the future seems uncertain. The changes have been too slow in coming, and there has been a proliferation of "fake" participatory processes that have no effect on decision-making and public action. In particular, she fears a loss of the authenticity of participatory processes and an increase in public cynicism. Similarly, Mazeaud and Nonjon deplore the reduction in the contestatory scope of participatory democracy as promoted by the militants of the 1960s and 1970s. But others see in professionalization a source of innovation and the potential for the dissemination of good practices. Escobar, for example, describes public participation professionals as agents of change with the capacity to transform an organizational culture, so that their role goes far beyond that of simple deliberation practitioners. Likewise, Quick and Sandfort demonstrate how these professionals learn their craft and become pragmatic, reflexive, and critical practitioners that help to improve practices in this field. Finally, Kahane and Loptson show that in the collaboration between academics and practitioners there is a strong potential for learning, critical reflexivity, and the transformation of practices. In this context, the question that arises is the following: do the institutionalization and professionalization of public participation and the enthusiasm for participatory processes guarantee greater democratization? The answer to this important question is not evident. As several of the contributions in this book show, the professionalization of the field involves risks that threaten democratization: fake participatory processes, loss of authenticity, instrumentalization, and a reduced contestatory scope (in terms of the capacity for change and real and significant effects on decision-making). Nevertheless, professionalization seems to have had major and positive effects on the standardization of innovative practices: the formation of epistemic communities of "facilitators," "mediators," and "pragmatic, reflexive, and critical practitioners," the development of learning processes, etc. Professionalization has also led to tensions and conflicts between the emergence of this new professional category and other, more traditional professional categories. Ultimately, the professionalization of public participation raises a number of issues in regard to the democratization of public action, which are tied both to the risks of the instrumentalization of practices (activation politics) and to new opportunities for the development of a democratic ethos.

Note

1 See the Acknowledgments at the beginning of this book.

Reference

Chilvers, J. (2012). Reflexive engagement? Actors, learning, and reflexivity in public dialogue on science and technology. *Science Communication, 35*(3), 283–310.

CONTRIBUTORS

Nina Amelung is a Sociologist, currently finishing her PhD thesis, "Democracy Under Construction: The Micropolitics of Coordinating Transnational Public Engagement," at the Technische Universität Berlin, Germany. She is a Research Scholar in the EXCHANGE project, funded by the European Research Council, at the Center for Social Studies (CES), University of Coimbra, Portugal.

Laurence Bherer is an Associate Professor of Public Administration and Policy in the Political Science Department at the Université de Montréal. Her research focuses on participatory democracy, local democracy, and urban politics in Canada and Europe.

Jason Chilvers is a Reader and Chair of the Sciences, Society and Sustainability (3S) Research Group, University of East Anglia, UK. His work focuses on relations between science, democracy, and society. This includes pioneering studies of public participation expertise and developing critical studies and reflexive practices of participation. He is co-author of the recent book *Remaking Participation* (Routledge, 2016).

Oliver Escobar is Lecturer in Public Policy at the University of Edinburgh and Co-Director of What Works Scotland, a research program to improve public services and inform public sector reform. His areas of research, teaching, and practice are democratic innovation, public dialogue, and deliberation and collaborative policymaking. He is co-editing the forthcoming *Handbook of Democratic Innovation and Governance*. Blog: https://oliversdialogue.wordpress.com; Twitter: @OliverEscobar.

Mario Gauthier is a Full Professor of Urban Studies in the Social Sciences Department at the Université du Québec en Outaouais. His research work concerns urban and regional planning, environmental impact assessment, and sustainable development.

Louisa Grabner is a Master's student in the Department of Sociology at Technische Universität Berlin. She holds a BA in Sociology and Technology Studies. Her interest lies in social movements and political innovation. Recent publications include "Challenging Futures of Citizen Panels" (research report from the Innovation in Governance Research Group, with C. Mann et al., 2014).

David Kahane is Professor of Political Science at the University of Alberta. He specializes in democratic theory and practice, especially as these relate to the design of public dialogues and consultations and to questions of sustainability and systems change. From 2010 to 2016, he was Project Director of Alberta Climate Dialogue, a community-university research alliance funded by the Social Sciences and Humanities Research Council of Canada.

Caroline W. Lee is Associate Professor of Sociology at Lafayette College. Her book *Do-It-Yourself Democracy: The Rise of the Public Engagement Industry* was published by Oxford University Press in 2015. She co-edited the volume *Democratizing Inequalities: Dilemmas of the New Public Participation* (NYU Press, 2015) with Michael McQuarrie and Edward Walker.

Rodolfo Lewanski is an Associate Professor at the School of Political and Social Sciences, University of Bologna, where he presently teaches courses in deliberative participation and policy analysis. From October 2008 to March 2013, as independent "Participation Authority," he was responsible for implementing the Tuscany Region's law No. 69/07 promoting citizen engagement. Recent publications include "La prossima democrazia," www.laprossimademcorazia.com.

Kristjana Loptson is a PhD student in the Department of Political Science at the University of Alberta. Her research mainly concerns housing politics and housing insecurity in Canada. She has worked as a researcher with Alberta Climate Dialogue since 2011.

Alice Mazeaud is a Lecturer in Political Science at the University of La Rochelle (France). In 2010, she defended a PhD on the uses and effects of participatory democracy in the context of change in regional power. Recent publications include "L'instrumentation Participative de l'Action Publique: Logiques et Effets" (*Participations*, 2012).

Magali Nonjon is a Lecturer in Political Science at Sciences Po Aix (France). In 2006, she defended a PhD on the professionalization of participatory democracy in France ("Quand la démocratie se professionnalise," Université de Lille 2). Recent publications include "De la Militance à la Consultance: Les Bureaux d'Études Urbaines, Acteurs et Reflets de la Procéduralisation de la Participation" (*Politiques et Management Public*, 2012).

Kathryn S. Quick is Associate Professor in the Humphrey School of Public Affairs at the University of Minnesota. Formerly a public manager, she now centers her research and teaching on civic engagement, collaborative management, and enhancing resilience to address complex public problems. Through interpretive and engaged research, she studies a diversity of approaches to stakeholder involvement and community capacity building.

Stefania Ravazzi is an Assistant Professor of Political Science at the University of Turin, Italy. She teaches policy analysis and urban governance. She has published several contributions on public participation and deliberative democracy. Recent publications include "Flexibility, Argumentation and Confrontation. How Deliberative Minipublics can Affect Policies on Controversial Issues" (with Gianfranco Pomatto, *Journal of Public Deliberation*, 2014).

Jodi R. Sandfort is Professor and Chair of the Leadership and Management Area of the Humphrey School of Public Affairs, University of Minnesota. Her research, teaching, and practice focus on improving the implementation of social policy, including through stakeholder involvement. She works with and studies leaders, organizations, and networks of public, private, and philanthropic organizations that develop and deliver social programs.

Louis Simard is an Associate Professor in the School of Political Studies at the University of Ottawa. Louis Simard holds a PhD in Sociology from the Institute of Political Studies in Paris. His research work focuses on public participation, instruments of public action, social acceptability, and organizational learning in the environmental and energy sectors.

INDEX

Italic page references indicate charts and tables.